"Root has made a career out of challenging the youth ministry industry, but this is his most important youth ministry book to date. The end of youth ministry? Hardly. This is where it starts."

—**Kenda Creasy Dean**, Princeton Theological Seminary; author of *Almost Christian: What the Faith of Our Teenagers Is Telling the American Church* and coauthor of *Delighted: What Teenagers Are Teaching the Church about Joy*

"Andy calls us back to the cross by inviting young people to identify with Christ's death and thus experience 'God's action' in their lives. Rather than busyness, silence and humility make way for gratitude, and genuine joy erupts."

—**Sharon Galgay Ketcham**, Gordon College; author of *Reciprocal Church*

"Sometimes the riskiest questions we ask return us to the most basic ones. Andy's quest to answer 'What is youth ministry for?' invites us to join his own journey of theological and self-reflection. This book dares us to reorient our youth ministry approaches away from cultivating happiness and toward Christ crucified."

—**Steven Argue**, Fuller Theological Seminary

"There are nagging questions in youth ministry, many of which we hesitate to name out loud. 'Does what I'm doing matter?' 'Is any of this making a difference?' In *The End of Youth Ministry?*, Root manages to put his finger on these concerns and bring them into the light. He doesn't just name these questions, he explores them at length and then returns them to the youth worker in such a way that the questions become gifts."

—**Amanda Hontz Drury**, author of *Saying Is Believing: The Necessity of Testimony in Adolescent Spiritual Development*

"Root's many books evince a learned and sustained engagement with some of the most important thinkers in biblical studies, theology, philosophy, social theory, and more. His latest work, *The End of Youth Ministry?*, is no different, though its methodology is refreshingly new."

—**Bryan C. Hollon**, Malone University

Theology for the Life of the World

Jesus Christ is God come to dwell among humans, to be, to speak, and to act "for the life of the world" (John 6:51). Taking its mandate from the character and mission of God, Christian theology's task is to discern, articulate, and commend visions of flourishing life in light of God's self-revelation in Jesus Christ. The Theology for the Life of the World series features texts that do just that.

Human life is diverse and multifaceted, and so will be the books in this series. Some will focus on one specific aspect of life. Others will elaborate expansive visions of human persons, social life, or the world in relation to God. All will share the conviction that theology is vital to exploring the character of true life in diverse settings and orienting us toward it. No task is greater than for each of us and all of us together to discern and pursue the flourishing of all in God's creation. These books are meant as a contribution to that task.

The End of Youth Ministry?

Why Parents Don't Really Care about Youth Groups and What Youth Workers Should Do about It

ANDREW ROOT

B

Baker Academic

a division of Baker Publishing Group
Grand Rapids, Michigan

© 2020 by Andrew Root

Published by Baker Academic
a division of Baker Publishing Group
PO Box 6287, Grand Rapids, MI 49516-6287
www.bakeracademic.com

Printed in the United States of America

Library of Congress Cataloging-in-Publication Data
Names: Root, Andrew, 1974– author.
Title: The end of youth ministry? : why parents don't really care about youth groups and what youth workers should do about it / Andrew Root.
Description: Grand Rapids, MI : Baker Academic, a division of Baker Publishing Group, [2020]
Identifiers: LCCN 2019027617 | ISBN 9781540961396 (paperback)
Subjects: LCSH: Church work with youth. | Church youth workers. | Youth—Religious life.
Classification: LCC BV4447 .R65265 2020 | DDC 259/.23—dc23
LC record available at https://lccn.loc.gov/2019027617

ISBN 978-1-5409-6269-0 (casebound)

20   21   22   23   24   25   26   7   6   5   4   3   2   1

To Skip Masback:

In gratitude for your friendship
and for a career of championing youth ministry

Contents

Warning for the Reader!
(Read before Using)

As you pick up this book and page through it, a good question is, *What is this?* I'll be the first to admit that it's weird. I've written it in the first person, as a story that I, Andrew Root, am going through. And in a real way, I am. Writing this book has forced me to think in new ways, connecting new thoughts to my earlier projects. In no small way, this book is the outworking of the implications of my *Faith Formation in a Secular Age*. It even offers a vision for how I think attention to the good life and the practices of faith connect to place-sharing and the theology of the cross, both of which my earlier thoughts rest on so squarely.

That said, the story that unfolds below is a parable, a kind of thought experiment. The best way to say it is that this book is written in the spirit of the Christian philosopher Søren Kierkegaard. All of my works have more than a hint of Kierkegaardian influence. Like Kierkegaard, who Karl Barth called "the melancholy Dane," I sometimes feel like I could be called a "melancholy Minnesotan." Perhaps both Kierkegaard and I have spent far too much time in snowdrifts and bone-chilling winds to see the world in any other way than through the crucifixion. So with Kierkegaardian irony, you'll be surprised to discover that this book is fundamentally about *joy*. It sketches out how I see joy as central to ministry, and how I see joy in the resurrection as essential to a theology of the cross.

But in this book I go further in my Kierkegaardian directions than I have before, taking on the Dane's style, using stories that mix factual occurrences and made-up characters to articulate larger points about reality. For half a second I even thought of using a Kierkegaardian pseudonym (Crash Adams would have been cool), but I resisted the temptation. So instead I'm calling the protagonist of the tale ahead Andrew. The character Andrew is on a nine-month journey to figure out what youth ministry is for. Just as Kierkegaard's two characters Judge Vilhelm and A in *Either/Or* serve as a way for the philosopher to push forward new ideas, so my characters do as well.

In homage to Kierkegaard I have nicknamed my sage youth worker J—which stands for Janna. But because she's the creation of my own imagination (and the many conversations with youth workers I've learned from), I've called her J also because she is part of my own consciousness (my middle initial is J). In a sense, J is a real youth worker—I've met many like J across the globe—but the overall arc of her story is for the sake of the parable. As a matter of fact, almost everything in these pages happened, just not quite in the order or with the direct existential immediacy that is relayed here.

That said, I did interview some parents for this book. These interviews show up in the middle chapters. So while the whole of the book is a Kierkegaardian parable, it does draw directly from real conversations that inspired each of the stories of the parents I relay. I've changed their names and circumstances, both because I promised to and to fit the parable. So in the end these interviews are more illustrative than scientific, more like a screenwriter doing a drive-along than a sociologist or political scientist honing question protocols. I ask the reader to judge them on the merit of the cultural philosophical ideas they illustrate, rather than on the scientific precision they provide.

Let me offer one final word about the mechanics of the book: *maybe* I've watched too much TV and am too influenced by flashback techniques of storytelling in *The Handmaid's Tale*, *Westworld*, or *This Is Us*, but I've decided to use flashbacks as well. Eventually, we get to the present and stay there for the second half of the book. It's rare to read a theology and ministry book that is told as a storied parable, much less one that uses flashbacks. So enjoy!

Preface

It's never a good thing to be spotted crying on an airplane. In those tight confines, it's best to be steady—neither too high nor too low. But I couldn't help it. I'd just finished a beautiful and convicting film called *The Florida Project*, about a little girl named Moonee living in a dark shadow cast by Disney World. Moonee and her mother live on the throwaway material of the tourism giant, having nothing but the scraps of those living the "good life"—for a week or two—in the Magic Kingdom. Moonee and her mom's only option is to call home a two-star motel made for, but now discarded by, tourists. She has nowhere to play except the busy highways laced with strip malls and next to a helicopter pad that promises visitors majestic views of Orlando. They are poor and overlooked, locked out of The Happiest Place on Earth.

The movie ends in the most shockingly beautiful and heart-wrenching way, which I won't give away. The ending starkly communicates that some have to live in these desperate kinds of situations not necessarily because others are coldhearted or don't care but because their own imaginations of the good life support or concede to pushing others to the edges. It's as if the movie says that some get to throw things away and others have to live off the throwaway; some get to bathe in happiness and others get the dirty water.

When the credits rolled, I cried not only because it was beautifully sad but more so because I knew white Protestant youth ministry has overlooked, or looked past, children living in economic and cultural crisis. Kids like Moonee have been as invisible to white Protestant youth ministry as they have been to the larger culture.

It seems fair to say that white American Protestant congregation-based youth ministry is mostly a middle-class phenomenon (its funding, resources, speakers, and ideas come from this demographic). And in turn, it seems fair to say that American Protestant congregation-based youth ministry is in crisis, not sure of what it is really for, feeling at this moment somewhat directionless.

To face this challenge, this book takes a fundamentally different approach than most other youth ministry books. It focuses not on how to do youth ministry but rather on why to do it at all. It asks the reader to wrestle with this most fundamental question.

This is a big question. Any "why" question tends to be large. So, to begin answering the why of youth ministry, this book focuses most directly on parents, examining how their conceptions of a good life affect their children and, in turn, affect youth ministry. For decades now, we've added "family" to youth ministry, often calling ourselves "youth and family ministry." Yet often when we ask the most fundamental questions of "why" in youth ministry, we stick with youth. In no way will young people be ignored in this book, yet as we explore what youth ministry is for, we'll also think about the ways parents' conceptions of the good life direct their children's lives, and how youth ministry often gets pushed off balance because of this.

An important point as you wade into this book: because congregation-based youth ministry remains mainly a middle-class phenomenon, I'll locate my story there, introducing you to youth workers and parents living in this cultural milieu. I do this because my goal in seeking to answer what youth ministry is for is to challenge some of the misguided conceptions of a good life embedded in this middle-class milieu, to which youth ministry has sought to respond and by which it has too often been unhelpfully captured. My hope is that examining and challenging the middle-class conceptions of the good life will open up imaginative space that not only frees middle-class young people and parents for a new vision of God's calling, but also directs youth ministry as a whole to young people like Moonee, living on the edges, who too often are casualties of our shared misguided conceptions. So I'll challenge what youth ministry is for by directing my cultural critique (and reconception) at congregation-based youth ministry that often, particularly in middle-class settings, contends that "youth ministry" equals only "youth group."

We have a big job ahead of us in youth ministry. Our modern lives are now going so fast that a common middle-class response has been to *slow down* young people's growing up, delaying things like dating and driving, which just a few decades ago were common in early teen years. As I'll show, this slowdown has caused youth ministry to be rudderless, leading many to feel unsure what it is really for. Through the parable that you're about to read, I'll offer a diagnosis of the challenges we face—and have been unclear about—and then provide a new way to think about what youth ministry can be for.

I'll assert that youth ministry is for joy. I'll contend that only if youth ministry is for joy can we avoid the traps that have led to a cultural slowdown and our misguided conception of a good life—namely, the need for recognized identity and the goal of happiness. These cultural pursuits have made youth ministry just another activity, and one that can't match the importance of piano lessons, test prep, soccer, volleyball, and debate club. The moral dimension, exploring what's a good life, becomes central in this book. I believe this book is unique among ministry texts for fronting a moral philosophy. I've moved into this moral philosophy because Charles Taylor's thought has become important for me in understanding why youth ministry feels, at times, aimless. I'll be applying Taylor's moral philosophy directly to youth ministry. This book, then, will offer a vision for how youth ministry can be reimagined in a time when young peoples' schedules are being overmanaged. As strange as it may seem, making youth ministry for joy may just be the answer.

Truth be told, I never would have stumbled into these thoughts without the work of the Theology of Joy and the Good Life project at the Center for Faith and Culture at Yale Divinity School, funded by the John Templeton Foundation. This project has been more than an inspiration; it is the fruit of many conversations at the meetings and consultations, in which I've been fortunate enough to participate, that have directly affected the ideas. I've served on two boards within the grant and have learned much. A look at my footnotes will reveal that I've been influenced at multiple points by the findings and research of the grant. The grant produced hundreds of papers, essays, and lectures. I've read most of them, allowing them to mold my imagination. I'm overwhelmed with thanks to Skip Masback for inviting me into the project. Skip particularly advocated for part of the project to focus on young people and youth ministry. Skip has been a champion for youth ministry and youth workers. Over the past six years, he has become a good friend. There is almost no one I enjoy talking with more than Skip. His passion for youth ministry and Yale Divinity School is contagious. It was Skip who commissioned me to write this book for the grant. His encouragement and inspiration have meant so much.

I'd also like to thank the grant's primary investigator, Miroslav Volf. Miroslav and I enjoyed some very rich conversations over the grant period, and his help on the ideas in this book are clear. Others from the Center have become good friends. I'm thankful for the support and wisdom of Sarah F. Farmer and Angela Gorrell. Ryan McAnnally-Linz, the managing director, was kind enough to read the first half of the manuscript, offering very helpful feedback. Drew Collins also read the first half, offering helpful insights on David Foster

Wallace. Drew and I had more than one good night of eating, drinking, and laughing at grant meetings.

Over three springs, the Joy and Adolescent Faith and Flourishing group of the grant met in some beautiful places. We joked that Skip was trying to hit all the destinations of the Beach Boys' song "Kokomo." We made it to Key Largo and Bermuda before the grant was finished. My wife, Kara, called these trips "scholar spring break." Yet what made them so great was less the location and more the people. I offer thanks to David White, Almeda Wright, Caroline Ainsworth, Mark Berner, Fred Edie, Mark Gornik, Dave Rahn, Rodger Nishioka, Anne E. Streaty Wimberly, Pam King, and Kenda Dean for support and inspiration. Additional gratitude goes to Kenda, who took the time to read the whole manuscript and offered wonderfully insightful feedback. Kenda deserves thanks for so much in my academic life.

Trusted and beloved friends David Wood, Blair Bertrand, Wes Ellis, Abigail Rusert, Jon Wasson, Bård Eirik Hallesby Norheim, and Mike King were kind enough to read through the manuscript. These people both understand the trajectory of my previous work and are some of the best readers I know. Their feedback was excellent, and I'm thankful for their important friendship. I'd like also to thank Nancy Lee Gauche for her friendship and brilliance in our mutual work at Luther Seminary. Working again with Baker Academic, particularly Bob Hosack and Eric Salo, has been an amazing gift. They, in every way, made this book better.

Finally, as usual, I need to thank Kara Root for wading through the whole manuscript, editing it for public exposure. She always asks the best questions. Her astute mind and able editing have been an amazing gift to the projects I've been blessed to share.

One

Toward a Journey to Joy

LATE MARCH

There's a palpable feeling of connectedness and warmth. I'm sitting in a youth group gathering, but not really. There are as many adults, and even children, as adolescents. I sit in the corner just soaking it in, trying hard to put my finger on what I'm experiencing. I'd heard about this supposed youth group, or whatever it is, and its youth pastor, Janna, from a friend. Janna, or J as all her friends call her (a nickname that has stuck since she was a first-year camp counselor), was nice enough to invite me to this weekly gathering.

I've been on a journey for the past six months, and now, in early spring, with winter slowly melting away and the days growing longer, all my trails have led here. I've been teaching and training youth workers and writing about youth ministry for over fifteen years. And yet six months ago I had an encounter that made me question what youth ministry is really for. I realized I was not sure how I'd answer if I were given a fill-in-the-blank question, "Youth ministry is for _____."

This realization brought a sinking feeling that would send anyone searching either for an answer or for a new vocation. I chose the former. Now, six months into my search, I am sitting in this nondescript church fellowship hall. The warmth and connection bring up a sense of anticipation, like I am close to receiving the key I've been looking for.

Over the next hour, three people—a man in his fifties, a woman in her early thirties, a boy in tenth grade—get up and tell stories. Their stories all are in response to the same text and prompt. The text is Matthew 19:16–30, the story

1

of the rich young ruler, and the prompt is, "Tell about a time when the good was a difficult or confusing surprise." Music, laughter, tears, and friendship encase the stories as much as the four walls of the fellowship hall. It's beautiful, an example of a youth ministry that is much more than an adolescent religious holding pen. It's something unique I haven't experienced before. But this alone isn't the key I've been searching for over the past six months.

With the last fifteen minutes, J comes forward and laces these three stories together, drawing people deeper into the text, teaching on it through these three stories of faith and witness. She focuses in on the rich young ruler calling Jesus "good" and Jesus telling him that only God is good. She then invites the room to gather into groups of three or four, making sure each group has at least one young person and one not-so-young person. In these groups they end the night by praying for one another.

As people slowly prepare to depart, I wait awkwardly at the back of the room. J and I have agreed to talk afterward. When nearly everyone has gone and J is able to take a breath, she motions me to a table. To my surprise a young woman joins her. As we sit J says, "This is Lorena. She's in twelfth grade." I'm not sure why Lorena has joined us, but I'm happy to meet her.

I start with the obvious, asking, "What made you think of this kind of gathering?"

J starts somewhere else, needing to give me context. "About two years ago I was days from quitting or, more likely, being fired. It was miserable. I was just a few years out of college, and my only youth ministry experience was a summer at camp. I was pretty good at the whole counselor thing, so I thought, *No problem. Youth ministry in a church is just being a camp counselor year-round.* I'd been the chief counselor of fun that summer. And so this church seemed like a perfect fit. The church wanted someone who'd create events and an overall program that kids would find fun. I knew it was deeper than just entertainment. The idea was that if young people were having fun, then they'd have positive feelings about church and stick around."

"I could see that," I say.

"But nine months into it, it started eating me up," J continues. "I mean, it's one thing to be the chief counselor of fun for a week, then reboot with totally different kids for another week. But how do you do that in the day-to-day of church life? I knew things weren't going well. And the more I tried to make things fun, the more energy left the youth ministry and me."

"So what happened?" I ask.

"Well, a few people on the personnel committee started hinting that things weren't working, and my senior pastor took some steps to both encourage me and hold me accountable. But they all just kept coming back to fun: 'Teach them the Bible in a fun way,' 'Connect with them and have fun,' 'Make church a fun experience for my ninth-grade son.' As if fun were freedom instead of a chain around my whole body."

Intrigued, I ask again, "So what happened?"

"*She* did," J says, pointing to Lorena.

Surprised by the response, but now clear on why Lorena is sitting with us, I inquire of the teen, "What did you do?"

With a cutting, dry sense of humor that makes her seem older than twelfth grade, Lorena responds, "Oh, I just got some fluid around my heart and almost died."

I can only hold my breath.

J then says, with equal measures of sincerity and sarcasm that nevertheless reveal a deep truth, "Having a kid in your ministry fighting for her life after some freak infection—*that* will change things for the chief counselor of fun pretty quickly. That will make youth ministry for something very different than just fun."

Without realizing it, J has referenced the phrase that I've been journeying to answer. My heartbeat quickens. I had not anticipated that I'd ask this question so early in our conversation, yet here it is. "If youth ministry isn't for fun—because you watched Lorena almost die—then what is youth ministry for?"

J and Lorena look at each other and smile. Then Lorena says with bright eyes, "Joy."

I let this odd response run over me. It isn't quite computing. I'm not aware in the moment that it's indeed the key for which I've been searching. Instead, I'm only confused. *Youth ministry is for joy*, I say silently to myself with incredulity. Over the past fifteen years of teaching and writing, I've focused on the cross and the experience of suffering. And here it is again—Lorena almost died, and J nearly burned out. But when they answer what youth ministry is for, J and Lorena don't say *support* or *commiseration* but, oddly, *joy*.

What does joy have to do with the cross? More concretely, what does joy have to do with youth ministry? These questions push me further into confusion. Yet I'm aware that throughout this journey moments of confusion have been the birth pains of new insight. So, like swimming with a current, I don't fight the confusion but let it have me. As I do, I flash back to early fall.

I can feel, even taste, the sensations of school being back in session, the still-warm weather reminding me of the summer now over, and the trees showing no signs of change. I'm arriving at a youth ministry conference, the place this intellectual and vocational journey began. There's a young man. I can clearly see his face. But I can't remember his name.

Two

Don't Waste Your Life

Youth Ministry and the Good Life

SEPTEMBER

I'm bad with names. I think it was Graham. But while his name escapes me, his statement shook me. Something about it moved me. What was behind the force of emotion, I wasn't sure. It just caught me. Now snared, I couldn't tell if I agreed or disagreed with what Graham said. In those moments when we feel like a statement, perspective, or idea unexpectedly hits us, we often go primal. So I started to size Graham up, planting him in categories I shouldn't have, wondering if he was more conservative or liberal than I was, if he was brilliant or an idiot, a friend or looking for a fight. But even with my primal Sorting Hat to protect me, I couldn't shake it.

Graham, this young youth worker I had just met, told me over coffee at a youth ministry conference that, for him, "youth ministry is for helping kids not waste their lives."

It felt like such an odd statement. *Not waste their lives?* I repeated it in my head. It just seemed weird.

Aware of my internal reaction, I tried to hide the skepticism that had entered my nervous system. I worked hard to keep my face from contorting like I had just tasted something icky. I decided my best option to keep this from happening was to freeze. So as if I were a cold stone statue, I shamefully sized Graham up, trying to discern where this odd statement was coming from.

Without much of a reaction from me, Graham had to pick up our conversation. His face showed that he worried his statement didn't connect, not realizing it had done the opposite. So he asked, "What do *you* think youth ministry is for?"

Unfreezing my body and shaking the Sorting Hat from my head, I found myself saying, "God."

Reading Graham's face, I now assumed that he had put on his own Sorting Hat.

The rest of the long weekend his statement kept haunting me: *Youth ministry is for helping young people not waste their lives.* Could that be true? I had to concede: it is an amazing fact that we are the kind of animals—the only animals—who can waste our lives. Deer or even dogs don't seem capable of this kind of misuse. Of course, it's such a waste for a young healthy dog to be put down because we haven't heeded Bob Barker's pleas and had our pets spayed and neutered, controlling the pet population. But we'd never blame this on the pet, contending that Max the beagle had wasted his life. We'd never be tempted to judge poor Max for the shame of wasting his days.

But this is not true with human beings. For us it is more than possible. It's an always lurking threat that one of us, or maybe a whole society of us, will waste our lives. The possibility that we're wasting our lives can awaken us in a cold sweat in the middle of the night. Regardless of period or place in human history, it has always been possible for a human life to be misdirected and therefore mis-lived. There seems to be nothing more tragic than to recognize a life squandered. Midlife can be a crisis because halfway through we wonder if we've missed life. Nothing seems to haunt us, especially us late modern people, more than the thought of wasting our *own* lives and living in regret.

I was starting to think Graham had a point. Yet later that same day I met a college student. (I do remember her name; it was Kathryn.) Kathryn told me that she was a youth ministry major on the cusp of graduation. She was conflicted about going to seminary and wanted to talk. She asked me earnestly, with a stab of panic, "How do I know if God wants me to go to seminary? I'd just hate to miss what I'm supposed to do with my life."

To be human is to sense—is to deeply *believe*—that there is a direction to our lives, that there is indeed a *good* way to live and, in turn, a real possibility of missing it. That's what led Kathryn to want to talk. To assume that a life can be wasted is to admit that there is a bad way, a way in opposition to the good way. To not waste your life is to live a good life. We don't hold deer and dogs accountable for wasting their lives, because their way of living is bound not in visions of the good but in instinct. A goose flies south not in a direct quest for the good but because it's instinctual. It may be good for the goose to fly south, but it is not a quest for the good that fuels the goose's motivation.

Human beings, on the other hand, are always directly pursuing some kind of good, deciding to move south because it seems good, because it opens the possibility of living a good life, and therefore welcoming other goods. For a human being, the good of moving south promises more goods like leisure, or time with family, or experiences in nature, or less income tax, or more lucrative employment, or more enjoyable weather, or more meaningful work—or maybe all of these goods in different measure.[1]

Of course, unlike a goose, a human being knows that a move south will also cost her something. She'll have to give up things in her old city that made her life good. She'll have to say goodbye to (the goods of) old friends and her favorite restaurant. She'll miss the changing seasons and leave her church community. But although she'll grieve the loss of these goods, she'll let go, because she senses that she is moving toward a better life ("a gooder life," to talk like a four-year-old).[2] She leaves one constellation of goods for another because she senses (even wagers) that these other goods are better; they give her a real possibility of living a good life, a full or fuller life,[3] ultimately a life

1. "When Taylor argues that there is an inescapably 'moral' dimension to human subjectivity, he is not saying that all human agents must be concerned with the welfare of others. His claim is that recognizable human agency involves some grasp, however inchoate or inarticulate, of the contrast between mere life and good life. It is the loss of this sense that Taylor relates to an identity crisis." Nicholas H. Smith, *Charles Taylor: Meaning, Morals and Modernity* (Cambridge: Polity, 2002), 94.

2. "Taylor is convinced that an orientation to the good is not something that we can do without because the direction of our lives is not static; in fact it is more properly understood in terms of 'becoming.' Analogously, the good that orients us is also something not fully realized. The good that orients us and indicates the direction of our lives is something of a heuristic. Thus, my understanding of the good has to be woven into my developing understanding of my life as an unfolding story, a narrative. Simply put, the shape of this good stands in relation to the unfolding narrative of our life. As a heuristic, the good can be 'some action, or motive, or style, which is seen as qualitatively superior.'" Brain J. Braman, *Meaning and Authenticity: Bernard Lonergan and Charles Taylor on the Drama of Authentic Human Existence* (Toronto: University of Toronto Press, 2008), 38.

3. James McEvory explains, through Taylor, what I mean by fullness: "A fundamental claim about human existence . . . concerns what Taylor calls 'fullness,' by which he means that we humans live in relation to some place, activity, or condition in which lies a fullness; in relation to which 'life is fuller, richer, deeper, more worthwhile, more admirable, more what it should be.'" *Leaving Christendom for God: Church-World Dialogue in a Secular Age* (Lanham, MD: Lexington Books, 2014), 6, citing Taylor, *A Secular Age* (Cambridge, MA: Belknap, 2007), 5.

that is flourishing.[4] She leaves the good of Ohio because she believes her life will flourish, will be fuller, in Florida.[5]

So we human beings fly south never out of pure instinct, but rather because we have an explicit or implicit sense of the good.[6] It is toward a good that we're moved.[7] And this means, whether expressed or unexpressed, that we want to live a good life, and we desperately don't want to waste it. Every human being wants to taste the good life.[8] Every parent wants their child's life to go well, wants their child to flourish. Maybe Graham was right, maybe youth ministry is for helping kids not waste their lives. Or to say it more positively, youth ministry is for helping young people live a good life; youth ministry is to help young people flourish.

Yet, to be honest, once I shifted his statement toward the positive, from *not wasting* to *flourishing*, I quickly got a stomachache. It was like sucking down a candy-cane milkshake. The first few sips were amazing but were quickly replaced by a sweet, sugary overload, leaving me more repelled than satisfied. I found myself refuting myself by returning to my awkward response to Graham. When he asked me what I thought youth ministry was for, I said, "God" (*duh*). But now I wondered if my stupidity didn't have a point. Why would you need God to *not* waste your life? Can't you flourish without God?[9] Aren't many people doing just this? To see youth ministry as ultimately for flourishing would seem to make it little more than a form of group therapy or life coaching for teens.

As I talked with Kathryn, the youth ministry major, about seminary, she triggered these concerns in me. With the same earnestness, but now more confidence, she said, "Plus, youth ministry is so *hard*. I experienced that in my

4. Miroslav Volf defines *flourishing*, saying, "The good life consists not merely in succeeding in one or another endeavor we undertake, whether small or large, but in living into our human and personal fullness—that, in a word, is a flourishing life." *Flourishing: Why We Need Religion in a Globalized World* (New Haven: Yale University Press, 2015), ix.

5. Alasdair MacIntyre supports this: "We learn what our common good is, and indeed what our own individual goods are, not primarily and never only by theoretical reflection, but in everyday shared activities and the evaluations of alternatives that those activities impose." *Dependent Rational Animals: Why Human Beings Need the Virtues* (Chicago: Open Court, 1999), 136. He adds, "So humans are goal-directed in virtue of their recognition of goods specific to their nature to be achieved" (23).

6. The whole of Charles Taylor's philosophical anthropology is to make this point. From his dissertation and first book (*Explanation of Behaviour*) on shortcomings of behaviorism to *The Language Animal* nearly fifty years later, he has been making this very point.

7. We are "moral, believing animals," to quote Christian Smith. See *Moral, Believing Animals: Human Personhood and Culture* (Oxford: Oxford University Press, 2003).

8. See Iris Murdoch, *The Sovereignty of Good* (London: Routledge, 2013), for more on the ranking of goods.

9. The fact that it is now assumed possible to have a flourishing or good life without God is the story that Charles Taylor seeks to tell in *A Secular Age*.

practicum class this fall. I volunteered at a church by my school." I paused, looking for clarification on what she meant by "hard." Kathryn continued, "I mean, families are so busy, and parents seem to prioritize so many things above church." I nodded, which gave her confidence to continue, so she leaned in harder to her point. "I don't blame them. In high school, gymnastics was so important to me, and I always missed church during our final meet season in March and April. So sometimes I wonder if I'd have an impact on more young people by being a coach. At least you're not begging them to come and pushing them to be passionate about something they're not." I nodded my head quickly, affirming that she was onto something important.

I was now feeling torn. Watching Kathryn wrestle with these questions clearly showed that she was desperate to not waste her life. She was comparing goods, probing for what it means to live a good life. At the same time, Kathryn revealed that this quest for a good life can be met by all sorts of means, and for many—even this youth ministry major—church is not judged to be the highest good in embracing a flourishing life. Youth ministry is nice but not an essential component in having a life that's going well.

Sitting with Kathryn, I started to ask myself new questions, like, *If we're to assume that youth ministry is for helping young people live a good life, to flourish, then what makes youth ministry different from gymnastics or an after-school program or AAU basketball? And can youth ministry really compete with these activities in the game of flourishing?* Kathryn didn't think so. I thought she might be right. Do we really naively assume parents would choose youth group, a mission trip, or confirmation over nationals, first chair, or a state championship?

I'd assume most parents, let alone young people, wouldn't, and Kathryn knew it for sure, making her wonder if she'd be more impactful (and flourish more in her own vocation) if she pivoted into coaching instead of youth ministry. Walking the halls of the conference convention center, I realized that to see whether Kathryn's and my assumptions were true, I'd need to think more closely about activities like gymnastics, after-school programs, and AAU basketball, seeing how these activities play their part in producing a presumed good life (a life not wasted) for young people.

Competing for the Good

As I said above, I believe that all parents (with only the most grotesque exceptions) want what is best (or good) for their children (as Jesus said in Luke 11:11–12, "Which of you fathers, if your son asks for a fish, will give him a snake instead? Or if he asks for an egg, will give him a scorpion?"). Ask any parent and they'll say that the reason they invest a lot of time and money in any of their kids' activities is for the sake of flourishing. In an economically challenged family, a parent works two jobs, exhausting herself, because she wants her children to flourish—to have full stomachs and freedom to play their sports and to make it to college someday.

Parents believe that ballet, piano, hockey, and debate provide their children with goods to flourish. The goods of making friends, developing skills, learning hard work, staying active, finding their passion, and being happy become the motivation for a parent to get up at 6:00 a.m. on a Saturday and drive the carpool. This parent is up, coffee in hand, because she, too, wants to live a good life. She wants to be a good parent. And a *good* middle-class parent, who is living a good life, gets her kids involved in a menu of activities so that they might flourish and she might feel good about being a good mom.

But as I said above, human beings not only seek to live a good life now but also have a deeply intuitive sense that flourishing is something to seek. It's a quest, an aim—there is always a future dynamic to it. Wasting our lives is such a huge fear because we not only can waste present moments and opportunities but also worry that such opportunities will never come again. Missing these opportunities, we can get stuck in a rut, which means a wasted future. And, of course, we don't know exactly when these opportunities to enter the currents of a good life will arise (we often don't even know in the middle of them!). But we do know that it is a deep shame to miss your opportunity and be cursed with regret—which is why Kathryn wanted to talk in the first place.

So parents drive the carpool at 6:00 a.m. not only so their kids can have the goods of friends, skills, confidence, and fun now, but also so they can flourish in the future. Ballet, hockey, and traveling boys' choir, it's believed, place young people on a certain path that promises flourishing in the future. It's worth fighting and paying for your kids to be on the AAA team or have a renowned coach because not only can parents take some pride in their kid's achievement (giving him a sense of his own flourishing) but, as a higher good, parents can feel like they have opened doors and set their kid up to flourish in the future. They have made it possible for their kid to have a good life (maybe even a great life) by going to a top college on scholarship, meeting the right people, and playing in the NHL.

If youth ministry is for helping kids not waste their lives, if we even contend that youth ministry is to help young people flourish, then it appears that youth ministry has lost. The cultural goods have been set up against youth ministry. Anyone running a confirmation program senses this.

Confirmation is an interesting case study because, at least in some traditions, it remains an activity that demands commitment, while also having a clear end point that provides a symbolic marker of accomplishment. In other words, in most confirmation programs, if you want to be confirmed on Confirmation Sunday, you *have to* show up, go on the retreat, and write a faith statement. To receive the good of being confirmed, you have to meet even a minimal bar of commitment.[10]

The Confirmation Case Study

Most parents in churches with confirmation programs want their kids to participate and be confirmed. Confirmation remains a good. But because we are finite beings with limited time and energy, goods must always be tacitly ranked.[11] No human being can escape the necessity of this ranking. Some goods are better, more valuable than others—why else would a human being from Ohio relocate to Florida? What makes some goods more valuable is our perception that these goods more directly help us in our quest to live a full life.[12] It would be good to live in Hawaii, but the taxes and a Christmas flight back to Ohio are way more costly; therefore it feels better—gooder—to live in Florida. Often, when it comes to parents' decisions about their children, the goods that promise flourishing in the future are weighted more than those that might support, but not drive us into, future horizons of living a full and good life.

What's so frustrating about leading a confirmation program (or any youth ministry activity that calls for commitment) is that confirmation remains a good. Confirmation hasn't been rejected as evil or even meaningless. This gives the

10. This is what Kathryn was feeling. A Barna study reports, "Comparing responses of youth pastors in the 2013 study with today's research, Barna found that major ministry challenges had dramatically changed in three years. Although kids' busy schedules remain the top concern, slightly fewer leaders mention it today (74%) than in 2013 (86%). Lack of interest from parents (34% vs. 41% 2013) and the breakdown of families (24% vs. 31% 2013) are also a bit less pressing than three years ago. However, the percentage of youth pastors who say they are taxed by a need for adult volunteers has increased; in 2013, about one in five youth pastors expressed that the lack of adult volunteers was the main challenge facing their ministry (22%), compared to about three in 10 today (29%)." Barna Group, *The State of Youth Ministry: How Churches Reach Today's Teens—and What Parents Think about It* (Ventura, CA: Barna, 2016), 33.

11. Taylor makes this point with his discussion of hypergoods (i.e., goods that are more important than others and that become the standard by which all goods are judged). To say that goods must be ranked is not to fall into rational choice theory but is to assume that all evaluation is done for a moral horizon, for the sake of living a better, *gooder*, life.

12. "One of the problems for individuals in the modern world is that, according to Taylor, we face a wider array of different goods." Ruth Abbey, *Charles Taylor* (Princeton: Princeton University Press, 2000), 12. Abbey continues, "The term 'strong evaluation' captures Taylor's belief that individuals rank some of their desires, or the goods that they desire, as qualitatively higher or more worthy than others. The term refers, therefore, to distinctions of worth that individuals make regarding their desires or the objects of their desires" (17).

youth worker a sense that confirmation has value—a positive valuation in the intuitive ranking of goods.[13] But while confirmation is still a good, its ranking has slid. This is exasperating. Parents are committed enough to add it to the list of activities, even willing to come to a September meeting and pledge their commitment. *It would be really good*, they think, *for Theresa to be confirmed.* This is something they want. But when the good of confirmation collides with other goods, like the need for piano practice, a hockey tournament, a Thursday morning test, or even a night off before a big swim meet, confirmation is relativized as less important. Better (gooder!) to not go to confirmation so you're ready for the test or rested for the meet. The test and meet are intuitively ranked as higher goods. They are activities that deliver more important goods today. But what gives them even more weight is their perceived ability to provide essential goods for living a good life tomorrow—like producing the social capital and work ethic needed to get into a good college and make a good living.

Of course, a higher-ranking good would not experience the same evaluation, and therefore fate, as confirmation. Sleep, or study of the Bible, is not as *good* and therefore as necessary as a playoff game or big concert. And because of our cultural ranking of goods, it is very rare (and becoming more so) for a parent to say no to a championship game because "we have church." Even rarer is for parents to assert that their son will need to skip Tuesday night's late practice so he's rested and ready for confirmation. (That's almost laughable, which shows how intrinsic this ranking of goods is within us; even devoted Christians and church professionals would giggle at the thought.)

Spiritual engagement and religious ritual are still regarded as good, but parents (again, often intuitively) have to ask themselves, "Is it a higher good than seeing my daughter happily engaged on the court, or gaining confidence and pride by mastering the piano?" And, just as powerfully, "Do I feel like a better parent, like I'm closer to a good life, if my kid is happy, passionate, confident, and skilled?"

But even if the parent were to go countercultural and rank the goods of confirmation and basketball as equal, believing that confirmation provides

---

13. Charles Taylor explores this ranking of good: "The man who flees seeks a good, safety. But we condemn him: he ought to have stood. For there is a higher good, the safety of the polis, which was here at stake. The judgment involves ranking goods, hence ranking motivations (since these are defined by their consummations, which is what we are calling 'goods' in this context). It is because this involves ranking motivations that speak of it as strong evaluation. It means that we are not taking our de facto desires as the ultimate in justification, but are going beyond that to their worth. We are evaluating not just objects in the light of our desires, but also the desires themselves. Hence strong evaluation has also been called 'second order' evaluation." *Human Agency and Language: Philosophical Papers 1* (Cambridge: Cambridge University Press, 1999), 166. We will get back to strong evaluation later in the book.

connections, character development, hope, and faith, she'd still have to contend with the ranking of goods next to the horizon of the future. She'd wonder whether skipping a violin lesson or basketball practice in order to attend a confirmation class would hurt her child's opportunities to get into a good college and therefore live a good life in the future. To add to this, what if her child is meant to be a professional musician or basketball player? These are highly esteemed vocations, promising to deliver a full life.

So each parent has to ask, "Is my kid flourishing more (feeling like her life is going well) when she is learning about the Small Catechism or jubilantly jumping on a pile of teammates after winning a tournament? Where is she happier? And what would a good life for my child even look like if I chose confirmation over hockey or the piano recital? How does spiritual engagement and a religious tradition prepare my child for a flourishing life more than playing in the Pee Wee A Regional Two championship game?" The marks of flourishing today and tomorrow seem so much clearer next to a Pee Wee championship than confirmation.

The Big Feel

A big task for parents, then, in an overly scheduled middle-class America where there are more opportunities than time, is to rank these activities.[14] And this ranking of activities happens not through committee hearings or even some equation. It is seldom a directly rational, calculated decision at all.[15] Yet because the decision is made for the sake of goods—to live a good life—it is, fundamentally, a *moral* decision.[16] In other words, pouring more energy, time,

14. It would take a whole other book to explore why over the past few generations we've shifted from the good of young people having free space and time to an overly scheduled existence, leaving some to push back against the perceived good of overscheduling with a competing good, like free-range kids, that tries to return to the good of childhood space, freedom, and roaming. See Lenore Skenazy's book *Free-Range Kids* (San Francisco: Jossey-Bass, 2010).

15. James Davison Hunter adds, "Needless to say, children and adults alike rarely relate to moral cultures as full-blown ethical systems. Who has time to master the intricacies of philosophical traditions and their evolution? Most people are too busy, pressed by the practical realities of daily life, to reflect much on how their personal opinions are shaped by larger cultural influences. Yet moral culture still frames their lives. More often than not these moral cultures exist for people as perhaps crudely formed assumptions about what is true and false; what is right and wrong; what is honest and corrupt and so on. Yet, however crudely formed in our minds, however inarticulate we may be about them, our personal grasp of these assumptions relates back to larger moral traditions or styles of moral reasoning in the culture." *The Death of Character: Moral Education in an Age without Good and Evil* (New York: Basic Books, 2000), 25.

16. Paul Bloom points to how deep this sense of the moral goes: "Even a pleasure such as the satisfaction of hunger is affected by concerns about essence and history, moral purity and moral defilement. There is always a depth to pleasure." *How Pleasure Works: The New Science of Why We Like What We Like* (New York: Norton, 2010), 53.

and money into piano rather than confirmation just feels like the right thing to do. It feels so right that many parents don't even stop to imagine that there is a choice to be made. And, in turn, this *feels* depressing to youth workers, enough to make Kathryn wonder if she should do something else with her life.

The moral decisions that shape our actions and reveal our deepest-held goods are not cold, rational computations but most often reflexes. It's not that reason and rational evaluation don't play a part. We add up the costs all the time, counting the hours and dollars. But even this rationalizing gives us a feeling. Whatever decision we make has to *feel right*. That's what makes things so frustrating for Kathryn. If asked, most parents wouldn't come right out and say, "Oh, yeah, basketball and piano are *way* more important than confirmation." And yet, like a reflex, this is what they find themselves choosing. Most, if asked to really think through which activities are most important, would access some insulated, rational evaluative zone and admit church should be a priority.[17]

But this is not how people make decisions. We don't make moral evaluations in sanitized rational zones. Rather, we decide what is good by *feel* (I'm leaning on Jonathan Haidt's important work on how people make decisions).[18] Parents choose piano over confirmation because it feels right, period. And that last sentence shouldn't be read as a pejorative statement of shaming, as if to say, "These evil parents are so shallow or corrupted by the world that they make moral decisions by feel." We *all* figure out what's right by feel.[19]

For example, imagine being on a cross-country flight. About halfway through, after a short snooze, you wake up to see that the man in the middle seat next to you has taken off his shoes and socks. You quickly realize that he's not only barefoot but has one foot on his knee and is cutting his toenails, unconcerned that the debris from discarded nails are flying all over your row. Most North Americans would assert that this is bad—dare I say, immoral.

---

17. For instance, we ask parents to say youth group is as important as their child's sport, but my argument is that this is exactly the evaluative-free zone that leads them to overreport the importance of youth ministry. The Barna study says, "In the constellation of non-school activities, Christian parents generally consider involvement in youth group to be of equal importance with extracurricular activities (55%), while three in ten say it is more important (8% much more, 22% somewhat more). In general, higher education levels correlate to a higher value on youth-group involvement." *State of Youth Ministry*, 30.

18. See Haidt's *The Happiness Hypothesis: Finding Modern Truth in Ancient Wisdom* (New York: Basic Books, 2006) and *The Righteous Mind: Why Good People Are Divided by Politics and Religion* (New York: Vintage, 2012) for more on this moral feel.

19. "Thus, even when we are inarticulate about the moral cultures we live in or operate by, when their principles, maxims, and habits are internalized deep in our consciousness, they act as moral compasses, providing the bearings by which we navigate the challenges of life. Far from a philosophical abstraction, moral culture guides our behavior, thinking, and expectations of others. Consciously or not, we refer to these compasses constantly, not only when we are confronted by moral dilemmas but in the rhythms of everyday life." Hunter, *Death of Character*, 25.

It is *never* a good—it never gives you a feeling of living a good life—to be sprinkled with some stranger's toenail clippings. When you get off the flight, you'll recap the incident in moral terms: "It just isn't right for someone to do that. It's so gross! I was totally repulsed. I mean, seriously, who does that! Why didn't the flight attendant stop him? That's just wrong!"

These are all deeply moral assertions ("it isn't right," "who does that," "that's just wrong"). But you're pushed into these moral assertions not through taking a philosophy class on moral reasoning or reading an article in the *Atlantic* on the capital costs of toenail litter, but rather because you feel repelled ("it's so gross," "I was totally repulsed"). You can only wonder, *Who does this?*—essentially asking, *What kind of person thinks it's right or good to cut their toenails on a flight?*—because through *feel* you are making judgments about what is good. It isn't right to cut your toenails on a flight, and the flight attendants should intervene, because such acts keep those in the toenail cutter's row from feeling like life is going well (from having an unreflective sense of things being good). You want someone to act, or end up acting yourself, because you *feel* a sense of moral violation.

All this toenail business is just to highlight that in very practical ways we're always making moral decisions, choosing what is right by *feel*. And this is what's so hard about leading confirmation. From some rational and emotion-free space, parents might reason that confirmation is just as important as ballet (or even more so). But they don't make these rankings here. They make them more intuitively as they *feel* dimly for the walls that shape a good life for themselves and their children.

If there is a concrete place where these decisions of ranking are made, a location where the *feel* gets practically implemented, for most parents it's through Google Calendar. Google Calendar is the place that both necessitates and allows for the ranking of goods through feel.

Say Hello to Our Overload: Google Calendar

What I mean is that parents *feel* their way into ranking their kids' activities through scheduling. They decide (better, they find themselves deciding) which activities are essential, and which are secondary and can be skipped, when schedules conflict. That's why it isn't helpful to ask parents which activities are more important in some hypothetical space disconnected from the feel of the weekly schedule. All these activities parents consider to be good (they provide ways for their child to live a good life now and in the future). But when there is a scheduling conflict, goods are quickly ranked.

Parents worry, as much as (probably more than) their kids, that their children will miss the opportunities to live a good life. Parents are under amazing pressure in our time not only to not waste their *own* lives but also to make sure their children don't either. To be in charge of the calendar, then, is to be responsible for ranking the goods and setting the trajectory for a life not wasted. So parents set the schedule by what feels right. This is an incredible amount of responsibility and pressure to place on mom's or dad's shoulders.

Parents of tweens and teens spend a lot of time feeling their way into which activities their children will partake in. There seems to be a never-ending multitude of sports, clubs, lessons, divisions, and tutors to choose from. But the pressure doesn't really stem from the menu of options. The tension is around how to schedule them all. And when it becomes clear that not all desired activities can be scheduled and some must be peeled off, which ones do we choose? Which ones are the *best* (the *goodest*) for our son or daughter?

"It would be good for Erik to go to confirmation, but not if it means missing a lesson with Mr. Sutton. He's one of the *best* piano teachers in the country, and Erik has a really *good* opportunity he can't miss. I'd *feel* terrible if we had to reschedule. I'd *feel* worse if we missed this opportunity to be one of Mr. Sutton's regulars." Or another parent might say, "It would be *good* for Amanda to go on the confirmation retreat—she'd make better friends, learn about the Bible, be more engaged spiritually, and feel more connected to church. But Saturday is volleyball tryouts, and she has a really *good* chance to make varsity as a freshman. I'd *feel* terrible if she missed the opportunity to make better friends, learn how to compete and work hard, stay active, and feel connected to her school. Plus"—and this is where even if the present goods of confirmation can somehow rival those of volleyball, the projection of future goods can't—"if she makes the team as a freshman, she might be on the road to a scholarship. That *feels* exciting, and I'd hate for her to miss that chance. I couldn't live with myself, I'd *feel* guilty, if we squandered this *good* opportunity."

And of course this is even more complicated, because many variables are involved. Some activities cost more in a sense of time and money, some are better for the mind and others for the body, and some your son is just plain more passionate about—which makes it more possible to feel that the investment is worth the cost. For instance, you may prefer that your kid go to confirmation, but he may hate it, especially if it means missing an activity he likes more. So you concede, because it is *no good* and *feels* terrible to fight with him every Wednesday night. The constant arguing keeps you both from feeling like life is going well.

So weighting the goods by feel, you choose piano over confirmation. Or, to contrast similar activities, you choose swimming over hockey (two activities your daughter enjoys). You pick swimming over hockey because while they are about the same price, swimming is only three nights a week and fewer weekends. This allows time to do one night of karate and piano lessons, while still providing enough time to get homework done. "That feels right." And to finalize the decision, "it's what Jackie wants," meaning she'll be more committed to the activity, which will allow her the best chance to harvest the activity's intrinsic goods, which will make the financial and time investment feel worth it.

But even after the decision, parents feel stuck and wonder, *Did we make the right choice, picking swimming over hockey?* Once this decision is made, there is no going back. *One winter without hockey and Jackie will never again have a chance to play on the AAA team. Does she really know what she's picking? What if she changes her mind? What if she could have been a great player, and now we allowed her to miss that opportunity? What a waste! That would feel terrible!*

The pressure is so heavy because once the activities are ranked through their goods, we question if we've made the right decision, if our *feel* was right. What if lacrosse or Spanish lessons—no, wait, maybe Mandarin—would be better? Because these activities are to prepare young people not just for present but also future flourishing, the parent who makes these decisions is squeezed with pressure. And it feels at the time like acute pressure, because the parent isn't just making a schedule but doing a moral act of ranking goods that have deep and long ramifications—the consequence of setting up children to flourish and keeping them from the dangers of a wasted life.

Yet what is interesting, and what gets us back again to confirmation, is that rarely do parents feel this same stuck anxiety when it comes to deciding between a youth group retreat and volleyball tryouts. They feel this when choosing between hockey and swimming, but often not hockey and church. This reality is what led Kathryn to consider other career options. It would be one thing if parents often came to youth workers conflicted, feeling stuck between the goods of basketball and confirmation. But this is rare. Most parents don't feel anxiety, because the goods of basketball are assumed to so outstrip the goods of confirmation that it feels right to choose it (and rarely with any accompanying anxiety). When practice and confirmation conflict, it is obvious which to choose. It feels like an easy decision.

To say that a choice between hockey and swimming could cause anxiety and ignite worries about wasted opportunities (and with too many wasted opportunities, a wasted life) is to reveal further how much these are moral decisions. It reveals that parents are searching for a *right* way to live, for a full life for both themselves and their children. But then to say that there is no choice, no conflicted feelings, when choosing between the confirmation retreat and volleyball, is to claim that for most parents confirmation is not essential in living a good life, not important in helping guard against a wasted life.[20]

I had the sense that Graham was onto something after all. Both young people and their parents are seeking for ways to not waste their lives. But Kathryn, too, was right. When it came to assessing which goods would add up to a good and full life, church and youth group were consistently downgraded.

Conclusion

As I left the conference, I was stuck. If youth ministry was for helping young people not waste their lives, what did that mean? And how could youth ministry possibly compete with all these other activities? The more I thought about it, the more I wanted to agree with Graham: youth ministry should have something to say about a good life. But the issues raised by Kathryn kept me in limbo. It seemed unfair to pit youth ministry against all the other activities in young people's lives, making youth ministry a defeating vocation.

That's why I wasn't quite ready to abandon my own stupid answer: that youth ministry was about God. Whether Sunday-school-lame or theologically presumptuous, such a statement allows us to opt out of the cultural competition. Young people, and more directly their parents, might not see (or better yet, feel) youth ministry as a high good. But who cares? We're about God. Yet I knew that without more attention my statement about God would be just a theologically arrogant way to justify meaningless ministry. Still, all this talk about goods, feel, and wasted lives did make me wonder about God's action and if youth ministry had always found itself in this pernicious place next to parents' and young people's vision of the good life.

So when I got to the airport, I decided to call Wes.

---

20. There is another layer to this I can't dig into. This sense of moral decision also has something to do with our sense of time. Hockey, basketball, and the school play all seem sped up. If you don't hurry to their activities, you lose the chance to gain their goods. Church seems slower and more long-term. Its goods aren't connected to speed. We do hockey now because it calls for us committing now. Church will always be there. Church may slide into the category of a family reunion. Most parents would choose the basketball tournament over the reunion, because another reunion is coming and there is no time crunch to participate. But if grandma is sick, if there is a crisis of time, then it would be assumed to be better (gooder) to miss the tournament. I'm thankful to Mike King for pointing out this sense of judgment being made next to the feel of time. In the upcoming third volume of the Ministry in a Secular Age series, I go more deeply into this (Baker Academic, forthcoming).

Three

Are the Kids OK?

Goods and Youth Ministry

SEPTEMBER

I met Wes years earlier at another youth ministry conference. But instead of talking to me about what youth ministry was for, Wes wanted to talk about Jürgen Moltmann. We sat on a bench outside Stuart Hall at Princeton Seminary on a beautiful spring day, two nerds in conversation for more than an hour. Since that spring day Wes had become a friend and helpful dialogue partner. So at the airport, I called him.

Wes was now a youth pastor in New Jersey and was still working on his dissertation. When he answered, I asked, without any pleasantries, "What do you think youth ministry is for?" He responded just as quickly, "To help young people encounter God." I was relieved that my "God" response to Graham wasn't without company.

But my conversation with Kathryn led me to respond, "And if they don't?" I knew my response opened me up to theological problems, and Wes didn't disappoint in pointing them out.

He said, "I'm not sure the focus should be on us and our ability to encounter God. God is the primary actor. I think this is the depth of the gospel. God moves to us, even when we can't, even when we're stuck; God arrives, bringing new life. I think the focus should be on God."

I knew this. I've tried as much as anyone to return youth ministry's attention to God's action that comes to us when goods seem absent and life *feels* nothing but empty—as opposed to full. It's a reality of every human life that we suffer. And in turn, for me, it is a deep theological commitment that God is a minister who meets us in these moments, turning what is dead into life. But this theological commitment doesn't obscure the fact that every human being, while experiencing nothingness, reaches for fullness. In these moments of suffering and nothingness we thirst so deeply for someone, for God, to meet us in our emptiness, because we yearn for fullness, for a good life. We pray for the nothingness (the sin we've done or has been done to us) to *not* render our lives a waste.[1]

Having been checkmated by Wes's theological response, I tried to find a better way to get at my concern, lit like a fuse by Graham. So, with Kathryn's words framing my imagination, I said, "But what about the parents connected to your ministry? What do they think youth ministry is for?"

Just as immediately, Wes responded with two words: "seeds" and "tools." I paused, confused, assuming for a few seconds that he was talking to someone else.

"What?" I said. "Is that for me? Is that your answer?"

"Yes," Wes responded, "that's what parents think youth ministry is for—seeds and tools." He expanded. "I mean, that's how I describe it. When parents talk about the importance of youth ministry, they say things like, 'I want them to understand God's acceptance; I want values like that planted in them. So, then, even if they leave the church, these seeds, these certain values, have been planted that can grow and maybe someday they'll return.' And then they add, 'I hope they learn some things they can use when things get tough in the future.' These are the tools. They hope these tools can help them avoid bad decisions."

I put my conversations with Graham and Wes together in my head: youth ministry is for helping young people not waste their lives by giving them seeds and tools. I wasn't sure that this understanding helped with the tensions that Kathryn had expressed. For these particular parents, youth ministry was still important, worth sliding up the scale of their intuitive ranking, even making room for it on the calendar, because of these seeds and tools. But this all seemed to add to Kathryn's concerns; youth ministry appeared subjugated to a secondary supportive role in the pursuit of a good life.

I wondered whether the parents in Wes's ministry assumed that without youth ministry, young people (and society as a whole) were at risk of wasting their lives. Probably not. But these parents seemed confident that youth ministry could provide seeds and tools on this quest for a good life. The seeds could become plants, which—even if they were not growing and blossoming—at least

---

1. This is all to say that the *theologia crucis*, which is at the heart of my work, is not in principle in opposition to this focus on fullness or a good life.

would give spiritual roots to a flourishing life delivered more directly through the goods of sports and college. And if a young person ever found herself caught in a rut, if despite all the good intentions of her parents and coaches she came frighteningly close to wasting her life, she could draw on the tools learned in youth ministry to find her way back to a good life.

"So it's totally utilitarian?" I asked Wes. "Youth ministry is in a supporting role? It's a safeguard or seatbelt. Totally worth it . . . if you have time."

"No, I don't think so," Wes replied, surprising me. "I agree that the wish for seeds and tools does have an overtone of safeguard and seatbelt, and if you asked, most parents couldn't access a deeper reason for youth ministry. But I think it's wrong to say that for them youth ministry is just utilitarian. These desires for seeds and tools touch something deeper."

I was intrigued, so I told Wes my thoughts about parents' and young people's quests for a good life. I explained how they feel their way into ranking goods and what that means for youth ministry. I concluded my minilecture by throwing things back to Wes, asking him, "So, how is this desire for seeds and tools something deeper than a safeguard or seatbelt on the drive to the harvesting of the goods from all these other activities, which more compellingly promise a good life not wasted?"

"Yeah, I see what you're getting at," Wes said. "But I think your point about this search for the good, for a full life, means that seeds and tools are deeper than just safeguards and seatbelts."

"How?"

"Because I think when parents say 'seeds,' they mean something connected to identity. I think parents recognize that the biggest task before their children is to construct an identity for themselves. And while parents can provide a bunch of activities as raw material their children can use to construct an identity, in the end it is solely up to the children. They know their children need to come to some understanding of who they are. I think parents simultaneously recognize that this is the core task for their children and sense that they have less control and influence on it than they'd hoped."

Wes continued, "Added to this, they're very aware that how their kids answer the identity question will affect their behavior. So the seeds the youth ministry sows are planted in the soil of their individual identities, making certain that particular values sprout. These sprouted values keep the soil of identity from erosion, keeping it fertile for a good life.[2] So it is a safeguard, but a deeper one than assumed."

2. James Davison Hunter defines and explores values, saying, "Values are truths that have been deprived of their commanding character. They are substitutes for revelation, imperatives

"And the tools?" I asked.

"Same kind of thing," Wes responded. "On the positive or productive end, these tools give young people ways to be happy. Parents want the youth ministry to provide the tools to avoid bad decisions so their kids can be happy by avoiding injury in venues other than church."

Wes paused and then continued, "To be honest, I often think this is the real driving force behind parents' involvement. They're so concerned about their kids being hurt that the youth ministry provides tools to avoid emotional injury. I often see that parents want kids to be safe more than even resilient. I guess getting the tools to avoid emotional injury will motivate you to come on Wednesday night!"

"Actually," Wes continued, "this is a big issue I see, and few youth workers are talking about it. I see parents and society as a whole slowing down young people's growing up, so afraid they'll get hurt and therefore be unhappy."

I hadn't thought of this before. But if the good has shifted to an overscheduled parenting style, in which parents work hard to give their children goods through multiple activities and full schedules, then it would make sense that growing up would, in some sense, slow down.[3]

---

that have dissolved into a range of possibilities. The very word 'value' signifies the reduction of truth to utility, taboo to fashion, conviction to mere preference; all provisional, all exchangeable. Both values and 'lifestyle'—a way of living that reflects the accumulation of one's values— bespeak a world in which nothing is sacred. Neither word carries the weight of conviction; the commitment to truths made sacred. Indeed, sacredness is conspicuous in its absence. There is nothing there that one need believe, commanding and demanding its due, for 'truth' is but a matter of taste and temperament. Formed against a symbolic order made up of 'values' and differing 'lifestyles' is the Self—malleable, endlessly developing, consuming, realizing, actualizing, perfecting—but again, something less than character." *The Death of Character: Moral Education in an Age without Good and Evil* (New York: Basic Books, 2000), xiv.

3. Jean Twenge describes this slowdown through Chloe, a young person she interviewed: "Chloe is more typical of her iGen peers than you might realize; fewer and fewer drink alcohol. Nearly 40% of iGen high school seniors in 2016 had never tried alcohol at all, and the number of 8th graders who have tried alcohol has been cut nearly in half." *iGen: Why Today's Super-Connected Kids Are Growing Up Less Rebellious, More Tolerant, Less Happy—and Completely Unprepared for Adulthood* (New York: Atria Books, 2017), 36. She continues, "Beginning with Millennial and then going full speed with iGen, adolescence is becoming shortened again—at the lower end. Childhood has lengthened, with teens treated more like children, less independent and more protected by parents than they once were. The entire developmental trajectory, from childhood to adolescence to adulthood, has slowed. Adolescence—the time when teens begin to do things adults do—now happens later. Thirteen-year-olds—and even 18-year-olds—are less likely to act like adults and spend their time like adults. They are more likely, instead, to act like children—not by being immature, necessarily, but by postponing the usual activities of adults. Adolescence is now an extension of childhood rather than the beginning of adulthood" (41). She adds, "Instead, it's more informative to employ the terms of life history theory, discussed earlier: teens have adopted a slow life strategy, perhaps due to smaller families and the demands wrought by increasing income inequality. Parents have the time to cultivate each

As the cabin door on my flight closed and the flight attendant gave me a stern look, I said to Wes, "If there is a slowdown happening for the sake of protection, this makes youth ministry for something very different than it was in the past."

"Sir, can you please put your phone in airplane mode?" the flight attendant said with a chipper tone but eyes of frustration.

"Got to go. Later, Wes."

Poop Bags and Hair Shirts

It's possible that youth ministry always shifts in response to moral transitions. It's beyond the scope of this project to give more than some snapshots of this transition below, but it would be interesting to map more extensively how new perspectives and forms of youth ministry are born in response to the shift of moral imagination. When the supposed goods that deliver a perceived full life shift, so does the form of youth ministry.

The moral—the feeling that there is a right way to live—is embedded in our humanity and the cultural structures we've built. Unlike geese, deer, and dogs, we are moral animals, always living out moral visions, always feeling our way into the world by seeking the good, by aiming for a full, well-lived life. And we are moral animals because we are believing animals.[4] Parents fill the family schedule and find themselves choosing piano lessons over confirmation because they believe it is good. It is what a good parent does, because it is good for her child. We believe that there is a right and good way to live. And not to find it is a waste. The moral constitution of our world is so deep, accessed through feel, that we often miss how much it affects us.

For instance, when I buy milk at Speedy Market, the corner store in my neighborhood, the college-aged checkout clerk will ask, "Do you want paper or plastic?" I often take this as a moral question. However I answer provides a narrative for this college-aged clerk to assume something about me and

---

child to succeed in the newly competitive economic environment, which might take twenty-one years when it once took sixteen. The cultural shift toward individualism may also play a role: childhood and adolescence are uniquely self-focused stages, so staying in them longer allows more cultivation of the individual self. With fewer children and more time spent with each, each child is noticed and celebrated. Sure enough, cultural individualism is connected to slower developmental speeds across both countries and time. Around the world, young adults grow up more slowly in individualistic countries than collectivistic ones. And as American culture has grown more individualistic from 1965 to the present, young adults have taken longer and longer to enter adult work and family roles" (42).

4. See Christian Smith, *Moral, Believing Animals: Human Personhood and Culture* (Oxford: Oxford University Press, 2003).

my ability to access a good life. He might be thinking about some YouTube video when I respond, but I assume first and foremost that he is interpreting me through moral categories.

If I say "plastic," I immediately feel an urge, which I've succumbed to more than once, to add awkwardly, "I reuse them as poop bags for my dog." As I hear myself say it, a wave of embarrassment comes over me, and I wish I could shovel the words back into my mouth. I'm impelled to add this piece of gross editorial so that I can communicate to this twenty-year-old I've never formally met that I'm not the kind of person who doesn't know that plastic bags are bad for the environment. I tell him I'm going to reuse them, not because I imagine he's interested to know that I have a dog who poops a lot, but because I want him to know that I know what's right, that I'm the kind of person who knows it's *good* to care about the earth. I don't want him to think I'm a bad person.

Yet this moral constitution goes deeper. After he ignores my awkward details about reuse—leaving me to wonder if he innocently didn't hear or is just the kind of spoiled brat who doesn't care about the environment (now I do the moral interpreting)—he hands me my bags and says, "Have a good day."

This is only a throwaway idiom, but it's constituted through an unthought moral imagination that assumes there *is* a good way to have a day.[5] If I doubled down on my awkwardness, stopped with the heavy plastic bags of milk swaying at my sides, and said, "What do you mean, 'Have a good day?' What would make my day good?" he'd be shocked. But after the surprise he would be able to give some detail. He might say something like, "Well, I mean, I hope you have a fun night, or are able to see your family, or make some money." Or probably, looking at the five cartons of milk, he'd say, "I hope you really enjoy your Fruity Pebbles!"

As I walk out the door, I might see a neighbor. We'd exchange hellos, and she'd ask, "Things good with your kids?" This, too, would be a moral statement, and a deeper one than that of the college-aged clerk's, because the topic would have shifted from plastic bags and idiomatic goodbyes to my children. My neighbor assumes, as do I—which is what makes the phrase work—that there is a good way for my kids to be, and at some level we share this good; it's what, in part, makes it morally right.

---

5. As this is developed below, it's debated whether these throwaway departing words are truly moral in constitution. It could be argued that there is no strong evaluation (as we'll discuss in the second half of the book). That may be true, but if indeed I confront him on what he meant, causing him to reflect, he may have to connect his unthought farewell with some evaluation of a good life. So it is debatable, but I use this as a way of showing how deeply moral categories are connected to human actions.

It would be super weird for even me (the theologian and husband of a pastor) to say, "Yes, they're doing very good. Owen fasted all week and saw two visions. And Maisy felt the deep conviction of the Holy Spirit and has entered a time of confession and penance. She wore our family hair shirt to school today. It made gym class difficult, but that's the point: doing penance for sin isn't easy!"

There was a time in history when this might have been exactly how a person would respond. But not today. The moral imagination has changed, and if I did respond like this, even a churchgoing neighbor would make all sorts of moral interpretations about me. She might create narratives about who I am and what my kids' life is like. My neighbor might even call social services, assuming that I'm some crazy religious freak, because my sense of the good feels wrong to her. And what would give her the moral high ground is her assumption that my poor kids are being kept from living a full life.[6]

But that's not how I respond. I say, "Yes!" and then rattle off all the activities they're involved in or a few of the accomplishments they've recently achieved. I'll say, "Yeah, they're well. Owen just added guitar to his piano and loves it. Maisy is in fencing. She's working hard and hoping to win a sword at the end of the term."

I'd respond this way because, in part, it is true (as compared to wearing a hair shirt), but I'd make this response without much thought, as a near reflex, ignoring last night's argument and all the unfinished homework, because of our shared moral imagination. I know without thinking about it that this is how *good* parents respond, speaking about activities, successes, happiness, and togetherness.

Youth Ministry on Moral Ground

Now imagine broadening the question and asking the church, "Things good with your kids?"[7] Our answers reveal the shape of the moral ground we

6. Nicholas Wolterstorff offers a broader articulation of where this sense of good comes from, exposing some of its problems. "The understanding of the good life that is dominant in the modern world is that of what might be called the *experientially satisfying* life. The native home of this conception of the good life is the modern utilitarian tradition; it is this conception that is employed by most economists, by most social scientists, and by most social planners." "God's Power and Human Flourishing" (unpublished consultation paper, Yale Center for Faith and Culture, 2014), 3, http://faith.yale.edu/sites/default/files/nicholas_wolterstorff_-_gods_power _and_human_flourishing_0_0.pdf.

7. Hunter points out that this moral question directed at the condition of our children has been common and is more complicated than we presume. "Is there a 'crisis of character' in our day? I am agnostic on this question, if only for the historical reason that every generation

presume. And this gives us interesting visions of what youth ministry is assumed to be for. In snapshot form, this shows how youth ministry has often
been a response to our shifting sense of the good.

If in eighteenth-century England you had asked a churchgoing acquain-
tance, "Things good with your kids?" you'd have heard about a moral threat
to the empire. Industrialization was producing a generation who couldn't
read—particularly their Bibles. This was a danger to the good of society, as
many children were unable to access a full life promised through education.
So Robert Raikes started the Sunday school movement.

In the late nineteenth century, we would have received a few different answers to "Things good with your kids?" Some might have said, "We're worried.
They just don't seem to be taking their Christian faith seriously enough. They
have a sense of apathy that keeps them from pledging their commitment."
Others might have said, "We're worried that the goods of the countryside are
gone. So many children are living in our new urban centers, wandering the
streets aimlessly. That's not good." These moral concerns birthed the Society
of Christian Endeavor and the YMCA.

In the twentieth century, particularly in its second half, when asking, "Things
good with your kids?" you'd hear worries about them growing up too quickly.
Congregational youth ministry had not only its birth but also its clearest objective in this time. Young people were growing up too fast, using all the free
time and space of the suburbs to experiment with drugs and sex. Youth ministry was for slowing things down, giving them something more positive, even
wholesome, to do.

The good of free childhood and adolescent space birthed in the 1950s and
early 1960s became a major concern in the 1980s and early 1990s. A staple
of youth ministry was to offer programs and outings to fill this open time,
giving young people something to do óther than drive fast, drink peppermint
schnapps, and score. Youth ministry was all about activities and outings because other than an after-school sport and a little homework, young people
had little else to do than hang out with peers.

In the second half of the twentieth century, many parents *felt* it good for
kids to be free, able to roam the neighborhood and do what they wanted
with their time. A good parent not only provided this space but also kept her
distance. If you need an example of this, think of Mr. and Mrs. Wheeler on
Stranger Things. Their son is hiding a paranormal child in the basement in

---

for the past two centuries has seen its youth as being in such a crisis. Hearing these claims
generation after generation tends to make one numb to this particular cry of distress." *Death
of Character*, 79.

season 1, and then off fighting Demogorgons from an alternate dimension in season 2. But they're oblivious, watching TV and reading trashy romance novels. This is not necessarily because they're bad parents. Actually, they're good 1980s parents, which means they stay out of their kids' affairs, giving the goods of free time and family dinners.

The show can only work as a period piece set in the 1980s. In 2010, cell phones, traveling baseball, and the constant hovering parental presence would have left no time for Demogorgon fighting.[8] And all those classic 1980s movies that *Stranger Things* is drawing from are coming-of-age tales. Think of Spielberg's *E.T.* and *The Goonies*, or John Hughes's *Pretty in Pink* and *Sixteen Candles*. They are all about young people, by themselves, with little to no adult involvement and massive amounts of free time, who use that time to come of age, to grow up, encountering and awkwardly finding their way into adultlike situations. These movies were epic tales in the 1980s and 1990s because they scratched young audiences' passionate desire to grow up quickly.

If you need a starker example than Spielberg and Hughes, try rewatching *Fast Times at Ridgemont High*. You'll be amazed at how old each character feels and how few parents are around at all. The movie starts with fifteen-year-old Stacy working at the pizza parlor in the mall. There she meets Ron Johnson, a twenty-six-year-old stereo salesman. Stacy lies about her age, wanting so badly to grow up and have her first sexual experience. The sex, dating, and work life of the characters throughout the film makes it seem like they're much older. And of course the actors are, but the screenplay is based on Cameron Crowe's year of going undercover at Clairemont High School in San Diego.

In this period, which in many ways is still so deeply nestled in our imaginations, youth ministry was synonymous with youth group. Parents and the larger society believed young people needed space and time. Yet this space and time most often produced self-enclosed peer groups in which the task was to grow up quickly by experimenting with all sorts of adult activities. This is why it was rare in the 1980s and early 1990s for youth ministry to have much concern for parents—it was a *youth* group, after all. Parents were often unseen. It wouldn't be until the late 1990s, when a new moral vision was being birthed, that youth ministries began adding "family" to their titles (youth and family ministry).

The youth group gave young people something else to do than try on all these adult behaviors. Unlike the flow of the larger society, the youth group

8. Not surprisingly, the parent who is involved, Will's mom, Ms. Byers, is a single parent living in a bad part of town. Outside the center of suburbia, she has different goods that mobilize her action.

encouraged young people to slow down. That was its appeal. You came to play games, hang out with a cool, young youth worker who was gross and funny, and have some wholesome fun (like eating ice cream out of a trough and carrying eggs in your armpits) without the worries of sex and cigarettes.

The youth group responded to the excesses and dangers that grew from the cultural goods of free adolescent time and space, when a 1980s San Diego fifteen-year-old like Stacy thought a good life was quickly growing up by dating much older men. The youth group was there to slow her down by giving her other things to do.

Maybe not coincidentally, the great youth group resource providers of the 1980s and 1990s were based in Southern California—the place young people seemed to be growing up most quickly. Youth Specialties, which did more than anyone to shape late twentieth-century congregational youth group life, was located in San Diego, not far from Clairemont High School. Youth Specialties had its finger on the pulse of what youth groups needed to slow young people down and give them Jesus.[9]

The Flip

As my imagined remarks to my neighbor reveal, we've shifted into a new moral imagination. Giving young people free space is no longer a central good. This has radically changed. In no way do I think it is good to stay out of my kids' business. Rather, unlike Mr. and Mrs. Wheeler, I feel it's good to be deeply involved in it. Filling my kids' time with activities, I diligently watch. Now a good parent is always monitoring his children, knowing at all times where his child is and what she's doing (unless she's slipped into a digital space he doesn't understand, which totally freaks him out). It takes a lot of emotional work, a real grind against my deeper *feels*, for example, for me to back off and let Owen be responsible for his own homework. This shows I'm operating from within a moral vision.

This shift in moral imagination began to occur with the arrival of the new millennium. For young people raised in the 2000s, the sense that free time and space was a high good started to quickly disappear. As the children raised in the teenage fast times of the 1980s and 1990s became parents, they imagined a very different way of helping their children flourish. It's no longer good to give young people loads of free time for experimentation, allowing enclosed peer environments in which to experiment. Parents no longer believe that the

---

9. Again, this is only a snapshot. Things are actually much more complicated. But I'll leave it to someone else to flesh this out.

best way to love their kids is to leave them alone. Rather, that old good is now seen as a moral violation. The new good is diligent involvement. The good offered to kids is no longer free space to enjoy *today* with little obligation other than a nightly family dinner. Now parents point young people mostly to *tomorrow*.[10] The offered goods are a menu of activities, opportunities, and oversight so that young people might get the most out of their lives and not waste their future. The moral ground has shifted hard from Mrs. Wheeler to Lorelai Gilmore (the mom on the television series *Gilmore Girls*).

Parents in the twenty-first century have embraced an opposite moral vision, flipping from a permissive parenting style to a monitoring one. Yet there is danger in this flip. One of the felt problems with the permissive parenting style, and the moral good of free teenage space, was that while kids were free, they felt little direct connection to their parents, and when parents needed to discipline them, it was often authoritarian and even harsh. To turn to the controlling impulses of the monitoring parent style of the new moral imagination could run the same authoritarian danger. For close monitoring to not feel punitive, the parent needs to be an intimate friend. It was rare, and very uncool, for a teenager in the 1980s or 1990s to say that their mom was their best friend. Yet this is now ubiquitous with the shift from a permissive to monitoring parent style (see *Gilmore Girls* for a clear example). Mom knows everything about you, but that's OK, because she's your best friend.[11] This is indeed a new moral vision.

Youth Ministries' Old Moral Vision

And yet many youth ministries still function, in form and purpose, on a twentieth-century moral conception that is no longer broadly present. In the late twentieth century youth ministry was for slowing down the fast times of growing up by giving kids an alternate group of youth to hang out with—by giving them a youth group led by an older youth. The youth group was essentially synonymous with youth ministry. Youth ministry was the youth group doing activities and going on outings. Youth ministry gave young people a group at church that encouraged them to slow down the fast rush into adulthood.

10. This has much to do with the acceleration of modernity. I'm convinced that Hartmut Rosa is right about this acceleration; see *Social Acceleration: A New Theory of Modernity* (New York: Columbia University Press, 2015). I'll engage more deeply with Rosa in the forthcoming vol. 3 of the Ministry in a Secular Age series.

11. For more on this, see Twenge, *iGen*, 44, 47.

In most of our churches today, this sense that youth ministry is one and the same as leading a youth group hangs on as a remnant. If we accept this assumption that youth ministry is just about getting kids to show up at youth group meetings, then it's fair to say that youth ministry was much easier and more dynamic in the 1980s and 1990s than it is today.

Yet if we see things through a moral imagination, then youth ministry isn't being done more poorly, but the moral ground youth ministry stands on is shifting. Goods have been redefined, and youth ministry has not caught up, making those of us who sense this transition unaware of what youth ministry is for. We know it can't be just for running a youth group.

But this "not yet caught up" of youth ministry goes deeper. The redefinition of goods has meant a complete flip in more than just parenting style. But the flip in parenting style points to the more pervasive change. This more radical flip is what Wes pointed me to at the end of our conversation.

The goods of organized activity, constant monitoring, and being your kid's friend are present because underlying these are a more overachieving and directing good. This kind of good is what Charles Taylor calls a hypergood.[12] It is a more active good, it buzzes at a higher frequency, because we hold it up as a primary good. What this means is that if we find out, say, that traveling soccer is violating a hypergood, we'll choose to keep our kid home, risking all

12. Taylor explains more about hypergoods: "Even those of us who are not committed in so single-minded a way recognize higher goods. That is, we acknowledge second-order qualitative distinctions which define higher goods, on the basis of which we discriminate among other goods, attribute differential worth or importance to them, or determine when and if to follow them. Let me call higher-order goods of this kind 'hypergoods,' i.e., goods which not only are incomparably more important than others but provide the standpoint from which these must be weighed, judged, decided about." *Sources of the Self: The Making of Modern Identity* (Cambridge, MA: Harvard University Press, 1989), 63. He continues, "Hypergoods are generally a source of conflict. The most important ones, those which are most widely adhered to in our civilization, have arisen through a historical supersession of earlier, less adequate views—analogous to the critical supersession of premodern by modern science. . . . Hypergoods are understood by those who espouse them as a step to a higher moral consciousness" (64). Nicholas Smith adds, "Generally, we resort to practical reason to help us cope with incommensurability in the ends we pursue. At least in some cases, this can lead us to reflect on the strong values that mean most to us. It can involve a ranking of the goods we recognize. Hypergoods are 'second-order' goods because they enable us to discriminate between goods or strong values. The task of choosing between goods, in Taylor's view, is often a matter of interpreting the requirements of a hypergood. But hypergoods themselves, as Taylor stresses, are sources of conflict. On the one hand, one might recognize several higher-order goods, that is, different standpoints from which to evaluate or rank first-order goods. On the other hand, the single-minded pursuit of a hypergood has its own costs. Those who aim at the highest good must sacrifice other goods. There are occasions when those who do have such an aim find themselves asking whether the sacrifice required by the hypergood is really worth it, and such moments also precipitate practical reason." *Charles Taylor: Meaning, Morals and Modernity* (Cambridge: Polity, 2002), 104.

other goods for the sake of this hypergood. In our time a hypergood is keeping kids safe so they can be happy now and in the future.[13] The highest moral good for parents in our time is to protect their children through oversight, helping prepare them for the competitive rat race of modern society, finding happiness with who they are in this fast-paced life. That's why activities and monitoring are so important. By filling up the calendar and joining them in all their activities, a good parent keeps his kids from growing up too quickly. Your life becomes your kids', because this not only gives you meaning but also promises to provide a hypergood of their safety, which will produce the ultimate hypergood of happiness.

But we have to ask, keep them safe from what? We've already answered this—we're keeping them safe from wasting their lives, from being unprepared to perform in a fast-paced world. But actually it is more urgent than this. Many parents feel that there are unseen dangers lurking in the weeds. Yet nearly every statistic of teenage risk is down over the last few decades[14] (except depression and self-mutilation, which may have something to do with a loss of meaning even inside this safety).[15]

While most neighborhoods are safer, the emotional state of the young person is not. Parents must give constant oversight to protect their children, not necessarily from bodily danger, but from emotional injury, from feeling unsafe and overwhelmed by the pace of life. It's hard to know if happiness is the end or the means. Yet, regardless, when a hypergood is emotional safety, then being happy is the clearest sign that you and your child are doing well. Again, it's hard to know if parents hold on to the hypergood of safety so

13. See Twenge, *iGen*, 157, for more.

14. "Like many generational trends, the interest in safety has trade-offs. iGen'ers are, by all accounts, the safest generation in US history, partially due to their own choices to drink less, fight less, wear their seat belts, and drive more safely. . . . Their caution helps keep them safe, but it also makes them vulnerable, because everyone gets hurt eventually. Not all risks can be eliminated all the time, especially for a generation that believes someone disagreeing with you constitutes emotional injury." Twenge, *iGen*, 167.

15. For more on this, see Alain Ehrenberg, *The Weariness of the Self: Diagnosing the History of Depression in the Contemporary Age* (Montreal: McGill-Queen's University Press, 2010). Hara Estroff Marano explains, "No one is sure why self-mutilation was rare just a generation ago but seems commonplace now. . . . Today students are more inward-turning; the self is seen as the primary arena for action. . . . Here lies perhaps the ultimate paradox of scarification: self-harm reflects the inability to find something else to do that makes one feel more alive. Earlier generations sought meaning in movements of social change or intellectual engagement inside and outside the classroom. . . . So constrained and stressed by expectations, so invaded by parental control, today's students have no room to turn—except against themselves. Their self-absorption makes it logical that they would use themselves as a stage of operations. Emotional well-being directly suffers when there are few distractions from egocentric concerns." *A Nation of Wimps: The High Cost of Invasive Parenting* (New York: Broadway, 2008), 173–74.

their children can be happy, or if happiness is the outward sign that they've met the hypergood and their kid is safe from emotional injury. I tend to think that happiness is the aim (the top-ranking hypergood), and I'll have more to say about this in chapters 8 and 10.

Nevertheless, a hypergood of parenting is to protect their child, which produces a hypergood in young people of feeling safe. Because they meet the world through the good of their parents' protection, young people's *feel* of the good is interlaced with feeling safe. Life cannot be good if they feel unsafe or at risk. Happiness is essential because it means you feel safe. Inside this hypergood, happiness and avoidance of emotional injury become interlaced.

The More Radical Flip

Pushing forward, what seems to happen when avoidance of emotional injury becomes a hypergood is that the fast times of growing up come to a screeching halt. Affected by this new moral imagination, the more radical flip we referenced above occurs. Inside this new moral ecology, middle-class young people are no longer at risk to grow up too quickly; they're at risk to grow up *too slowly*.

The desire to protect children has meant a radical slowing of their cultural passages into adulthood. It only makes sense that when watching *Fast Times at Ridgemont High* today, we're shocked at how old the teenagers seem. In a real sense (a cultural one as opposed to a biological one) they are. Objectively, young people in the 1980s grew up more quickly than young people do today. When the church was asked in the 1980s and 1990s, "Things good with the kids?" the concern was that they were growing up too quickly. Not so much today.

Research supports the notion that kids are growing up much slower. Researcher Jean Twenge says, "Contrary to the prevalent idea that children are growing up faster than previous generations did, iGen'ers are growing up more slowly: 18-year-olds now act like 15-year-olds used to, and 13-year-olds like 10-year-olds, teens are physically safer than ever, yet they are more mentally vulnerable."[16] Where in the 1980s and 1990s young people were rushing the doors to partake in adult-sanctioned behaviors, today many young people seem in no hurry at all. Compared to past generations, many wait till very late to get driver's licenses and start dating—even to have a first kiss. And overall, they are spending much less time with peers and much more with

16. Twenge, *iGen*, 3.

parents. Twenge, whose research exposes this trend, found to her surprise that high school kids in San Diego today, just like the characters in *Fast Times*, often go to the mall. But unlike Stacy and slacker-surfer Jeff Spicoli, they are *rarely* there with their friends and almost never without an adult.[17] Add to this other economic and educational factors—the expense of college and anxiety about the job market—and we enter a society as a whole slowing down young people's growing up.

The youth group was youth ministry, and youth ministry as the youth group was there to encourage young people to slow down and avoid the fast times of high school life—that's what it was for. But what is youth ministry for if young people aren't growing up too fast, but too slowly? And what is youth ministry for if young people's highest good (hypergood) is not the adventure of adultlike behaviors but the deep desire to always feel safe? What is youth ministry for if parents' high good is protecting kids by keeping them close and active, so that emotional injury doesn't put them at risk for wasting their lives? What is youth ministry for when fast times have given way to slow times?

Conclusion

Thinking this all through at thirty thousand feet, with a little bag of almonds to fuel my contemplation, I was convinced that Wes was right. There was a great slowing down that shifted the moral ground on which youth ministry was operating, making us less sure than ever what youth ministry is for. But as the Upper Midwest appeared in the window and our wheels hit the runway, violently jerking and shaking the jet-propelled energy out of the plane, I wondered how this connected to seeds and tools. Wes may have been right about the slowdown, but was it true that parents really thought youth ministry was for giving their kids seeds and tools? And if this desire for seeds is engendered by the task of identity construction, and if tools are related to happiness, then how does this connect with the moral shift to slow down?

As I flipped airplane mode off, my phone shook with notifications. It was mostly junk emails about pending meetings and new Netflix releases, text messages from the school district about late school buses, and updates from home that we were out of milk. So I opened Twitter. A few seconds into my scroll I saw tweets by two local youth pastors I knew. They worked at two

17. "iGen teens are less likely to go out without their parents. The trend began with Millennials and then accelerated at a rapid clip with iGen'ers. The numbers are stunning: 12th graders in 2015 are going out less often than 8th graders did as recently as 2009. So 18-year-olds are now going out less often than 14-year-olds did just six years prior." Twenge, *iGen*, 19.

very different churches in basically the same Minneapolis neighborhood. I wasn't sure they even knew each other, but I knew them both. The plane slowed into the gate, and we awaited the jet bridge. I found myself wondering, *In this slowdown, what would parents at these two churches say youth ministry is for?*

So I decided to ask them.

Four

Three Sets of Parents

Things and Happiness Emerge

LATE OCTOBER

I t was the time of year in the Upper Midwest when the seasons stutter from one to the other. Winter previews with a few windy, cold days, the air sharp, stabbing your face with the sensation of a thousand tiny toothpicks. But the next day might bring warm, welcoming air that feels more like spring breaking than the creeping up of winter. Yet as I walked this city neighborhood on a mild afternoon, the signs were clear. The trees were stripped of leaves, and the lawns had gone brown and looked almost gray against the overcast twilight in the painfully shortening days. And the people? There was a rush in their step, a hurried directness to their pursuits.

No one would confuse this tucked-away Minneapolis neighborhood for Manhattan, but still, at this time of year there is a kind of urgency in people's strides, a focus to their movements. Few people linger on the corner or mill around on their front walks. Minnesota Nice is still operative—we continue to smile and nod and say hello, even to strangers—but it becomes more abbreviated as a kind of primitive muscle memory kicks in that readies us for the snow and subzero temps. People hurry like ants on their well-worn paths, readying their yards, getting leaves raked, gutters cleaned, and summer lawn furniture stored.

The houses that sit on these yards are a mix, built between 1900 and 1990. They come in all shapes and sizes. For the last two decades, housing prices have steadily and sharply climbed as young families leave the suburbs, seeking a return to the city. To live in one of the bigger, refurbished old homes takes means, and while even the smaller houses feel overpriced, there are a number of low-income housing options. This gives the neighborhood a sense of diversity. As a matter of fact, the many political signs on people's lawns seem to reveal that diversity is a core good to most.

As for location, this neighborhood is the perfect middle ground. It has a feel of a self-contained town, with corner shops, good schools, a Fourth of July parade, and metro access to Minneapolis's urban center. And yet a large suburb with all manner of Targets, Starbucks, and Chipotles is just a mile or two away. Because of a lake, though, the neighborhood seems hidden from the ambient pulsing of soulless strip malls. Both city and suburb are kept at arm's length but easily accessed. People love the neighborhood because it allows for a feeling of something lost, a time when life was more embedded in and ordered around neighborhood and civic involvement, but never in a way that restricts your freedom or feels unsafe.

I was in the neighborhood to meet three families: two arranged by my two youth pastor friends I'd seen on Twitter, the other by a friend deep in the youth-sports scene. Going into these conversations, I was more than aware that they were far from representative. That thought hit me as I walked past the ice cream parlor. I was here looking for snapshots—conversations that would help me get clearer on what youth ministry is for. So I decided not to interview any of the young people. I decided I'd stick to exploring how parents were operating from within their feels of the good, what they saw youth ministry as being for, and what they hoped for their children.

As I searched for the first house and became more acquainted with the neighborhood, I became even more aware that the families themselves weren't representative. For example, all three were two-parent homes, though one is a blended family. Two of the three families were racially diverse. All three were situated squarely—though to different degrees—in the middle class. But I was sure that they could teach me something, helping me in my journey.

Three Families

The Rodriguez-Eriksons

I spotted the house of the first family from across the street. It was big and old, and the yard was meticulously prepared for winter. The three trees in the front yard were bare, but there was no sign of as much as a single leaf on the ground. The shrubs were covered with burlap, and the sidewalk and walkway to the door were freshly edged. I spotted a beautiful eight-foot cedar fence lining the backyard. A little sign next to the door read, "Friends are welcome, because friends are a gift from God."

I knocked on the door and was welcomed inside by Linda and José. Linda, an executive at a big company in Minneapolis, exuded not just professionalism and competency but also warmth. José worked in the chemistry department of the university, writing and administering grants. He treated me like we'd met many times before. He was so friendly and familiar I wondered whether I was missing something, if indeed I'd met him but couldn't remember it. They were at such ease I couldn't help but be also. Quickly my eyes were drawn to the house. From the outside it was clear that it was at least eighty years old, but inside it was modern and open, with a huge kitchen that wonderfully flowed into almost all the main floor rooms. The colors and furnishings were warm and soft. I thought, *Yes, friends really are welcome here!* and *I wonder if this house was on "Property Brothers" or "Love It or List It."* It was a marvel of renovation.

Linda and José have been married fourteen years and have three children. Maria is twenty-five, Jessicah is nineteen and a sophomore at a local liberal arts college, and Manny is thirteen and in eighth grade. Maria and Jessicah were each from Linda's and José's first marriages. Maria never lived permanently with Linda and José, only spending a month or so with them in the summers and during Christmas breaks. Jessicah was five when they married, and about a year later Manny was born. Linda explained that for all intents and purposes, José has been Jessicah's father. Her biological father disappeared before Jessicah could remember him, and only in the last year had he reached out to her.

Linda grew up in the large evangelical church just outside the neighborhood. Her parents were part of the core that saw the church move quickly from less than a hundred members to over three thousand. To this day the church names its focus on youth ministry as the secret to its quick growth in the 1980s and 1990s. And Linda concurred.

She told me over a hot cup of tea at her beautiful kitchen island, "Some of my best times growing up were on youth group trips. I loved my youth pastors, and so many of the volunteers had an impact on my life."

When Linda's first husband had left her with a two-year-old, she headed back home—as much to the church and its youth ministry as to the neighborhood. The home the Rodriguez-Ericksons welcomed me into was just six blocks from the house she grew up in. She explained that she found her footing and put her life back together while volunteering in the youth group. "So youth ministry has meant so much to me," she said.

José grew up Catholic and stopped going to Mass sometime in college, but when he met Linda through a friend and they started dating, he joined her at church. Now over fifteen years later, he felt it was as much his church as hers. He explained that moving from being a Catholic to an evangelical was very challenging. But when he saw the youth ministry, he knew right away that he wanted his kids to be part of it. "It just seemed so positive, so much energy," José explained. "I thought to myself, wow, if I'd been in a group like this, maybe I wouldn't have wasted those ten years I did after high school."

My eyes must have opened wide when he said "wasted." I was connecting José's words to my conversation with Graham. But José didn't know this, assuming instead that I thought it wasn't right to make such statements. He stopped and rephrased, saying, "I'm sorry, I shouldn't say it like that. It wasn't a waste. I mean, my first daughter was born in those years. But honestly, I was far away from living well." His rephrasing connected even more to this sense of the good and the drive to avoid a wasted life.

Sensing that my body was communicating something more than I'd wished to, I turned the conversation to their children. "Are your kids having the experience you'd hoped for? Do they feel connected to the youth ministry?"

Linda jumped back in. "Jessicah didn't, and honestly, that was hard for me. But it was a weird time. When she was going into the high school group, our youth pastor left. And probably because we were in the middle of this transition, a group of girls just started to manifest some really cliquey—honestly, mean—behavior. So Jessicah just didn't feel safe in the youth group, and I wasn't going to make her go."

I'd learned my lesson: I kept my eyes from widening as Linda's comment connected with Wes's assertions about emotional safety. I paused and then said, "Wow, that's intense."

"It was hard," José added.

"But the good news," Linda continued, "is that she got involved in other places in the church. Jessicah is just that kind of person. She's a self-starter and really wants to make a difference. So when she didn't feel comfortable in the youth group, she just found another way to be engaged. She'd put in like ten volunteer hours a week in the nursery."

"There really are just so many options," José inserted. "Plus, Jessicah really is a strong person; she has such a handle on who she is and what she's about."

Intrigued, I asked, "What do you credit that to?"

"Her mom!" José said immediately. Linda, looking both embarrassed and flattered, met eyes with José and smiled shyly.

"No, seriously," José continued. "I think she has these strong values, and she's gotten them from her mom."

". . . who got them from youth ministry," Linda quickly added.

"Right," José said, returning to his point. "These values just help her know who she is. We had some tough times, like during those years when the youth group felt unsafe. Jessicah was just so unhappy for a year or so. But she's really found her stride now. I mean, we have new problems. We have a freshman in college without any interest in dating, who doesn't even have a driver's license. She picked this small faith-based college, probably because it felt safe and not overwhelming. But still, I think she knows who she is."

"Manny is another case in almost every way," Linda added.

"What do you mean?" I asked.

"He loves middle-school youth group. That's the good news," Linda answered. "But we worry he just doesn't have a sense of who he is. When Jessicah felt unsafe, she detached and found other outlets. Manny, on the other hand, just tries so hard and wants so badly to be included. Seventh grade was hell for us. We had to find our way through his inability to get his schoolwork done, next to some intense bullying. His phone became a major issue; it distracted him from what he was supposed to be doing, while serving as a portal for twenty-four-hour bullying. And yet we needed it to get him back and forth from all the sports, tutoring, and youth group activities."

Thinking about my conversation with Kathryn, I asked, "How do you guys make decisions when schedules conflict?"

José shrugged and said, "Those decisions are made for us."

"What do you mean?" I responded.

"Well, like hockey. If you miss, you let a lot of people down."

"You let down some people if you miss youth group too," Linda quickly added, signaling that this was a return to a conversation they'd had before. "I was a volunteer for a long time. If kids don't show and you've put a lot of time into something, that's a major bummer."

"Right, right, I understand that," José said, "and honestly I'd rather Manny go to youth group or Sunday school than a Sunday morning game. But if he doesn't show and they're down a guy—or maybe down a few guys—and they have to forfeit or just get creamed . . . that'd be bad. Those kids and parents are passionate about their hockey."

"How would you define bad?" I asked.

"It'd just feel terrible," José responded, sure of his sense but not sure how else to describe it. Stretching for something more substantive, José shifted to more solid ground. "I guess it comes down to Manny. Manny wants this; he wants to be on that team. I mean, he wants to be at youth group too. I'm just trying to help him figure out who he is."

"And honestly," Linda said, "we're worried about that. We were with Jessicah as well. We just want to help our kids figure out who they are. That's why I love youth ministry so much, because it gives parents another—I think, better—resource to help their kids figure out who they are and who God wants them to be."

"But what are you worried about?" I asked, finishing my cup of tea.

"Manny just seems to really struggle with figuring out his *thing*," José said. "You know, something he's really passionate about. He just bounces back and forth. I just really want him to have peace with who he is, to feel good about himself, about being Manny. In ten years, I want him to know who he is and just be happy."

"And you think those things go together? Being happy and knowing who you are?" I asked.

"Yes, for sure," José said confidently, "and I think if he could just find his thing, then knowing who he is and being happy will all come together. I just so want him to find his thing. But he seems too scattered. Really, we're always directing him."

I was struck with how Manny finding "his thing" was connected to finding himself, which in turn delivered happiness, and how, in the slowdown of growing up, parents were directly responsible for this work of helping their kids safely figure out who they are so they can be happy. I think I understood better what Kathryn, the youth ministry major, was sensing. The full schedule wasn't purely about capital. Young people weren't carrying full schedules just because their parents wanted them to make more money in the future or meet the right people. This was part of it. But more foundational was the working out of an identity. And this identity is something that you seem to discover, finding who you are by knowing your *thing*. These activities provide direct opportunities to know who you are. And what could make someone happier? Happiness is assumed to be knowing and living out of who you truly are. But was that really what Linda and José meant?

So I asked, "For you two, is figuring out who you are the most important thing?" I was wondering if this sense of finding who you are was a high good, and if it had any connection to God. They gave an affirmative nod.

"Yes," Linda and José said in unison.

"And we think for Manny to figure this out, he needs to know that he's loved, that he belongs, that Jesus is always with him," José added.

"Then what's youth ministry for?" I asked, getting to the heart of my reason for meeting with them.

"To help him know that he's loved and belongs. To know Jesus. And I hope that by helping him know this, youth ministry gives him values, and that these values can support who he is. I really hope that church, overall, gives him a place where if he fails—"

"When he fails," Linda interjected.

"When he fails," José continued, "he can feel supported. It can be a safe place."

Wes was right: at least for Linda and José, youth ministry appeared to be for seeds. Youth ministry didn't appear to be able to provide the *thing* that a young person would use to construct an identity; it couldn't give a distinct way of life. But it could, in Linda and José's mind, plant values that could be a support in this identity journey, even providing a safe place when the search for who you are becomes bumpy.

The Tuckers

As I left the Rodriguez-Eriksons' house, my stomach was warm with tea. According to my phone it was about a nine-minute walk to the Tuckers' home. My warm belly encouraged me to go the long way so I could pass the Tuckers' church. I'd been there before, almost a decade ago now, teaching in their Sunday morning adult education hour.

If the evangelical church that the Rodriguez-Eriksons attend seems to hover like a spacecraft just outside the neighborhood, pulling city neighborhood dwellers into the suburbs, the Tuckers' Lutheran church does just the opposite. In an odd way it feels like a bunker deep beneath the skin of this neighborhood. This is both its strength and its weakness. It remains a truly neighborhood church, its property part of all sorts of neighborhood events. But because of this it can be overlooked. It doesn't feel that different from the post office across the street. I noticed two signs on the post office door. One was an official-looking alert telling the neighborhood that because of lack of use, the post office would close right after Christmas. The other was a homemade sign to the neighborhood from a neighbor, pleading to keep it open. It appeared that some liked the idea of having the post office in the neighborhood but didn't necessarily visit it. Post offices and churches were part of the quaint Americana that made this neighborhood great.

Like the post office, the Tuckers' church could be overlooked, though unlike the post office, there was no threat of it closing. Even covered with a coat of civic religion, it remains a vibrant mainline church. It has a growing confirmation program and a booming summer VBS, and the leadership is always open to trying new things.

The Tuckers lived just four blocks from the church. Unlike the Rodriguez-Eriksons', the Tuckers' yard was not ready for winter. Far from it. There were piles of leaves, and remnants of summer activities could still be spotted as I approached the door. I knocked and waited, staring at a big camper trailer set up in the driveway.

After a few seconds Sue invited me in and introduced me to her husband, Ted. Sue was a part-time accountant for a company in Minneapolis. Ted ran a small heating and cooling business his family had owned for seventy years. Their house, too, had a warm feeling, but it wasn't nearly as put together as the Rodriguez-Eriksons'. It felt like a more private space, set up not for guests but for family. Sue and Ted had been married for twenty-five years and had three boys. Their oldest had just joined the military; the other two were in eleventh and ninth grades.

The Tuckers had moved to the neighborhood just over ten years earlier and immediately joined the Lutheran church. Both Sue and Ted had been confirmed in a Lutheran church and wanted all three of their boys to do the same. Over the years their commitment and participation ebbed and flowed. Ted didn't hesitate to tell me that for long stretches they were absent from church. But never because they didn't *want* to be there, he assured me; rather, things just got busy. The boys' schedule, coupled with their commitment to family time, would keep them away.

Ted explained, "As a matter of fact, you probably saw our camper out front. We're heading to South Dakota on Friday for our annual family pheasant hunt. That kind of stuff is really important to us."

"Yep," Sue added, "family time is really our main commitment. And our boys love it. We feel really privileged that all three of the boys always choose to be with us and do things together more than anything else." This was at a different pitch than the Rodriguez-Eriksons but nevertheless the same song of slowdown. The Tucker boys weren't racing away from their parents, rushing themselves into adulthood, but instead chose to make being with their parents central.

"How did you do that?" I asked, impressed.

"Well, it isn't easy," Sue responded. "The boys, as they've gotten older, are so much busier. We have a lot to balance with soccer, Boy Scouts, and just all the homework. But we refuse to not take time together to get out and do things."

"What about church?" I asked. "How does it fit in?"

"Like I said," Ted answered, "we get there when we can. It's important to us. I'd say it is a major element of our family. But sometimes you miss one family activity like church for the sake of being together as a family. We think that's OK." Ted laughed and added, "Not sure what our pastor thinks about that, but that's how I make sense of everything."

Wanting to know more, I asked, gently pushing Ted, "How about when it comes to deciding between a soccer game or confirmation? Which one do you pick?"

"Usually we choose soccer," he said, looking at Sue. "I'm not really sure why."

Now it was Sue's turn to let out an uncomfortable laugh. She concurred: "I'm not sure either. I guess it's just how things work. Like our middle son, Trevor, got his black belt in jujitsu right in the middle of confirmation. I loved watching him work so hard. He was so passionate, and it took a lot of work. I mean, a lot. I know I couldn't have done it. But it was all him; he wanted it. And that meant working at it every night and going to advanced classes on Wednesdays. So for a few months there he missed confirmation. But that's just how it works. The skills in jujitsu don't come if you don't show up. And it was just so amazing to watch him work so hard for something. I could, like literally, *see* his confidence grow. He just had this sense of who he was."

"Yeah," Ted jumped in, "it was totally his thing."

So finding your *thing* was important, a high good, for the Tuckers, just like for the Rodriguez-Ericksons. I followed the trail.

"I've heard other people say that—'finding your thing.' What does that mean?"

"Never thought about it," Ted responded.

We sat in silence for a few seconds. Then Sue ventured, "Well, we just really want the boys to figure out who they are and what they offer the world. Knowing who you are and being useful is important to us. We think if the boys are going to be happy, that's what it will take."

"Do confirmation and youth ministry help with that?" I asked.

"I hope so, yes," Ted said. "We have so many friends whose kids are in high school or whatever who just went off the deep end. Lucky for us, that's never happened. But these kids are just trying so hard to figure out who they are, trying all sorts of crazy things. Sometimes they get overwhelmed with anxiety and even do hurtful stuff to themselves. I mean, that scares the crap out of me. There are a lot of cruel people out there, so we hope they get support. We hope the youth ministry supports the boys, giving them a safe place when they fail."

"Because we know they will," Sue added, just like Linda had. "I'm the same," she continued. "I just want them to know that the church is there. The world is hard, and when they feel lost or hurting, I hope they know the church is a place they can go. And I hope it's something we as a family can continue to do together. When the boys have their own families, I think going to church will make those families stronger."

It appeared that for Sue and Ted, youth ministry was a gateway into an experience with the church, and the church was a tool—even a safe zone— that could stabilize their children's search for happiness through their own family. It was interesting that youth ministry didn't seem to play the lead role for either the Rodriguez-Eriksons or the Tuckers in finding identity. That would happen through finding their children's *thing* in and through all the other sorts of activities available to them. No wonder these activities were ranked above confirmation or youth group. It seems that youth ministry can't provide or be the *thing*, even for evangelicals like Linda and José. If it did, it would be strange, like me telling my neighbor at Speedy Market that Maisy was wearing a hair shirt for penance. But if it couldn't be the *thing*, it could be a safe zone, a place to return to when beaten up by the battles for identity in all sorts of other pursuits of your *thing*.

"So what do you think youth ministry is for?" I asked Sue and Ted. Linda and José wanted Manny to *know* that he was loved, to *know* Jesus as *the* seed in his search for his identity. For the evangelical Rodriguez-Eriksons, youth ministry was for knowing and belonging.

Not so for the mainline Tuckers. For Sue and Ted, youth ministry was for supporting the larger ideal of family and togetherness. When it came directly to what youth ministry does, Ted said, "It can provide opportunities for service."

"Say more," I returned.

"Well, earlier this fall, part of the men's group and a group from youth ministry went down to southern Minnesota to help people who had lost their homes in the floods. It was an amazing experience. When you see the faces of people who've lost everything and you help get them back into their homes . . . man, that really impacted me. And to make it better, the fact that I could do it with my youngest two boys, that it was like a family thing—it was just awesome."

"Right," Sue added. "So for us youth ministry is for giving our kids a sense of helping others—I guess, of doing service."

"That's right," Ted followed. "I think it gives them a sense of how they can be useful, giving them ways to find happiness in helping others. Not just thinking happiness is found in video games and Twitter followers."

Wes seemed to be as right about the tools as the seeds.

The Dahls

About halfway through my conversation with the Tuckers, when we were talking about their middle son's jujitsu, as good Lutherans, they offered me a beer. But as a good Minnesotan, I refused, claiming that I didn't want to be any trouble.

But Ted knew this game and said, "It's no trouble; you'd actually be helping me out. I've got some leftover summer beers, and I need to clear them out."

I'm a sucker for a good wheat ale, so I couldn't refuse.

As I left the Tuckers, the beer warmed my stomach in a different way than the Rodriguez-Eriksons' tea. I had one more stop to make. Through a friend, I'd connected with the Dahls. As far as I knew, they had no connection to a church. My friend knew them through the local sports scene.

The Dahls lived just a few streets away from the Tuckers. Not only was their yard far from ready for winter; it looked like a Play It Again Sports had vomited all over it. There were balls, nets, and paddles everywhere. There were some leaves raked, but only in the backyard, clearing the way for the layout of an ice rink that would be flooded when the temperatures dropped.

At the door, I was met by two excitable girls who looked about ten and eight, and two dogs, all four jumping in celebration of my arrival. I felt like a celebrity. I was quickly brought back to earth when the ten-year-old said, "And who are you?"

"I'm here to see your parents," I returned with a giggle.

Just then Holly appeared, shooing the girls off to do homework and welcoming me to sit down at their dining room table. The dogs, having no mind for homework, continued with the friendly welcome, sniffing and nosing me as I took a seat. James appeared and shook my hand. He was a graphic designer who worked from home. Holly had just returned to work, teaching fifth grade. Until that fall she had chosen to only substitute, wanting to be present at home for her girls. Their four daughters ranged in age from eight to fifteen.

I started by asking Holly and James to tell me about their family. They looked at each other, their eyes communicating that they were not sure where to start.

James broke the silence. "B-U-S-Y . . . yeah, that's how I'd describe us."

"Busy, but loving it!" Holly added with a bright smile. James was a stoic type, and Holly was all energy and positivity.

"What makes things so busy?" I asked.

"Four girls!" James said, continuing his role as straight man.

"Well, we're really involved in basketball," said Holly, offering commentary to James's directness. "All four girls are on traveling teams, and we're really involved in that. James is the head coach of three of them—with a lot of help. And I coach the other."

"Wow, that is a lot," I responded.

"Yep," James said. "We've got a game or practice every night of the week this time of year. And on weekends we'll have at least three games each day."

Both James and Holly played in college. Holly was a Division III All-American, and James the captain of his Division II team. Not only was basketball a major part of Holly's and James's lives, but it stretched deeper. Holly's dad coached high school basketball for over thirty-five years. Basketball even was how they met, both attending an elite camp their senior year of high school. They went to different colleges but stayed in touch and reconnected when both played one year professionally in Europe.

"So basketball is just in your blood," I responded, stating the obvious.

"Yes," Holly answered, "it totally is. But we've been really intentional with our girls. I didn't work and James worked from home because investing in our kids is really important to us. I came from a strong family, and basketball was the ligaments that kept us together. James didn't come from a strong family, and basketball was his escape. So both of us, coming from those different experiences, want to really spend time with our girls—to really invest in them. So we're into basketball, but that's because our kids want that. We're not pushing it at all."

"But," James added, now warming up, "we are really committed to our kids being active."

"True, true," Holly said, calling on her coaching voice. "We don't want our kids just sitting around. Activity is key! When we don't have basketball, we want them outside. That's why we built the skating rink. We're not hockey people, but I *hate* the idea of them sitting around watching TV or on their phones or whatever, so we really push doing something."

Getting inside their lives, I was both impressed and exhausted, but mostly intrigued, so I asked, "Why is activity so important to you both? That's a lot of work."

"Well, for instance," James said, "basketball provides all sorts of positive impact on our girls. They make friends who tend to be positive, active, and come from good families. They develop skills like communication, hard work, and perseverance. And they learn how to set goals and accomplish them."

"And we get it," Holly added. "There is way more to life than basketball. So we don't care if one of the girls doesn't want to play or even be on a competitive traveling team. As a matter of fact, Lucy, our twelve-year-old, told me last spring that she didn't want to play lacrosse this year—for three of the girls, lacrosse is their second sport. And we said, 'Fine. But what do you want to do instead?' Lucy said, 'Nothing.' And we were like, 'Nope, not an option, find something else to do.' I told her I didn't care if it was tennis, guitar lessons, or a craft class, but it's not an option to do nothing."

"We just want them to be passionate about something," James explained.

I heard something very similar to this when talking with Linda and José and Sue and Ted. All three sets of parents seemed pulled to help their kids find their *thing*. This was a high good for them. Holly and James came with a huge history in basketball, but as they explained, the good they sought wasn't centered on that sport per se but on helping each of their daughters *find their thing* through activity. Having been over similar ground with the Rodriguez-Eriksons and the Tuckers, I sensed this activity focus was interlaced with pursuits of identity.

So I asked, "How are you helping your kids figure out who they are?"

"I guess the same, by staying active," James shot back. "I mean, that's the point. They can be whoever they want to be. I don't think they'll ever be happy if they don't live out of who they really are. But there are a lot of mean and cruel people out there who love tearing others down. So these activities, I think, keep them from being one of those cruel people and give them places to really find themselves."

"Right," Holly said. "Basketball teaches those traits James mentioned earlier, but it also builds skills like listening to others, teamwork, and sportsmanship. It demands—or at least the teams we coach demand—that each player respects others. We're really big on respect and tolerance. But you can only learn to respect and be tolerant by getting off your phone and being active by having fun with others. At least that's what we think. For me, the girls can be whoever they want to be as long as it makes them happy and helps them be good people who respect others."

We paused for a few seconds, for the first time allowing for silence. I noted in my mind that these people without any connection to church were the only ones to talk about tolerance. I'm sure something similar was operating within the other two sets of parents. But this conversation pointed to the fact that people were indeed picking up on an ethic—a right way of living—outside of any connection to religion or the church.

"As I think about this," Holly continued, now a little more reflective, "I know that each girl has to figure for herself who she is, but that's why I need to be there. I just need to be mommy bear as they figure that out."

The slowdown in growing up was in effect for Holly and James too. This wide openness in identity, coupled with the need to be tolerant and respectful—and the fear that not everyone was—called for a huge sacrifice. It asked Holly and James to be heavily involved in each of their daughters' lives, pulling each of them closer through a full schedule of activities. James even admitted that they had no life outside their girls' activities. He said, "We coach, sleep, do laundry, and repeat—that's it!"

I began to see that activities were the strategy that slowed kids down by speeding up the franticness of their schedules. The openness of identity—that you could be whoever you wanted, and yet others could be cruel when you broadcast that identity—led many parents to work hard to be present at every turn, overseeing the identity construction by protecting their children from the pitfalls of this radical freedom to be whoever they wanted.

All three sets of parents affirmed in their own way their deep wish for their children to be happy. And in turn they expressed that the only way for them to be happy was to be who they really are. The fear that young people could do this all alone, or in some digital space or with a group of questionable friends, leads parents to pull them close by overengineering their schedules. Because of this freedom in identity, the stakes were too high for parents like Holly and James to not spend nearly every waking moment overseeing their daughters' lives.

Identity, Emotional Injury, and Concerns

This pursuit of identity and happiness was present in all three sets of parents. All three of these couples assumed that a wasted life would be an unhappy one in which their children couldn't be who they really are. In different measure, all three sets of parents shared a hypergood of avoidance of emotional injury. To experience injury would upend happiness. Yet none of the three sets of parents worried too much about physical injury. Holly and James affirmed a little physical pain; a few bumps and bruises are badges of passionate engagement, proof of intense activity.

But in their own ways, all were concerned about *emotional* injury. Emotional injury was judged as a deeper risk than physical injury for these middle-class parents (no doubt a privileged place to be). They assume that emotional injury can more quickly upend happiness and risk a wasted life. The focus on the emotional is wrapped tightly around the depths of identity. If young people can't find their *thing*, receiving the affirmation and recognition of who they are through this *thing*, they will be lost in knowing who they are.

To some degree, each kid needs to be out there working this out for him- or herself, risking the emotional pain of negative recognition. Without this risk, a child could miss out on the highest good of happiness that comes from positive recognition. But this risk needs to be mitigated and controlled. Best to have mom and dad close when the recognition is negative, shielding you from some of the emotional pain that this negative recognition inflicts on your sense of identity. Better yet, have mom or dad present to help open doors of positive recognition so you can know who you are and be happy. (I'll have much more to say about all of this in the next few chapters.)

All three sets of parents had different concerns when it came to helping their kids through this *identity to recognition to happiness* process. The Rodriguez-Eriksons' concern was that Manny *knows* that he belongs, he is loved, and Jesus is with him. Knowing this, in the tension of working out an identity, could help him find happiness. The Tuckers' concern was different. While they, too, are centered on identity and happiness, their central concern was for family togetherness and usefulness. In the battles of recognition, the best option is to be useful and remember where you belong: with your family. Activity was the Dahls' concern. Activity is the stage and workshop of discovering who you are. Holly and James made activity their core concern because they could control, shield, and assist their daughters most directly inside of it.

Conclusion

By the time I walked back to my car, darkness had settled in completely. It was still early—not even 6:00 p.m.—and yet it was as dark as midnight. Even though the temperatures that day said otherwise, the early darkness was proof that winter was near. Now, finished with these conversations, I had to admit I was more confused than when I started. Talking with the Rodriguez-Eriksons, Tuckers, and Dahls was supposed to shed some light on what youth ministry was for. But I felt further in the dark. And like the time of the year in the Upper Midwest, it felt too early in my search for it to be so opaque.

I'd learned a lot since Graham kicked off my journey. I was with him that youth ministry has a dynamic of helping kids not waste their lives, because at the core we're moral animals, seeking goods. But Kathryn had led me to see that what counts as a good and avoids waste often puts youth ministry off balance, seeking for some justification in the franticness of scheduling. The way goods were now negotiated wasn't through traditions that carried with them ways of life, but through something closer to consumer interest.

Wes helped me add to Graham's assertion by signaling that there is a slow-down in effect; the busyness of young peoples' lives leads them, ironically, to grow up slower. Young people are moving more slowly into adulthood as a way to cope with the speed of modern life. My conversations with these parents confirmed it, revealing further that avoidance of emotional injury is a hypergood. I now saw how youth ministry is assumed to be for helping young people not waste their lives by providing seeds and tools. And Wes was right: most parents see these seeds and tools as connected to identity and happiness—but slowdown is also built on a moral framework with a more immanent vision, with few to no transcendent or even spiritual horizons.[1]

But this is where I was thrust further into the dark. The issues of identity and happiness seemed to ooze out from underneath all the concerns and actions of these parents. I just couldn't make sense of why this movement from identity to recognition to happiness was there, especially next to the slowdown. And what could youth ministry do about it?

That's when I heard her songs. Listening to them right after these conversations opened something up to me that I hadn't sensed or understood. I felt taken under the surface to see what I hadn't before. Who would've thought Demi Lovato would be my muse?

---

1. Paul Bloom provides a provocative discussion of why religion is important and is fused with moral codes: "The underlying reality of religion is different from that of science in a couple of ways. For one thing, science tells us, as the physicist Steven Weinberg once put it, that the universe is pointless. It has no interest in our success or happiness; it provides no moral guidance. In contrast, the deeper reality expressed in religion is full of meaning or love. For another, while science can tell us about the deeper reality (through tools like microscopes) and can sometimes even manipulate it (through techniques such as gene splicing), religion has even more powerful mojo, because it provides tools that work at an experiential level." *How Pleasure Works: The New Science of Why We Like What We Like* (New York: Norton, 2010), 213.

Five

Identity, Part 1

A Dance Party, Demi Lovato, and the Internal Quest

LATE OCTOBER

I used to wear it like a badge. It was a sign that youth ministry was central to my being: young people never annoyed me. I never wished them ushered away to some cordoned-off space apart from me. Sure, I got irritated with a few personalities here and there. But overall, I enjoyed being around young people.

That is . . . until I had my own.

It's one thing to enjoy tweens and teens at church, on a trip, or at a coffee shop. It's totally another to finish a long day, anticipating a mindless slide into Netflix, and be met instead by a house full of ten-year-old girls in the middle of a dance party. I feel the annoyance growing inside me just thinking about it. I'm no Holly or James. I'm happy with my kids' activities, but sometimes I wish I could take out their batteries.

When I came home from meeting with the parents, I encountered the noise, smells, and chaos of these young people clogging up my space, and I wished for a split second that I was a monk or a lonely bachelor bathing in the warm waters of silence and able to do whatever I wished. The shock of giggle-screaming and blaring Pandora, mixed with my thoughts about the conversations I'd just finished, made for a painful cacophony. *I'm too tired for this*, I thought.

All I could muster when entering the living room was a sarcastic and defeated, "Wow, hello. I didn't know there was a dance party here tonight," all in the tone of *Please, someone send me to Mars!* But no one heard me over the singing of "Sorry Not Sorry."

There's no competing with Demi Lovato's hit song. So I let go of my Netflix fantasy, grabbed a piece of pizza, and watched the train wreck of my night unfold as a tween dance party. Just one piece of pizza in, the song changed to one of Demi's earliest tracks. Back when she wasn't a revenge-seeking vixen but a Disney Channel star. It's called "This Is Me." In it Demi, not that much older than the girls dancing in my family room, sings, "This is real, this is me . . . No more hiding who I want to be." I found myself saying out loud to no one in particular, with a mouthful of pizza, "Now this is a song about finding your *thing*! It's all about being brave enough to broadcast your identity—your way of being you—so you can be recognized." Maisy gave me a look that screamed, *You're embarrassing me!* so I dammed the words from spilling out of my mouth and flooding Maisy with embarrassment by shoving another bite into my piehole.

While all three sets of parents I visited were very different, and they'd disagree on many things, they all tacitly confirmed that Demi is right. Each one felt that each of their children must state to the world, *This is me*, figuring out their own identity. This identity is interlaced with a sense of pursuing the good.[1] Your identity (how you define yourself) and your sense of the good (what is worth living for) are linked.[2] There are times that we live in opposition to who we are, but this is always classified as bad—as a waste. To live a good life, there needs to be some felt coherence between our self-definition

1. Charles Taylor explains, "Perhaps the best way to see this is to focus on the issue that we usually describe today as the question of identity. We speak of it in these terms because the question is often spontaneously phrased by people in the form: Who am I? But this can't necessarily be answered by giving name and genealogy. What does answer this question for us is an understanding of what is of crucial importance to us. To know who I am is a species of knowing where I stand. My identity is defined by the commitments and identifications which provide the frame or horizon within which I can try to determine from case to case what is good, or valuable, or what ought to be done, or what I endorse or oppose. In other words, it is the horizon within which I am capable of taking a stand." *Sources of the Self: The Making of Modern Identity* (Cambridge, MA: Harvard University Press, 1989), 27.

2. "This moral philosophy has tended to focus on what it is right to do rather than on what it is good to be, on defining the content of obligation rather than the nature of the good life; and it has no conceptual place left for a notion of the good as the object of our love or allegiance or, as Iris Murdoch portrayed it in her work, as the privileged focus of attention or will." Taylor, *Sources of the Self*, 3.

and our way of living.[3] We're always reaching for, searching for, pursuing this good, and because of this we are also always searching for our identity itself.[4] As parents think about their child, they assume that identity is a necessary and weighty individual pursuit. Identity is something that each individual child journeys to discover.

Each set of parents has different staples they believe their child must pack when going on this journey for identity. Whether the staples are *knowing, togetherness*, or *activity*, they're like a toothbrush and clean underwear. What's interesting is that, while different, none of the parents I spoke with questioned the presumption and necessity of this *individual* identity journey. All three couples, without question, affirmed that each individual child is on his or her own quest to figure out (and then state) who he or she is.

As each child goes on this journey of identity, the Rodriguez-Eriksons wanted their son to *know* he belonged to Jesus and his youth group, the Tuckers gave their sons family *togetherness*, and the Dahls provided their daughters with constant *activity*. These packed staples are core values. To switch the analogy and draw from Wes, *knowing Jesus, togetherness with family*, and *staying active* are seeds that can grow in the individual soil of the young person. They're indirect ways of influencing and assisting young people as they go on their *own* individual search for identity. These values can be drawn on while on the trail of the identity quest. But what's interesting is that these values can't in themselves be goods that you chase in figuring out who you are. They're just strategies or instruments that help in searching for the deeper good of being happy with who you are.

So while parents can directly plant these values, they nevertheless sense that this isn't enough. Values are important, and at least the Rodriguez-Eriksons and the Tuckers hoped youth ministry is for planting—or better, watering— some of these value seeds. Youth ministry, to switch the analogy again, is to help pack some important values for young people to carry on their individual quests for identity, to feel good about who they are.

3. Taylor tells us where this identity search comes from and how it has shifted: "The search for identity can be seen as the search for what I essentially am. But this can no longer be sufficiently defined in terms of some universal description of human agency as such, as soul, reason, or will. There still remains a question about me, and that is why I think of myself as a self. This word now circumscribes an area of questioning. It designates the kind of being of which this question of identity can be asked." Taylor, *Sources of the Self*, 184.

4. Nicholas Smith helpfully lays out some basic foundations of this point: "As Taylor often says, the most fundamental feature of a self is that things matter to it. The self is first and foremost a being with concerns. If my desires and purposes mean nothing to me, I suffer a loss of self in this sense." *Charles Taylor: Meaning, Morals and Modernity* (Cambridge: Polity, 2002), 96.

Yet these parents sensed that the journey for identity is too taxing to assume that a few staples would sustain their children. A little youth ministry
values-direction isn't enough. The stakes are too high to assume that a few
seeds of knowing, togetherness, and activity will sprout, producing the fruit
of a happy identity. So each set of parents encourages (even at times pushes)
their children, not to have this or that identity but instead to find their own
individual *thing*.[5] Each set of parents believes it is their parenting task not
necessarily to give their children an identity—that's up to their children, as
we'll see more fully below—but to help them find their *thing*.

They believe it's a high good to find your *thing*. This is so important that
if it means at times violating even the values, then so be it. For example, the
Rodriguez-Eriksons allowed Manny to miss youth group for hockey. The
thing is a high good, and even more important than values, because this thing
becomes a *station* in the journey to discover your true identity. Therefore, it
holds more weight on the identity quest. This sense of station possesses two
meanings. Your *thing* (basketball, piano, jujitsu, hunting with your family,
art, making YouTube videos, beatboxing, or graffitiing walls) is a station in
the sense of being a broadcasting mechanism in which you relay to the world,
"*This is me!*" (We'll have much more to say about this sense of station below
and in chapter 7.) But from the parents' perspective, the *thing* is a station, like
a soldier being stationed in San Diego. In this sense, the *thing* gives the young
person a particular marked trail to follow—a way of life—as she quests for
her unique identity and ways to express it. This *thing* is what you're about,
what you're reaching for. This phenomenon plays out very differently in communities under economic and racial oppression. For these young people, even
if your parents can't afford to get you on a travel team or debate team, you
still need a *thing*. That *thing* might be your art or hustle. Your *thing* is what
you're about, and to represent means to state your identity through your *thing*.
And what you're about is believed to essentially be who you are.

If parents can't directly construct their children's identities, then they
can intently (sometimes bordering on furiously) provide particular trails—
zones—in which they hope identity will be discovered. Hockey, traveling choir,
and debate club, if passionately embraced by the young person, become environments or semi-enclosed stations where identity is discovered. This zone
or station is not optional. All young people in all contexts will find some
environment to work out their identity. The only distinction is that it will

---

5. Taylor here tells us why the *thing* is so important: "So the issue for us has to be not only
where we are, but where we're going; and though the first may be a matter of more or less, the
latter is a question of towards or away from, an issue of yes or no." *Sources of the Self*, 47.

either be sanctioned and supported by parents or found on their own on the streets or online.

Parents who lived in the fast times of growing up, or were raised by folks who came of age in that era, understand that leaving this *thing* to children alone is highly risky. So parents like the Rodriguez-Eriksons, Tuckers, and Dahls sense that if they can make the *thing* constructive, positive, future-oriented, filled with skills—and most importantly, fun—the odds are heightened that the chosen identity will produce the ultimate goal: happiness now and in the future. As we said in the previous chapter, usually youth ministry isn't the *thing* for parents or young people, which is why it slides in the ranking of commitments.

Focusing on the Internal Because of the Ethical

Yet even with this *thing*, figuring out that *this is me* is assumed to be an internal pursuit. While it is indeed a quest, and analogically we can talk about trails and journeys, this shouldn't be confused for being anywhere other than hidden within the self. This is why Demi sings about not hiding her real self anymore. This has a sense of the identity being within, something hidden under the surface and deep within the self. So the journey is primarily internal; your true self is supposed to be found within you. It is identity's location deep within the self that makes parents so anxious. No matter how much a parent hopes to pass on values and put energy into their child finding a *thing*, identity nevertheless is assumed to remain up to the child, mysteriously worked out within the self. The Rodriguez-Eriksons particularly, because of the middle-school age of their son, exuded a palpable anxiety about who Manny would choose to be.

Because identity is something we suppose happens inside us, it is something we feel. And because we feel this identity, it is closely connected with our sense of the good; it's bound to a moral feel. Therefore, we now assume that the fastest way to waste your life—or for your child to waste hers—is to live dishonestly with who you feel like you are.

Or we could say it like this: the sources for discovering *this is me*, and therefore the impetus for broadcasting that discovery, come solely from within the young person. *This is who I feel like I am, this is—feels most like—me.*[6] This

6. Taylor adds, "The notion that each one of us has an original way of being human entails that each of us has to discover what it is to be ourselves. But the discovery can't be made by consulting pre-existing models, by hypothesis. So it can be made only by articulating it afresh. We discover what we have it in us to be by becoming that mode of life, by giving expression

sense of identity is assumed to be so locked within the young person's own subjective *feel* that parents like the Rodriguez-Eriksons can *feel* quite power-less in directing a child's sense of identity. To a parent, the young person's inner life can feel like a mud-bottom lake. It's hard to see beneath the surface, and during middle school it just gets murkier. But the parent waits (often in fear and trembling), even while frantically driving her child back and forth from her *thing*, looking into the murky waters, knowing that at some point soon, like a submerged buoy, the child will release her identity, allowing it to be pushed to the surface with a pop that states *this is me*.[7]

As a parent you have to face (or embrace) that even with all your best intentions and wishes, even with all the energy and money poured into help-ing your child find her *thing*, she's free to choose whatever identity she *feels*. And because this feeling is connected to the moral pursuit to not waste your life, it is a high good to "never change who I am," as Imagine Dragons sings. I'm (supposedly) never to be affected by any outside force that tries to shift my identity in a way that doesn't *feel* like me, conforming to someone else's desires or definitions.

This belief, that the pressure of outside forces should never change your internal sense of self, ties these thoughts together with those in the above chapters. Parents concede that identity is an internal—nearly self-enclosed—pursuit because of their own sense of what is good. What is good is to be authentically *your* self, feeling proud to sing, *This is me!*[8] We live in what Charles Taylor calls "the age of authenticity,"[9] a time when it's assumed that

in our speech and action to what is original in us. The notion that revelation comes through expression is what I want to capture in speaking of the 'expressivism' of the modern notion of the individual." Charles Taylor, *The Malaise of Modernity* (Toronto: Anansi Press, 1991), 61.

7. "This is the powerful moral ideal that has come down to us. It accords crucial moral im-portance to a kind of contact with myself, with my own inner nature, which it sees as in danger of being lost, partly through the pressures towards outward conformity, but also because in taking an instrumental stance to myself, I may have lost the capacity to listen to this inner voice. And then it greatly increases the importance of this self-contact by introducing the principle of originality: each of our voices has something of its own to say. Not only should I not fit my life to the demands of external conformity; I can't even find the model to live by outside myself. I can find it only within." Taylor, *Malaise of Modernity*, 29.

8. "Being true to myself means being true to my own originality, and that is something only I can articulate and discover. In articulating it, I am also defining myself. I am realizing a potentiality that is properly my own. This is the background understanding to the modern ideal of authenticity, and to the goals of self-fulfillment or self-realization in which it is usually couched. This is the background that gives moral force to the culture of authenticity, including its most degraded, absurd, or trivialized forms. It is what gives sense to the idea of 'doing your own thing' or 'finding your own fulfillment.'" Taylor, *Malaise of Modernity*, 29.

9. For the interested reader who cares about what came before the age of authenticity, Jason Blakely says helpfully, "Prior to an age of authenticity, identities were often fixed by custom and tradition and enjoyed a kind of a priori recognition. However, once we pass over into an

each individual expression of your own internal sense of your self is a high good.[10] "Authenticity is itself an idea of freedom; it involves my finding the design of my life myself, against the demands of external conformity."[11] It is so high a good that this pursuit of authenticity becomes an ethic. It is a moral good, a right, for everyone to define for themselves, from their internal self, what it means for them to be human. Whatever way any individual person defines what it means for *this* to be *me* must be accepted and affirmed—it's bad or wrong to do otherwise. Each set of parents acknowledged this, telling me again and again that no matter who their child decides to be—even if it means denying something as central to the family as basketball—they'll accept it.[12]

But until that happens, parents will give their children every opportunity to find their *thing*, asking youth ministry to play a supporting role. The *thing* does give parents a small (very small) bit of control next to a plethora of identity options. Parents cannot, without violating this ethic of authenticity,

---

age where individuals and groups seek to express authentic senses of self, there is no guarantee that the identity developed will receive recognition from others (Taylor often refers here to the examples of race, post-colonialism, feminism, or gender politics). If part of what motivates modern selves is a search for authenticity and recognition for their specific way of being human, then 'our identity is partly shaped by recognition or its absence' so that 'non-recognition or misrecognition can inflict harm, can be a form of oppression, imprisoning someone in a false, distorted and reduced mode of being.' Taylor thus has spent a considerable amount of energy advocating for a brand of multiculturalism that responds to the deep modern need for recognition. Sociobiological explanations are dangerous because they elide the need modern peoples have developed for group and cultural recognition. At worst, sociobiology's casting of nationalism as a kind of biological drive may even lead to reinforcement of non-recognition, thus exacerbating the problem." *Alasdair MacIntyre, Charles Taylor, and the Demise of Naturalism* (Notre Dame, IN: University of Notre Dame Press, 2016), 101.

10. Brain J. Braman explains this ethic: "Taylor's view of authenticity expresses the conviction that terms such as *self-fulfillment* and *self-realization* are not just cover stories for narcissism, nor are they terms that justify a stance that is labeled the 'liberalism of neutrality.' Authenticity is a moral ideal that ultimately answers the question of what constitutes the good life. In short, as with [Martin] Heidegger, Taylor understands that acquiring a proper understanding of authenticity is getting at the truth of human existence." *Meaning and Authenticity: Bernard Lonergan and Charles Taylor on the Drama of Authentic Human Existence* (Toronto: University of Toronto Press, 2008), 29.

11. Taylor, *Malaise of Modernity*, 68.

12. Ryan McAnnally-Linz says, "The ideal of authenticity demands, in contrast, that one's identity be forged through expression of something inward and therefore precisely *not* by a given social role. This demand puts recognition into question because an 'inwardly derived, personal, original identity' does not just receive recognition a priori, as a matter of course, in the way that an identity based on a taken-for-granted social category is apt to. As a human being whose identity is dependent on dialogical relations with others, one still needs recognition. But adopting the ideal of authenticity entails that one might not receive it. So, Taylor claims, 'what has come about with the modern age is not the need for recognition, but the conditions in which the attempt to be recognized can fail.'" "An Unrecognizable Glory: Christian Humility in the Age of Authenticity" (PhD diss., Yale University, 2016), 119.

impose (or rule out) their child's chosen sense of self-definition. A bad parent opposes and restricts her child's unique way of feeling, and therefore living out, *this is me*. So while parents can't impose head-on a child's self-definition, they can give him travel teams, computer clubs, and the best violin teacher in the state. But this will only work to impact identity if the young person is passionate about the *thing*, moving it from a hobby to a source of self-definition—a way of life. This is why parents are always checking in and even pushing their children to really invest and care about these expensive (in time and money) commitments. The child at some point has to *feel* like this is who he is—"I'm a hockey player," or "I'm an artist."[13]

So the ethic of authenticity makes finding your *thing* essential, because your *thing* becomes the stage and station to express this unique way of being you. It provides the patterns, practices, language games, way of dressing, and more that allow you to really express who you are. (Of course, this also reveals that our sense that identity is a completely internal reality is false. Nevertheless, some of the excesses—particularly, expressive individualism—of the age of authenticity encourage us to assume it is. More on this in chapter 7.)

Parents have a deep sense that it's wrong to impose any outside coercion on who someone, even their own child, feels he or she is. So parents have to walk a very narrow pass between providing opportunities for their children to find themselves and imposing a way of being that might, in the end, not be who they are. This means that to push a child too hard to make the invested money and time in Suzuki piano her *thing* and therefore part of her self-definition, when she has expressed that it's not, crosses a moral line. A parent needs to be careful; there's a delicate balance between too much and too little pushing. A single mother fears that if she doesn't push academic commitment as her son's *thing*, the streets will take him. At the same time, she fears that if she pushes this *thing* too hard, she'll actually push him right *to* the streets, the streets providing another way of life than academic commitment as his *thing*. So parents have to anxiously balance appropriate pushing and supporting. Parenting a teenager who is immersed in the internal pursuit of identity is an art in cajoling.

We can spot that this individualized internal sense of identity rests on an ethic because, as we said, it's bound in a feel. We always feel our way into

---

13. "It is choice itself that makes you significant. It doesn't matter what you choose. As long as you're happy and satisfied, nobody beyond you can judge. The moral horizon is obliterated. . . . So the point here is that when moral horizons are flattened, and the act of and power to choose becomes what makes us significant, then we have in essence created a new horizon of significance: *choice itself*. It is good to have the power to choose who you will become, and to seize that power; if you don't have or take that choice, you are not living life rightly." Robert Joustra and Alissa Wilkinson, *How to Survive the Apocalypse: Zombies, Cylons, Faith, and Politics at the End of the World* (Grand Rapids: Eerdmans, 2016), 90, 92.

what is good, as noted in chapter 2. None of the parents I talked with had thought about this ethic of authenticity, had never signed a contract to affirm that they'd live in an age of authenticity. Yet, though they came from different backgrounds, they could all feel that, indeed, identity is the core task of their child, and that identity's construction is bound internally. Once the identity has been released and emerges on the surface, the parents—to be good ones—can only accept, recognize, and support whoever and however their child decides *this is me*. If the child's definition of who he or she is changes, it's assumed that only the child has the power to change it.

Most parents are more than willing to follow this ethic, because they feel it. They feel that if they don't, the ultimate goal of their child's happiness will be called into question. Happiness, as we'll explore more in a few chapters, has its foundation in being content with who you are. Happiness may be more than this, but it's assumed to be impossible to be happy without some contentment and acceptance of who you really are. And what most parents want is for their children to be happy. However, ironically, this internal sense of contented happiness, which supposedly rests on an identity solely bound in the self, has a few contradictions, as we'll see—which makes this sense of happiness rarely free of turbulence. But before we can get there, we have to place these thoughts alongside the slowdown of growing up.

The Slowdown and the Deep Quest Inside

The move from the fast times of the late decades of the twentieth century to the slow times of the twenty-first century is interconnected with the sense that each young person *must* construct his or her *own* identity, and that this quest is a deep one with a surplus of options. It's much easier to look the other way and let your kids be, as do Mr. and Mrs. Wheeler from *Stranger Things*, if you have a sense that the environment provides only a few legitimate options for your child's identity. Even if kids are racing to grow up—drinking beer, dating older boys, and hanging loose with Spicoli—in the end, the options of future vocation, religious investment, and overall self-definition are few.

So in the fast times of seeking to grow up quickly, youth ministry was needed to reduce the speed with which young people were racing to grow up, making sure they didn't crash before getting to one of the well-worn identity paths of adulthood. These fast times are over. But the reason for their departure comes with a twist. They are gone not because identity options have narrowed and our overall culture slowed down but because these have sped up, exponentially expanding the identity options. It's very possible that the narrower the identity paths, the more wide-open free space is allowed for experimentation. For example, think of a medieval carnival or rumspringa in the Amish community. These cultural constructs allow for radically open, but rigidly bracketed, times for experimentation—allowing people to get things out of their system—because in the end the identity routes are few and worn, strictly regulating what are legitimate and acceptable identities. This may seem counterintuitive at first blush but actually makes good sense. The overall slowdown into adulthood is directly related to the expanding of identity options and the contention that one's identity is found solely through an internal quest.

Couple this with changes in the economy and the movement to later marriage, and the slowdown is here because, as we've said, parents feel *much less* control.[14] Mr. and Mrs. Wheeler can let their kids roam, caring little about their whereabouts, because in the end they sense that they have a great deal of control. This sense of control is justified—even with their minimal involvement—because the options for identity are only a well-known handful. In the end, a child will essentially take on something close to the identity of their parents. If there was a concern in the fast times, it was that with all this free time and space an accident, pregnancy, or crime could upend the young person. Youth ministry could protect from these dangers by mitigating the fast times with religious fun.

Today the slowdown is in effect because parents take extensive steps to control their children's lives. They take these radical steps for control (like spending fifty hours a week coaching basketball) because they ultimately feel like they have *very little* control. The identity options are so staggeringly open. And, more disorienting, parents are so bound to children's internal *feel* that the only option seems to be to pull their children as close as possible, managing children's stations and making children their life by being their closest friend.

And friendship becomes a valuable key, because a friend is allowed into the hidden space of the internal journey, helping the young person work out his or her identity. Children raised in the fast times, who now are parenting in the slowdown, recognize that friendship held an esteemed place because the

14. Hara Estroff Marano argues that this desire to slow down kids has to do with economic categories almost exclusively. While I think economic categories play their part, I believe it's a mistake to overplay this hand. The slowdown does have to do with this, but it also has to do with fear next to surplus identity options. "Nervousness about globalization has made parents so concerned about competitiveness they believe that they must do everything in their power to not let their kids fall behind. But they make the assumption that their kids have been hit, too. And meaning the best for their kids, they try to protect them." Marano, *A Nation of Wimps: The High Cost of Invasive Parenting* (New York: Broadway Books, 2008), 29.

friend was an invited guest on the adventure to figure out who you are. The friend served the purpose of echoing back to you who you are.[15]

These parents now raising their own children slow them down by taking extensive steps to be the kind of parent-friend who is invited on this more directly internal identity journey—"I can tell my mom anything; she's my best friend." The move to be your child's friend indeed points to a permeability in parenting style (as theorists like eminent psychologist David Elkind and others have argued).[16] Yet what I believe these theorists don't see is how this permeability and drive to be your child's best friend is not necessarily present because of permissiveness or immaturity on the side of parents. Friendship parenting is present because the identity journey is now an anxious internal quest with vast options. Friendship has direct impact on the identity journey without ever threatening to be coercive, which in the end could corrupt the pursuit of happiness.

This is good, even an advance; we should celebrate that some young people think of their parents as friends. But it reveals a change. Youth of the 1980s and 1990s could be left alone to go on all sorts of coming-of-age quests. Spielberg's Elliott returns E.T. to his ship on a flying bike, avoiding the FBI, while Mikey, Brandon, and Data, the goonies, journey for pirate treasure beneath their Oregon town. Adventure and quests were found in the overwhelming amount of free time and space that young people enjoyed. This often made a major part of the outward quest the trying on of all sorts of risky adult behaviors, like smoking, drinking, and sex. For these 1980s and 1990s youth, the journey was not necessarily as directly internal as it is today. For these past youth, there was more of an outward quest for adventure, which, like a wave, would wash them quickly into adulthood.

Yet in the slowdown of growing up, young people are much less free to roam and seek external journeys of adventure. Nevertheless, a quest remains. It has just shifted to being radically internal. The point of growing up isn't to go on adultlike adventures with your friends. Parents' hovering presence and the time spent mastering your *thing* won't allow for this. Nevertheless, the young person is on a quest into an inner world of expansive options, seeking to come to some unique sense that *this is me*.

With the well-worn identity paths to adulthood multiplied to the nth degree, young people now stand before an exponentially larger array of options

15. David Brooks points to this friendship reality: "Parents and children, even college-age children, communicate constantly. With only quiet qualms young people have accepted the vast achievement system that surrounds them. They submit to it because they long for the approval they get from the adults they love." *The Road to Character* (New York: Random House, 2015), 256.

16. See Elkind, *Ties That Stress: The New Family Imbalance* (Cambridge, MA: Harvard University Press, 1994).

when it comes to identity.[17] These options lead parents with economic privilege to pull their children closer, managing and minimizing the risk of their external activities, so that the radically open voyage of the internal is not damaged.

The coming-of-age quest is no longer out in the world, going on adventures with your friends, seeing a dead body on a railroad track as in the movie *Stand by Me*. Rather, the great quest, almost completely internal now, is a mission to discover who you most fully feel like you are. Now the young person does this alone, maybe with a friend, but no longer with a neighborhood group. Rather, she's now in her room under her parents' (friendly, constant) eye, searching the internet (which again shows that this isn't quite as purely internal as we assume).

The slowdown happens not because parents like the Tuckers and Dahls feel the external world is a more dangerous place but because they sense that the stakes of a chosen identity are much higher than when they were young. Parents keep their kids close, controlling all their external activities, because the voyage inward feels uncontrollable. If a child is confused or shamed, or overall feels unaccepted for her identity—getting the message that her feel of *this is me* is wrong or bad—then all roads to happiness seem closed.

This is why bullying is now, thank goodness, a top issue that demands the quickest intervention by teachers, youth workers, and coaches. Back during the fast times, bullying was rife; older kids picked on many of us all the time. To be a seventh grader or freshman was to always feel unsafe. But few adults intervened, because they assumed this experience was part of growing up. Unfortunately, they seemed to believe that bullying could actually serve a good purpose; it could, they wrongly believed, toughen you up for the external adventures that followed, readying you to be an adult in one of the well-worn paths of identity. Few would articulate it quite like this, but it was assumed that bullying could actually penalize odd behavior, making the well-worn paths appear the only identity option.

Thankfully this is not so in the slowdown. Bullying is now recognized as a hideous problem that must be dealt with immediately and swiftly, because it is a direct attack on the internal identity. Bullying violently opposes the unique expression of a young person's *this is me*. Because we no longer assume there are only a handful of identity paths, but perhaps as many as there are people, bullying can have *no* productive impact. It can only cause discontent and

17. Joustra and Wilkinson explain, "So when we're answering the big question—Who am I?—it's scary, but it's also freeing. Our lives, personally as well as socially, are full of possibilities. Our personal development, as well as our social development, doesn't have to be locked into one unswerving direction. It's a process of faithful compromise, of genuine (if fraught) exploration, and one that does not end." *How to Survive the Apocalypse*, 187.

shame about the child's self-definition, which absent intervention can lead to self-hatred, making it impossible for the young person to be happy. The response to bullying, then, must be zero tolerance, because we *feel* Demi is right, that each individual has to internally discover his or her identity.

The slowdown of growing up happens because parents feel like they must pull their child close, both to manage the stations in which identity will be discovered and, in turn, to make sure that, no matter how the identity becomes expressed, the child is protected from negative recognition of this identity.

Emotional Safety and Identity

The parents I talked with went out of their way to fiercely protect their children from feeling unsafe, because a good parent is aware that what's most important is their child's internal journey, her quest to embrace and express *this is me*. Sitting watching the ten-year-old dance party in my living room while I ate too much pizza, I was aware that I, for good reasons, do the same. I do it because avoidance of emotional injury has become essential to getting to the hypergood of happiness. I would never wish emotional or physical danger on one of my children. But I was becoming aware that my pursuits of emotional safety could keep my children from resilience and grit (as Angela Duckworth has famously written about).[18]

Even when parents understand the need for resilience, some have a very hard time allowing for the circumstances that would develop it. The fear is that if a child feels unsafe, it means she must hide her *this is me*, and perhaps even lead her to wonder whether her self-definition can't be embraced and is therefore wrong. This feeling, against the background of the internal identity quest, is very risky. Parents work hard to protect their children from such feelings because parents fear that these negative emotions will contaminate their child's inner life. And the young person herself interprets her chosen way of expressing *this is me* under threat.

It becomes a parent's primary job to protect the child from emotional injury so that the child never gets the idea that his chosen identity is wrong or bad.[19] Again, I don't intend this as a wholesale critique of this drive for safety.

18. See Duckworth, *Grit: The Power of Passion and Perseverance* (New York: Scribner, 2016).
19. Jean Twenge provides more: "iGen'ers' risk aversion goes beyond their behaviors toward a general attitude of avoiding risk and danger. Eighth and 10th graders are now less likely to agree that 'I like to test myself every now and then by doing something a little risky.' Nearly half of teens found that appealing in the early 1990s, but by 2015 less than 40% did." *iGen:*

Feeling safe is important; my description of how this drive for safety functions next to the pursuit of identity shouldn't be misinterpreted as criticism.
My point is to show why some parents, myself included, feel a need to take
decisive action when their child says he feels unsafe. We do so because it's assumed that too many episodes of feeling unsafe leave a permanent emotional
injury. To feel unsafe could make the young person feel like his unique identity
isn't affirmed. And in a world where identity options are exponential and
created internally, that's frightening. Emotional injury is terrifying because
it threatens to damage the internal self, like frying the internal circuits of
your computer's motherboard by plugging in too many unsafe USB devices.

To be emotionally injured brings a dark, stormy chaos to the internal quest,
making life much harder. Emotional injury can strike in two directions, both
of which frighten parents. First, emotional injury risks upending (or negatively redirecting) the construction of identity. It is assumed that because of
your emotional injury you can never be happy with who you are. Second,
emotional injury can happen when a young person who is expressing her
chosen identity finds no one to embrace it, no one who recognizes her unique
expressions of her unique self. She's emotionally injured because she feels like
her way of *being her* is recognized only by haters. It becomes a moral man-
tra, a therapeutic strategy, to just "shake, shake, shake it [the haters] off," as
Taylor Swift sings. Charles Taylor says, "The thing about inwardly derived,
personal, original identity is that it doesn't enjoy this recognition a priori. It
has to win it through exchange, and it can fail."[20]

Emotional injury is so risky because it ultimately witnesses to a discontent
with the inner feel of the self. To rise above the haters and find contentment
with her self—shaking, shaking, shaking it off more and more—the young
person must work much harder at forming and expressing her true self. But
this is nearly impossible when this self-chosen identity demands recognition,
that people see her unique way of being her. And yet it's believed that without some contentment or even satisfaction with her self, happiness—being
happy—will evade her, or at least be undependable. The ultimate objective for
parents, as we've said, is for their children to be happy, so providing emotional
safety becomes essential. With so much about the construction of identity
feeling uncontrollable, working hard to furiously protect a child—even a
twenty-year-old one—from emotional injury, slowing them down, constantly
overseeing them, and being their best friend are things parents can do.

---

*Why Today's Super-Connected Kids Are Growing Up Less Rebellious, More Tolerant, Less
Happy—and Completely Unprepared for Adulthood* (New York: Atria Books, 2017), 152.
    20. Taylor, *Malaise of Modernity*, 48.

Youth Ministry in the Slowdown of Internal Identity Quest

When youth ministry is in a supporting role, seen as adding to (or at least watering) the seeds of values that parents plant and offering tools for finding happiness, then youth ministry, too, becomes for protection from emotional injury. It's primarily the job of parents to do this protecting, but youth ministry can help, offering skills and perspectives that are affirming and supportive. Depending on the tradition—particularly if mainline or evangelical—the youth ministry will be permitted, in varying degrees, to engage the inner construction of identity.

Parents in evangelical traditions will expect the youth ministry to push *some* against the expressed identity, asking young people to correlate their *this is me* statements with the biblical tradition. But this pushing will have limits. And if it starts to feel (to a young person or a parent) like the youth ministry isn't accepting, and is therefore unsafe, it will be too much a risk to continue participating, due to fear of emotional injury. Mainline youth ministries will take on a disposition of never pushing against someone's identity, claiming to be tolerant of all. The mainline youth ministry will push emotional safety to a more central place, helping young people even see it as the ministry's mission to stand with all those who feel unsafe or who are emotionally injured for claiming their unique identity.

In some ways this is all very important. We should never harm another person or stand by idly if witnessing harm. Abuse, particularly, is always wrong, and the emotional injury from it must be respected and embraced. So the last thing we should wish for is that our youth ministries make people feel unsafe. But full acceptance of this internal sense of identity seems to inevitably push youth ministry and, more importantly, Christianity (or even religious ways of being and knowing) to the margins. As mentioned, some theorists are discovering that this most recent generation (often called Generation Z or iGen) is growing up more slowly than their predecessors. So it's no wonder—and I would say it is actually because of this—that they are much more individualistic and internally focused, and far less religious.[21] Some even claim that religion as a whole is unsafe. If youth ministry is going to be for anything deeper than watering value seeds and being a benign, safe place that serves as another tool for happiness, then it will have to affirm this sense of an identity quest—and also challenge it.

---

21. "Affiliating with a religion was once a near-universal experience for young people: In the early 1980s, more than 90% of high school seniors identified as part of one religious group or another, meaning that only one out of ten chose 'none' for his or her religious affiliation. As late as 2003, 87% of 10th graders affiliated with a religion. Then that changed. Beginning in the 1990s and accelerating in the 2000s, fewer and fewer young people affiliated with a religion." Twenge, *iGen*, 121.

What about a Little Romance?

Back in the middle of the dance party, as I grabbed for my third slice of pizza, I thought about Joey Chestnut. He's the professional competitive eater who holds world records in rib meat, chicken wings, and, most famously, hot dogs. Believe it or not, he consumed seventy-four hot dogs in a mere ten minutes. Sitting at the edge of the dance party, I wondered about his record for pizza. I was on slice three, and Demi's song was just half finished.

As I daydreamed of taking Joey Chestnut down, ripping his title belt away from his sweaty graphic tee, the girls in the room screamed, snapping me back to reality. Coming from the speaker was a boy's voice. None of us realized when it started that Demi's old song was a duet, but that wasn't why they were screaming. As I wondered whose voice this was, one of the girls giggle-screamed, "It's Joe Jonas. Nick's brother! Nick is so hot! I sooo wish he was my boyfriend!"

As the stereotypical dad on the fringe, a little tipsy with pizza, I shouted into the room, "No! Nooooo boyfriends! Maisy has to be twenty-five before she's allowed to have a boyfriend."

Maisy's eyes shot me a dagger, which communicated clearly, *Strike two!* Her derision sent me quickly back to the pizza box, now *sure* I'd be Joey Chestnut's worst nightmare. As I smashed into my next piece, I remembered that James Dahl had said something funny and insightful about dating and boyfriends. But I couldn't really remember it.

Six

Transformation in Youth Ministry

LATE MARCH

Youth ministry is for joy?" I repeat in confusion, sitting in that nondescript fellowship hall. Watching J and Lorena smile at each other, it feels like I'm on the outside of an inside joke. My tone of puzzlement only makes them laugh harder, assuring me that I'm missing something.

As I try to work out what this strange answer could possibly mean, I notice the setting sun spilling through a side window, and I flash back to Graham, Kathryn, Wes, and the three sets of parents. Thinking about them, I wonder how joy could be the answer for what youth ministry is for. It just seems so odd.

In those few seconds of silence, the setting sun through the window reminds me that it's staying much lighter now. It's always such a welcome relief when days are longer. March had come in like a lion in the Upper Midwest; a huge snowstorm arrived at the end of the first week, pulling us back deep into winter after it felt over. But now the late-staying sun and the temperature touching the sixties are assurance enough that March will end like a lamb and spring is here to stay. Thinking about the warmer evenings, the freedom from hats and heavy coats, and spring's overall transfiguration gives me the smallest but surest taste of joy.

This amuse-bouche is enough to rebalance me, helping me regain enough mental equilibrium to find a follow-up question. So I respond to J and Lorena: "You seem so sure that youth ministry is for joy—you answered so quickly— but why did you use the word *joy*? Clearly you've talked about it. And I know it's a biblical word, but it isn't a word we usually use, particularly connected to youth ministry."

"It's the best word we have for the experience of transformation," Lorena says, again responding in a way that makes her seem way older than twelfth grade.

I'm not sure this is exactly true, and J must be able to read that on my face, so she jumps in, returning to the subject of her near firing and youth ministry breakdown. "When I was trying to do youth ministry as the lead counselor of fun, it became really clear to me that youth ministry wasn't about change or transformation; it was about retention."

I nod, spurring J to continue. "People kept telling me to make it fun, so kids would choose to come. And that was a killer! When people tell you to *make* something fun, like telling you to be funny on cue, especially when you're feeling overwhelmed and exhausted, it's so hard. It just zaps you further. But there were times I was actually good at it. Usually it was when I stole some game or idea from a popular youth ministry website. But even when it went well, I wasn't sure there was any sense of transformation. They may have been having fun 50 percent of the time, but I'm not sure we'd met any kind of deep transformation."

J pauses, blinks quickly to hold back some emotions, and continues, "And honestly, the more I was failing at youth ministry, the more people were actually sending me to popular youth ministry sites and conferences, which took me farther away from this deep sense of transformation. Some even talked about transformation, but it was really all about what you did and what you got kids to do . . . which only made me *more* burned out and tired."

"*That's* when I came in!" Lorena interrupts, with a fragile confidence, breaking the tense moment with some silly humor.

J laughs and says, "It is! When Lorena got sick, everything changed. And not only with our youth ministry, but with me, with the whole church. We started to witness real transformation."

Moving to the edge of my seat, I ask, "What did your youth ministry look like? What did you do? What changed?"

"We didn't *do* anything, really. That's why it was joy, because it came as a pure gift, not as something we did," J responds. "We had a sick kid, not a program or strategy."

"You didn't do anything?" I ask, not sure that could be true, but now for the first time seeing how this focus on joy could be the key I was looking for.

"No, you're right," J says. "We did start doing a lot of things, but that wasn't the point. We could only get to joy when we focused more on receiving."

We sit in silence for a few more seconds, and I notice that sun from the window has shifted onto the floor and crept right up to our table. I'm not sure if I actually feel its heat or just imagine it, but its presence next to our conversation gives me an overall feeling of warmth. I'm no longer feeling outside the punch line but blessed to be part of it. Still, there is so much more I don't know, like really what this all looks like and how it connects to Lorena and her brush with death. But the moment calls first for silent reflection.

J finally breaks our stillness, saying, "So, for us, joy is a description of our experience of transformation. To say youth ministry is for joy is to say it comes from God's gifts, and when we receive them, we're changed."[1]

"That's about way more than pizza and a Christian boyfriend!" Lorena adds like a Flavor Flav rap hype man to J's Chuck D. The three of us laugh.

When Lorena says "pizza" and "boyfriend," it flashes me back to late October and Maisy's Demi Lovato dance party. I can hear in my mind "This Is Me"—it's playing on loop and will be stuck in my head now for the next day. I knew James Dahl had said something funny and insightful about dating and boyfriends, but I couldn't untangle it in my mind right then. Yet Lorena's comment is the serum that brings James's words to my memory.

---

1. David Brooks adds, "Joy is not produced because others praise you. Joy emanates unbidden and unforced. Joy comes as a gift when you least expect it. At those fleeting moments you know why you were put here and what truth you serve. You may not feel giddy at those moments, you may not hear the orchestra's delirious swell or see flashes of crimson and gold, but you will feel a satisfaction, a silence, a peace—a hush. Those moments are the blessings and the signs of a beautiful life." *The Road to Character* (New York: Random House, 2015), 270.

Seven

Identity, Part 2

Romance, Recognition, and Resentment

LATE OCTOBER

When I had asked the Dahls why they were willing to spend so much time coaching basketball, James had said with his dry sense of humor, "Because it will keep the boys away." I laughed, and mostly thought James was kidding, but there was enough sincerity in his statement for him to continue, "Seriously, I think the more basketball, the later dating starts. That's worth a hundred hours a week for a dad with four daughters."

Now starting to slow down on my pizza as I shadowboxed Joey Chestnut, I wondered why Demi, in this song that celebrates the individual internal *feel* of identity, needs Joe Jonas. Why is he needed in this internal quest to state *this is me*? But there he is, singing, "I gotta find you / You're the missing piece I need."

One of the clearest signs that we're in the midst of a major slowdown in young peoples' growing up is dating habits. In the fast times it was different. In the movie *Fast Times at Ridgemont High*, fifteen-year-old Stacy lies about her age to date twenty-six-year-old stereo salesman Ron Johnson. It's not that kids today don't want boyfriends and girlfriends, even being willing to lie and sometimes tragically finding themselves in criminal situations with older individuals. For a contemporary example that parallels *Fast Times at Ridgemont High*, in season 1 of the Netflix show *Ozark*, Martin Byrde's fifteen-year-old daughter is in an identity crisis. Like Stacy, she lies about her age to have sex at Party Cove with a man in his midtwenties. Yet even with these parallels, overall, things appear to have changed in the slowdown. Not only has courting shifted from one-on-one dates to group activities and text messages, but the obsession with having a boyfriend or girlfriend has also waned for most young people. Many parrot back their parents' proclamations that they're "just too young" or "too busy for that." In the fast times, Stacy couldn't wait to date and had loads of free time to do so, much like an adult—with as many fancy one-on-one dinners and fast cars and as much sex as possible. These were fast times, after all.

Yet today research reveals that American young people—particularly high-school-aged students like Stacy—are waiting much longer to have a boyfriend/girlfriend or even their first kiss[1] (though they're watching pornography much younger, but that's a whole other can of worms[2]). Many are reluctant to date. And when they finally do, having their first kiss for instance, it often doesn't happen beyond the knowledge of mom and dad. Stacy starts fully clothed under the blankets when her mom tucks her in, then sneaks out of her parents' house to meet Ron. She wants so badly to date like an adult and therefore must do so behind her parents' back. Today things have changed. Young people may make contact and flirt online or in text messages without their parents knowing, maybe even sending risqué pics. Yet if there is going to be a meetup, it most often happens through direct parental participation. For example, because so many young people are waiting longer to get a driver's license, mom or dad becomes wingman and friend with whom to debrief it all. And this shift is perceived, by both parents and kids, as a much safer way to do things.

1. Jean Twenge notes that kissing at skating rinks is "less common," as is dating among teens: "Only about half as many iGen high school seniors vs. Boomers and GenX'ers at the same age ever go out on dates. In the early 1990s, nearly three out of four 10th graders sometimes dated, but by the 2010s only about half did." She also notes, "The lack of dating leads to the next surprising fact about iGen: they are less likely to have sex than teens in previous decades. The drop is the largest for 9th graders, where the number of sexually active teens has almost been cut in half since the 1990s." *iGen: Why Today's Super-Connected Kids Are Growing Up Less Rebellious, More Tolerant, Less Happy—and Completely Unprepared for Adulthood* (New York: Atria Books, 2017), 20, 22.

2. See Gary Wilson, *Your Brain on Porn: Internet Pornography and the Emerging Science of Addiction* (Kent, UK: Commonwealth, 2014). While indeed it is a different can of worms, it connects to our overall movements into the good. Miroslav Volf considers pornography an example of a larger phenomenon: "Parched for meaning, we then project the power to give meaning onto the finite goods that surround us—the muscle tone of our bodies, steamy sex, loads of money, success in work, fame, family, or nation. But looking for meaning in finite things is a bit—in one regard and to a degree only—like experiencing sexual fulfillment from pornography: it isn't just addictively unfulfilling; as a crass simulacrum of a genuine good, it eats away at our ability to enjoy actual sex." *Flourishing: Why We Need Religion in a Globalized World* (New Haven: Yale University Press, 2015), 202.

Romance and Internal Quest: Let's Get Just a Little Genealogical

If it's true that James Dahl and other parents want to delay their children's dating for as long as possible—and if young people, too, believe it is safer not to date—then why does Joe Jonas show up in Demi Lovato's homage to the quest for internal identity? Why is it necessary for Joe, like a comet out of nowhere, to invade Demi's own internal quest for *this is me*? Some feminist cultural critiques can help us understand why a young woman is told she supposedly needs a man. These critiques point to something true about late modernity as a whole. Yet a short listen to the Top 40 and the voices of other young men like Ed Sheeran, The Weeknd, or Adam Levine of Maroon 5 reveal a similar longing for romance as an important (maybe essential) internal pathway to identity. So to answer why Joe needs to appear (seemingly inconsistently) in Demi's hymn of her *own* internal identity, we have to look back, decoding for just a bit the genome of our internal identity quest.

This journey for identity, as we've said, is lodged within late modernity's age of authenticity.[3] The age of authenticity has its origins in the thought and ethos of Bohemian Romanticism in the eighteenth and nineteenth centuries.[4] This sense that every human being has a right to define for oneself what it means to be *uniquely* human was something that only a small group of mainly artists, novelists, and poets in Berlin, Paris, London, and New York believed. Overall, it was a minority report, stuck in little artist enclaves in Soho or Le Bateau-Lavoir. Most, other than these avant-garde, organized their lives around duty and loyalty to larger structures like the state, the church, and the family. If you thought about your own identity at all back then, wondering who you were, you might go to war.

3. Jennifer A. Herdt provides a nice discussion of authenticity: "For [Charles] Taylor, authenticity at its best and most coherent does not imply ignoring all moral demands that transcend the self or instrumentalizing all relationships to the end of individual self-fulfillment. What it does require is that each person be true to himself or herself, in the sense of grasping the particular way of being that is properly and uniquely his or her own and living it out. The moral life is fundamentally one of self-discovery and self-expression, rather than conformity to external models. . . . Like [Jeffrey] Stout, Taylor advocates this ideal both simply because he believes it to be ours, at the root of our culture, and because of its intrinsic worth. He articulates this worth not in terms of a negative freedom from what lies beyond the self but rather in terms of a positive account of fuller selfhood: 'authenticity points us towards a more self-responsible form of life. It allows us to live (potentially) a fuller and more differentiated life, because more fully appropriated as our own.'" *Putting on Virtue: The Legacy of the Splendid Vices* (Chicago: University of Chicago Press, 2008), 7.

4. "The seedbed of the culture of authenticity lies for the most part among what Taylor calls the *Romantic* axes." Ryan McAnnally-Linz, "An Unrecognizable Glory: Christian Humility in the Age of Authenticity" (PhD diss., Yale University, 2016), 94.

The period from the nineteenth to the first half of the twentieth century was filled with young men in particular yearning for war so they could test their mettle and find out what they were made of. Ernest Hemingway, people longing for the Wild West, Teddy Roosevelt, and thousands of sixteen- and seventeen-year-olds who lied about their age to join the Pacific or European theaters in World War II come quickly to mind. War was adventure that revealed who you really were. Doing your duty, even to death, revealed your internal resolve, building a sturdy character—if you survived.

Roosevelt is a good example. Teddy felt like he'd never know what he was made of until he found himself on the battlefield. He felt as if he'd been cursed that no war had been available to his generation. So when one arrived, even though at forty he seemed too old, Roosevelt felt like he couldn't miss it. So, in the last years of the nineteenth century, he resigned from his important post as assistant to the secretary of the Navy to fight in the Spanish-American War. Forming the Rough Riders, he did all he could to place himself in the heat of the battle in Cuba, ready to die doing his duty. As a good father, he'd later encourage his own sons to fight too—to find out what they were made of by doing their duty in the trenches of World War I.[5]

However, in the late 1960s, with another war raging, now in Indochina, things radically changed. The Vietnam War in many ways was doomed because it assumed, both militarily and culturally, a continuity with World War II. Not recognizing that duty and war itself were no longer assumed to be costly but productive ways of finding what you were made of, a new journey was unfolding in our larger cultural imagination. And shockingly, this new perspective was coming from those who refused to carry a gun or dig a ditch. This new perspective was engendered by the small avant-garde enclaves of artists and novelists who spoke of individual uniqueness, nonconformity to duty, and the power of romance.

5. Of course, it is not that romance was completely absent. There were many wartime love affairs. And the troubadours had been with us for hundreds of years. Hubert Dreyfus and Sean Dorrance Kelly discuss the impact of the troubadours: "In his poem Dante does not neglect Jesus and seek access to an eternal disembodied God by way of his deepest inner self, as did Augustine. Dante was a totally outgoing person deeply involved in the politics of his city of Florence and also totally devoted to the woman who inspired his poem. Happily for him the early Christian mood of total devotion to Jesus had indirectly inspired a group of French poets called troubadours to develop a new understanding of love. It wasn't Greek erotic desire, but it wasn't Christian agape either. It was a new mood that came to be called courtly love. This new kind of love involved total devotion to a person who became the center of pure life. Indeed, in the troubadour tradition your beloved actually gives you your identity. Without her you would cease to exist as the person you have become in loving her. You understand who you are entirely in relation to her, and therefore you are ready to die for her. In short, the troubadours invented romantic love and Dante was a romantic lover." *All Things Shining: Reading the Western Classics to Find Meaning in a Secular Age* (New York: Free Press, 2011), 129.

Yet, of course, this isn't the whole story. These small groups of artists and novelists had no power to shift our cultural imagination. Their sense of being on a quest for a unique identity, to be truly authentic as opposed to dutiful, needed to meet the perfect carrier. It took the late 1960s youth counterculture and Madison Avenue's dissemination of this Bohemian ethos to the whole society to move the avant-garde to the mainstream.[6] The search for a uniquely authentic identity beyond duty now became a primary task across the culture. As the largest middle-class generation came of age in the womb of free time and space in the late 1960s, they embraced this ethic of authenticity, this individual internal pursuit of an identity, as their own.

Throughout the rest of the twentieth century, adventure would still have its place. Like a recessive gene, it would pop back up in the fast times of the 1980s and 1990s, but with a new twist: now adventure itself had to be molded around authenticity. Think again of Spielberg. The goonies sought adventure, even going to war with a country club, but their adventure was not for the sake of duty, and it was not related to structures like the state or family or school—or even an ideal like patriotism. Rather, adventure was connected to your self-chosen friends.[7] On these adventures with friends, the war was a way to find yourself. And romance—embraces, kisses, and overall sexual feelings—was essential to and interlaced with, becoming nearly one with, the adventure to claim your unique sense of self. Even in the fast times, the goal was your own identity, and at the end of these 1980s movies the kids not only won the day but did so by finding their most authentic selves. The romantic kiss was the potent empowerment that gave the individual the strength of identity to win the adventure and conquer the foe.

If we regard *Stranger Things* as fitting into the same genre as the 1980s Spielberg movies, then Mike and Eleven's romance must be as central to the plot as the search for Will. Eleven can only really find her authentic, unique self through her romance with Mike. And side romances, too, must be brewing under the surface, pushing the story forward, leading us to anticipate their revelation. They come to fruition at the very time the characters need them to find their truest selves. After season 2 we're all waiting in anticipation for Hopper and Joyce to admit their love and for Mike's sister, Nancy, to tell the world that it's Jonathan Byers (Will's outcast, unpopular, and therefore authentically unique brother) whom she truly loves. This confession of romance will reveal who Nancy truly is on the inside.

6. For more on this, see part 1 of my *Faith Formation in a Secular Age: Responding to the Church's Obsession with Youthfulness* (Grand Rapids: Baker Academic, 2017).

7. This is to echo Anthony Giddens, *Modernity and Self-Identity: Self and Society in the Late Modern Age* (Stanford, CA: Stanford University Press, 1991).

Romance and Identity

In the age of authenticity, instead of going to war to test your mettle, do your duty, and harvest adventure, you made love. "Make love, not war" was more than just a catchphrase of the late 1960s. It pointed to a major shift. It was more than just a middle finger to the establishment—though of course it was that too. More importantly, "make love, not war" was a new assertion about how the direct quest for identity could be achieved. Really finding out who you are would no longer happen on the battlefield of duty but in and through romance. You were no longer seeking to find your own dutiful part to play in the larger structures of society but rather your own uniquely authentic way of being human.[8]

This made love the new battlefield (yep, that's a Pat Benatar reference). If you need a more contemporary example, think about Pink. A common theme running through her albums, songs, and videos is the war of romance—even at times leading her to throw both verbal and physical hooks at her on-again, off-again lover Carey Hart. Romance as its own bloody battlefield next to the individual internal pursuits of identity can be seen most clearly in her album *The Truth about Love*, with singles like "Blow Me (One Last Kiss)," "Just Give Me a Reason," "True Love," and "Walk of Shame." (Or listen to the opening lyrics of her 2018 hit "Beautiful Trauma": "We were on fire / I slashed your tires / It's like we burned so bright we burned out.") Not surprisingly, Pink is also deeply insightful about the need for recognition. Her song "Raise Your Glass" is an anthem to the unique internal construction of identity.

In the age of authenticity, then, it's the romantic relationship that tests our mettle. It's here that we figure out who we really are. In the spirit of Bohemian Romanticism, we all, in one measure or another, contend that it's romantic love and the feelings of a sexual charge that move us to the authentic depth of the self.

Demi's song is all about the internal discovery of her unique identity because she is questing for *this is me*. If Demi is really to find her *truest* identity,

---

8. "The easiest way to see this is to consider how we often talk about romantic relationships today. Does your boyfriend not accept 'who you are'? Break off that relationship. Does your wife try to box you in with her expectations? It's time to seek counseling, or just get out of there altogether. We often advise teenagers of the importance of finding someone with whom you can 'be yourself'—that is, someone who accepts you for who you are, for better or worse. 'I finally found somebody who loves me for me,' characters say in movies, and that's when we know they've found The One." Robert Joustra and Alissa Wilkinson, *How to Survive the Apocalypse: Zombies, Cylons, Faith, and Politics at the End of the World* (Grand Rapids: Eerdmans, 2016), 109.

it will happen through romance.[9] Enter Joe (or Joyce or Justin or Johanna). Joe, then, isn't out of place at all. Rather, because Demi is questing to *feel* her truest self, romance becomes essential. Demi's song is the proclamation of her own internal sense of who she is. That Joe appears like a comet isn't inconsistent after all; it's logical, because a romantic interlude is what will take Demi to her deepest emotive depth. This romantic experience will reveal who she really is. As Robert Joustra and Alissa Wilkinson say, referencing Charles Taylor, "This validation of the individual within intimate relationships finds its most crucial home today in love relationships, particularly romantic ones. Relationships, for us, are the 'key loci' of self-discovery and self-confirmation, says Taylor. They are 'crucibles of inwardly generated identity'—in my boyfriend or girlfriend . . . , who I *think* I am is tested by fire."[10]

Romance and the Slowdown

This connection between identity and romance helps us understand why a major part of the slowdown of growing up revolves around dating habits and late first kisses.[11] The fact that young people are waiting to participate in these romantic realities, choosing to stick nearer to their parents and claim with them that they're too young, isn't contradictory to the centrality of romance in the identity quest but rather shows its ultimate potency. If love is a battlefield, then every parent will experience their child's entrance into the war of romantic love with a level of anxiety, even wishing they could dodge the draft. Some parents work hard to protect their child completely from it (or at least until they are twenty-five, as James Dahl joked). As we saw above, the slowdown doesn't stand in opposition to the surplus of identity options. Rather, the slowdown starkly shows how open identity choices are, and how deeply identity is connected to the feel of a romantic relationship.

In the nineteenth century, war was risky but was nevertheless the most direct way to discover what young men were made of. This shift to romance seems like progress. Better to find yourself heartbroken, deleting old photos and changing your Facebook relationship status, than bleeding out in a French hedgerow. Yet, while the mortal peril may be lessened, the emotional risk

9. Taylor adds, "This culture puts a great emphasis on relationships in the intimate sphere, especially love relationships. These are seen to be the prime loci of self-exploration and self-discovery and among the most important forms of self-fulfillment." *The Malaise of Modernity* (Toronto: Anansi Press, 1991), 45.

10. Joustra and Wilkinson, *How to Survive the Apocalypse*, 109.

11. See Kate Julian, "Why Are Young People Having So Little Sex?," *Atlantic*, December 2018, https://www.theatlantic.com/magazine/archive/2018/12/the-sex-recession/573949.

remains high. Heartbreak is a heavy threat because it not only hurts but, more, reaches deeper to "mess with your head," as young people might say. And it reaches to this depth because it's a primary vehicle for identity construction. Romance is an essential way to feel who you are. Then when romance turns acidic, it eats at your self-definition.

It's no wonder, then, that pop stars sing lyrics like "I'm lost without you / I don't know who I am when you're gone." My guess is that you can't put your finger on which particular song this is, because it feels like so many.[12] That same Demi Lovato sings in her 2018 hit "Tell Me You Love Me," "And all my friends, they know and it's true / I don't know who I am without you." Then the chorus shouts and repeats, "You ain't nobody 'til you got somebody." This shows clearly the centrality of romance to identity, particularly this internal identity quest Demi started in "This Is Me." For another example that shows the battle and pain of love, think of Shawn Mendes's 2017 hit song "Stitches." He sings, "I thought that I've been hurt before / But no one's ever left me quite this sore / Your words cut deeper than a knife."

Love is indeed a battlefield—for identity. It's no wonder that young people talk often about relationship PTSD. The pain of their lost love feels like battle wounds, because it leads them to doubt who they are, making them jumpy about ever opening up to anyone again. This is the central theme of season 1 of MTV's lowbrow reality series *Floribama Shore*. Nilsa and Aimee are haunted by their ex-boyfriends, not sure they can ever love again, but they need to in order to find their true selves. The theme shows up over and over again in more polished shows like Netflix's *Love*, produced by Judd Apatow.

Catching a Contagion

So love is now a very dangerous game. So dangerous that involved parents like Holly and James seek to protect their girls from it, hoping basketball and other passions, which become their girls' *thing*, will compensate, pushing the romantic relationship battlefield off until they're more emotionally ready for the carnage they're bound to see.

And it's not just parents who are uneasy about this romance risk. Some young people, too, fear its impact, recognizing that a romance will press in on their identity through deep feelings. A new idiomatic warning has surfaced in the culture. Young people say to one another, "Oh no, I think I'm catching

12. Here I'm actually thinking of Tegan and Sara and their album *Heartthrob*. It's filled with songs of love lost and the identity crisis that occurs because of it. Tegan and Sara are sisters from Calgary, both lesbians, which makes their music of love and identity particularly interesting.

feelings," or "Dude, I'm worried, because we've been hooking up and now I'm afraid she's caught some feelings," or "I hate when I catch feelings so early; it gives her the upper hand, and I get so afraid I'm going to get hurt."[13]

"Catching feelings" is a particularly interesting phrase, because it implies that emotions of romance are a virus that comes from the environment. But it impacts the inner constitution, always happening against the person's direct will. Young people catch feelings like an illness when they'd rather not. And to catch feelings is particularly risky because it means that this person has found his or her way into your internal feelings about your self. This other person now has the power to influence how you understand your self. Our identity is built around feel, and now that you've caught feelings for this person, he or she has the ability to influence your individual quest to state *this is me*.[14]

This power is why some young people call it "catching feelings" and fear these feelings will mess with their head. It's a risk not often wished for, like catching diphtheria on the front. It makes you susceptible to injury. Mainly, in this context, if the other person has not caught the same feelings, the same contagion, disappointment and pain are coming. It's not good to catch feelings that aren't reciprocal. It's a painful waste—even deeply embarrassing—to have your deepest feelings, which reveal your naked self, not embraced. As an example, Post Malone, in his 2018 hit "Let You Down," sings, "Never caught a feelin' this hard / Harder than the liquor I pour / . . . But I can't let go."

So young people join parents in slowing themselves down, avoiding catching feelings, so they're safer. However, they know that at some point they'll only really know who they are when they've risked the injuries of romance and entered the battlefield of love. But right now, many of them aren't ready for that.

Romance in Slowdown Youth Group

The youth group was one and the same with youth ministry back in the fast times of rushing to adulthood. And one of its great appeals was its ethos of romance. Not only were you invited into an enclosed coed group of people your same age, but you went on trips with them, played silly games, and did emotionally revealing things. It was hard not to fall in love with someone in

13. Twenge explains this phenomenon further, connecting to our discussion of internal identity: "Many young iGen'ers also fear losing their identity through relationships or being too influenced by someone else at a critical time." *iGen*, 215.

14. Taylor says it like this: "Love relationships are not important just because of the general emphasis in modern culture on the fulfillments of ordinary life. They are also crucial because they are the crucibles of inwardly generated identity." *Malaise of Modernity*, 49.

youth group! And that kept many young people coming back, making youth group exciting.

The youth pastor, most often unaware, set this romantic ethos and encouraged its flowering. For instance, it was just part of youth ministry for a college-aged leader to spend late nights talking with her cabinmates about who they had crushes on. But while tacitly encouraging this romantic ambience, the youth pastor also had to prohibit all direct sexual expression. So it was super great to find your girlfriend at youth group and have your first kiss on the seventh and eighth grade retreat (full disclosure: that's where I had my first kiss, smooching Kelly on the lakeshore beach!). But then, in turn, the youth pastor had to spend loads of time talking about "how far was too far" and how "true love waits."

This would eat up a good amount of youth group time and energy. The rest would be spent in romantic-style worship, singing tearful songs about our love for Jesus and about his strong arms that hold us (to get a little snarky). The more kids cried and showed emotions in worship, the more the youth pastor assumed—without thinking through the dynamics above—that faith was core to the individual young person's identity. This romantic encounter with Jesus set the terms of the internal quest for *this is me*. And forgetting Mr. Beaver's statement about the Christ figure Aslan in *The Lion, the Witch and the Wardrobe* ("He isn't safe. But he's good"), Jesus was assumed to be a safer option for identity, because he never lets us down or breaks up with us.

Recognition

The centrality of romance in the internal identity quest reveals something we've already pointed to in the chapters above, but it calls for more development here. In earlier chapters, we discussed how the three sets of parents sought to provide their children with their *thing*. Finding your thing, we said, was a station. And *station* here has two meanings. Chapter 4 articulated how a young person's thing (hockey, choir, hacking, cross-country) is like being stationed in San Diego. It provides a location—with practices, language games, fashions, and more—to possibly work out your internal feel of *this is me*. But we also said that station possesses a broadcasting meaning, like a radio or television station. To state *this is me* broadcasts it to others.

Our conversation on romance reveals how important this broadcasting dimension is to identity. And focusing in on this dimension reveals new strategies, other than just romance, for young people inside the slowdown. Yet romance remains so powerful because it puts your self-definition under fire (making it the best fodder for pop songs). It's a battlefield, which tests what you're made of. As with war, you often leave romance bruised, stitched, and traumatized (shell-shocked from all the drama), but also having lived and discovered more about who you are. You emerge more experienced. This reveals that while identity is assumed to be an internal feel of self-definition, it nevertheless necessitates a direct expression that others recognize. Romance is the most potent form of identity recognition, but what is of ultimate importance is recognition itself. All three sets of parents in chapter 4 pointed in their own ways to the centrality of recognition.

This starts to reveal that identity is not as internally bound as we often assume. Rather, there is a dialogical necessity to identity; it's bound within and is therefore ultimately a conversation.[15] We can only state *this is me* if there are others to hear it, recognize it, and respond (often making them either haters or fans—more on this soon). Taylor says, "Our identities are formed in dialogue with others, in agreement or struggle with their recognition of us."[16] I may have the freedom to construct my own identity, finding my *this is me* through my own internal feel.[17] But at some point I can only really truly have an identity by broadcasting it to others, who in turn recognize it.[18]

15. Charles Taylor explains, "This is the sense in which one cannot be a self on one's own. I am a self only in relation to certain interlocutors: in one way in relation to those conversation partners who were essential to my achieving self-definition; in another in relation to those who are now crucial to my continuing grasp of languages of self-understanding—and, of course, these classes may overlap. A self exists only within what I call 'webs of interlocution.'" *Sources of the Self: The Making of Modern Identity* (Cambridge, MA: Harvard University Press, 1989), 36. Ruth Abbey adds, "Taylor believes that existing within a web of interlocution, being in some sort of conversation with some others, is an inescapable, ontological feature of selfhood." *Charles Taylor* (Princeton: Princeton University Press, 2000), 69.

16. Taylor, *Malaise of Modernity*, 46.

17. Even to concede this point is an abstraction. You only feel something because your nervous system is connected to an environment. So any feel is dialogical from the start. In the case of the human being, the most poignant environmental reality is interaction and interconnection with other human beings.

18. Taylor adds, "My self-definition is understood as an answer to the question Who I am. And this question finds its original sense in the interchange of speakers. I define who I am by defining where I speak from, in the family tree, in social space, in the geography of social statuses and functions, in my intimate relations to the ones I love, and also crucially in the space of moral and spiritual orientation within which my most important defining relations are lived out." *Sources of the Self*, 35. Ian Fraser writes, "Taylor argues that when we try to work out our identity, we do so through dialogue with others in a process of recognition. He maintains that recognition on the intimate level of personal relationships has a powerful function in forming identities, just as on the social level it has shaped the politics of equal recognition." *Dialectics of the Self: Transcending Charles Taylor* (Exeter, UK: Imprint-Academic, 2007), 12. McAnnally-Linz importantly adds the layer of class and race here: "*While recognition of individuals is supposed to be neutral with respect to race, class, gender, etc., recognition of members of marginalized groups serves to reinforce culturally dominant scripts for 'appropriate' behavior.* Since there are

So there is a certain conflicted duality in our identity construction in late modernity's age of authenticity. We are to be whoever we *feel* we most authentically are. We're to listen to no outside authority imposing on us what it means for us, individually, to be human. And yet, to have this individually constructed identity, we desperately need others to recognize it. Our authenticity is dependent on others' attention, comment, and overall acknowledgment. This is why "cool," since the dawn of the age of authenticity, has been so culturally central.[19] Those who are cool seem the most adept at authentically receiving recognition.[20]

Ironically, the more the identity paths multiply and are assumed to be totally and fully bound in an internal feel, the more furiously recognition is sought— even demanded. It's common to hear nostalgic comments from middle-aged and young adults, like, "I wish I hadn't cared so much what people thought of me in high school." For instance, Macklemore's 2018 hit "Good Old Days" has him rapping,

> Wish I made it to homecoming
> Got up the courage to ask her
> Wish I would've gotten out of my shell
> Wish I put the bottle back on that shelf

multiple economies of recognition, it is not the case that some dominant group either gives or withholds recognition to excluded groups who themselves have no recognizing role. There are always communities of counter-recognition. Nevertheless, power in and between economies of recognition does accrue to some more than others, one result of which is that recognition can function as a disciplinary tool. Those who resist injustices might be 'recognized' as fulfilling a cultural stereotype—the angry black man or the shrill feminist—and summarily dismissed; those who adhere to scripts of the 'appropriate' behavior for their group might be recognized in the sense of public avowal of value." "Unrecognizable Glory," 159.

19. See Thomas Frank, *The Conquest Cool: Business Culture, Counterculture, and the Rise of Hip Consumerism* (Chicago: University of Chicago Press, 1998).

20. I lack the space to discuss money here, but McAnnally-Linz has shown that "money . . . is the single most powerful means of influencing what is determined to be worthy of recognition." "Unrecognizable Glory," 154. Following this, Yuval Noah Harari adds, "Money is not coins and banknotes. Money is anything that people are willing to use in order to represent systematically the value of other things for the purpose of exchanging goods and services. Money enables people to compare quickly and easily the value of different commodities (such as apples, shoes, and divorces), to easily exchange one thing for another, and to store wealth conveniently." *Sapiens: A Brief History of Humankind* (New York: Harper, 2015), 177. He continues, "For thousands of years, philosophers, thinkers and prophets have besmirched money and called it the root of all evil. Be that as it may, money is also the apogee of human tolerance. Money is more open minded than language, state laws, cultural codes, religious beliefs and social habits. Money is the only trust system created by humans that can bridge almost any cultural gap, and that does not discriminate on the basis of religion, gender, race, age or sexual orientation. Thanks to money, even people who don't know each other and don't trust each other can nevertheless cooperate effectively" (186).

> Wish I wouldn't have worry about what other people thought
> And felt comfortable in myself

This is a common wish projection for many of us. But ultimately it's only possible when you've received enough recognition to supposedly not care what others think. It is easy to look back and wish you hadn't cared what others thought, not needing their recognition. But that's only because you've now received recognition in other ways. These longings are actually not so much about transcending the need for recognition as about wishing you could transfer your accrued recognition back in time to when you felt overlooked and like you were losing in the recognition game. This shows how closely internal feel of self-definition and outside recognition are connected, even fused together. High school and junior high remain psychic spaces many Americans can't leave, because they are some of the earliest periods of our lives in which we expressed our identity and received back recognition (often not as we wished). Oddly, we now long to take the recognition we've received beyond high school, and the confidence in our identity that it has produced, and walk again the halls of our high school. We imagine that with this new recognition we wouldn't have to care what anyone in high school thinks—again, not because we're beyond recognition but because we would already have it. The American high school reunion is such a huge phenomenon because of this dynamic. Those who had little recognition in the teen years but now run companies, started an app, or discovered their style and sex appeal in their twenties, rush back to the reunion to show that they are deserving of recognition after all. The reunion is an illusion that somehow you can return to being seventeen, carrying back in time your post-high-school recognition.

Young People, Parents, and Recognition

This necessity for recognition, then, is what both frightens and mobilizes parents like the Rodriguez-Eriksons, Tuckers, and Dahls. Parents become hovering helicopters to both protect and assist their children in the recognition game. Those in the fast times didn't have a parent who moved like a military helicopter, giving cover to troops on a trail. Today many parents hover above their child to protect them from negative recognition.

As we've said, parents feel little direct control over their children's stated identity, conceding that it's internally constituted, born from the murky waters of the self. But once this identity has been claimed, popping to the surface, it now must be expressed. The child must go out into the world and assert *this is me*. She must bear the response of negative or positive recognition—showing, again, the dialogical nature of identity. Parents fear that too much negative recognition will be damaging, eating away at their daughter's confidence or, worse, leading her to hate herself and ultimately never be happy. So some parents hover to shield their child from this negative recognition, pulling kids from classes and teams that don't seem to "get" their kid and seem abusive because they don't recognize the child as the parent wishes.

But the hovering parent plays another role besides protection in the necessity of recognition. The parent works to blaze a trail (this is why some educational theorists have argued that we've shifted from helicopter to bulldozer parents).[21] To switch the analogy, some parents spend loads of time and money to make sure the broadcast identity of their children is a strong signal, seeing it as the parents' job to turn it up. Stories of dad cashing in parts of his 401(k) for his daughter to have the necessary resources to be a YouTube star, or mom quitting her job when her son is in ninth grade so she can give fifty hours a week to making sure he gets into an Ivy League school, abound in middle-class America.

Parents become coaches, managers, and financers who work to turn the signal of their children's broadcast identities up to eleven. Parents hover (or bulldoze) to make sure their children get all the recognition they can. And many young people appreciate this, calling mom their best friend, sensing that they need all the help they can to win recognition and therefore be happy with their self-definition. (Of course, there are direct cases when this bulldozing isn't done for the sake of acquiring recognition and esteem. Sometime the structures of a school, for example, are bent in a certain direction, causing the school to overlook and fail to assist a child. This happens often in the case of parents of children with disabilities.)

This harvesting of recognition becomes the new strategy for both parents and kids to delay the battlefield of romance. If young people are all working on their own broadcast identity, branding themselves,[22] to receive the recog-

21. "Other educators see them as 'snowplow parents': they work hard to clear the path for their kids, push obstacles out of the way, and make the traveling as smooth and safe as possible. . . . The names for pushy parents are proliferating [e.g., helicopters, snowplows]. But they all do the same thing: remove from their children opportunities for learning how to problem-solve. And so far there seems to be only one name for the children—teacup kids." Hara Estroff Marano, *A Nation of Wimps: The High Cost of Invasive Parenting* (New York: Broadway Books, 2008), 19–20.

22. "The rationale behind personal branding's claim to necessity is bound up with the highly competitive imagination that shapes contemporary (ideologically capitalist) economies of recognition. Augustine's claim that humility circumvents the deeply destructive agonism of the Roman glory ethic suggests humility's relevance here. The utopian ideal of perfect (and thus

nition they want (one hundred thousand Instagram followers, admittance to Yale), who has time for a boyfriend or girlfriend? Curating your brand for your watching fans, or responding to your haters, takes too much time and energy. Who needs romance for recognition when you have Instagram, Snapchat, Twitter, YouTube, and Facebook?[23]

Taylor Swift and *Ressentiment*

As Taylor Swift sings in her 2018 hit "End Game," "I don't love the drama, the drama loves me." (By the way, nearly every one of Taylor Swift's hits, other than those about an intense romance, are about drama with ex-friends in the battle for recognition.) And in a way this is true for many young people seeking identity recognition. As you work to broadcast your identity, haters and drama will proliferate. Swift doesn't love drama; she loves recognition—and with the broadcasting of her identity for the sake of recognition, so comes

---

non-competitive) brand distinction notwithstanding, the practice of personal branding is one of competitive distinction. The Personal Brander seeks to demonstrate her value to a market, and that value is always implicitly a matter of being better than some other persons. If humility is a mode of commitment to the mission of a God whose Kingdom knows no conflict, the humble person will reject (and be rejected by) the logic of the dominant contemporary economies of recognition. She will lift up others even when it does not conduce to her benefit. She will place no stock in demonstrating her superiority." McAnnally-Linz, "Unrecognizable Glory," 248.

23. "By the same token, Facebook has become a primer for promoting the self as the center of an extensive network of friends; the notion of 'friending' relates to bonds that may also exist in real life, but equally refers to weak ties and latent ties. In online environments, people want to show who they are; they have a vested interest in identity construction by sharing pieces of information because disclosing information about one is supposedly linked with popularity. Psychology researchers Christofides, Muise, and Desmarais have argued that 'identity is a social product created not only by what you share, but also by what others share and say about you. . . . The people who are most popular are those whose identity construction is most actively participated in by others.' Since Facebook is the largest social network, it offers the best potential for what Castells calls 'mass self-communication.' In contrast to other mass media, SNSs in general—and Facebook in particular—offer individual users a stage for crafting a self-image and for popularizing this image beyond intimate circles. Popularity and disclosure are two sides of the same coin, and they mirror the double meaning of 'sharing' as argued above. . . . Nursing a big following is not just a celebrity's privilege, however; for a lot of average users, Twitter has become a prime tool to advertise the self. The sheer number of followers has become a barometer for measuring popularity and influence, ascribing more power to few users in the twitterverse. Individuals quickly learned how to play the system. . . . According to *New York* magazine journalist Hagan, the 'impulse to make life a publicly annotated experience has blurred the distinction between advertising and self-expression, marketing and identity.' Users want large followings not just for reasons of vanity or self-esteem: they may actually cash in on their popularity rating by selling their influence to the highest bidder." José Van Dijck, *The Culture of Connectivity: A Critical History of Social Media* (New York: Oxford University Press, 2013), 51, 76.

the drama. Actually, the better and more successful she is at broadcasting her identity for recognition, the more haters come to the surface. This is why each of the three sets of parents talked about their fear of mean/cruel people. These mean/cruel haters appear because others, too, must broadcast their identity, often in opposition to your own. It's no wonder that *drama* is one of the most common words used by young people. It's an endemic social reality of the need for identity recognition. Broadcasting for recognition is a competitive game; the bandwidth is not exponential. Peoples' eyes can only be on so many people at a time, recognizing their unique selves. Both parents and young people sense the competitive nature of this recognition, hence the reason to mount an offensive helicopter or bulldozer.

Yet it's important to see that the endemic drama of the conflicting needs for recognition is deeper than just disagreement or tension. It stretches to a level that those growing up or raising children in the fast times would never have predicted. It's called "drama" because it feeds on *ressentiment*. This is a French word used by Friedrich Nietzsche.[24] He explained that *ressentiment*[25] is "grounded in a narrative of injury or, at least, perceived injury; a strong belief that one has been or is being wronged."[26]

The drama comes because a person (or group) feels like others are not recognizing him, and therefore his lack of recognition is wounding.[27] For how

24. Pankaj Mishra, in his weighty and brilliant book *Age of Anger: A History of the Present* (New York: Picador, 2017), traces the concept back to Kierkegaard. Mishra's whole book asserts that *ressentiment* has been a central underbelly of modernity, popping up again and again throughout the West. He shows how nineteenth-century German Romanticism is similar to the Oklahoma City bomber's, jihadists', and Trump voters' takes. They're all responding from deep narratives of injury, fueled by resentment.

25. James Davison Hunter explains, "[Nietzsche's] definition of this French word included what we in the English-speaking world mean by resentment, but it also involves a combination of anger, envy, hate, rage, and revenge as the motive of political action. *Ressentiment* is, then, a form of political psychology." *To Change the World: The Irony, Tragedy, and Possibility of Christianity in the Late Modern World* (New York: Oxford University Press, 2010), 107. Jeffrey Olick adds, "For Nietzsche and Scheler, *ressentiment* represented the victim's inability to move past his injury, and is thus a laming of the autonomous will. The man of resentment, Nietzsche wrote, is 'Powerless against what has been done . . . [an] angry spectator of all that is past.'" "The Return of the Repressed" (unpublished consultation paper, Yale Center for Faith and Culture, 2016), 5.

26. Hunter, *To Change the World*, 107.

27. Hunter puts this in view of the larger political and Christian culture; this helps us see the depth of his perspective: "Contemporary political culture in America is marked by a *ressentiment* manifested by a narrative of injury and, in turn, a discourse of negation toward all those they perceive to be to blame. Though each expresses this *ressentiment* differently, in different degrees and to different ends, it is present in all of these factions. It is especially prominent, of course, among Christian conservatives, which may be why they have been so effective over the years in mobilizing rank and file to political action. *Ressentiment* is also centrally present among Christian progressives and it is clearly a major source of their new solidarity and the

else can my self-definition be affirmed if it isn't recognized? I'm wounded and offended because the other's eyes are not on me, giving me no clear way to receive the feedback I need to express my truest self. I should have this privilege (my parents' efforts and support prove it), but this other person (or group) is taking it away. Therefore, I confront this other, whom I resent for eating up the recognition I desire. I claim that the other's broadcasting of their identity is a threat to me, overlooking or silencing my own need for recognition.[28]

Often, this other person's response is to say that I just love the drama. That's what I want, to make the drama hot, so that people put their eyes on me, not because I'm unique or worth recognizing, but because I'm loud and dramatic (I'm just a dramatic superhater). In the end, it will be the jury of eyes of recognition themselves who will judge.[29] And most often their means of doing so is to support whoever feels most injured by galvanizing the most eyes or, better, retweets, likes, and shares.[30]

The End of Romantic Youth Group

Particularly with the advent of social media, the avenues for recognition beyond romance play a major part in the slowdown of growing up. The fact that

---

motive behind their recent assertiveness in Democratic party politics. Both the Right and the Left ground their positions in biblical authority and they both appeal to democratic ideals and practices to justify their actions. But the *ressentiment* that marks the way they operate makes it clear that a crucial part of what motivates them is a will to dominate. The neo-Anabaptists are different in this regard. It is true that they too participate fully in the discourse of negation but domination is not their intent." *To Change the World*, 169.

28. Jean Bethke Elshtain explains Taylor's position. This is what I'm pushing for here. I'm not completely opposed to recognition, but I do worry about its essentialist and deconstructionist excesses. Elshtain says, "A Taylorian politics of recognition, in other words, can, and should, be brought to bear against that form of identity and recognition politics that pushes either in strongly essentialist or strongly deconstructionist directions. The heart of the matter is our understanding of the human person and in what the dignity of persons consists." "Tolerance, Proselytizing, and the Politics of Recognition: The Self Contested," in Abbey, *Charles Taylor*, 128.

29. See Jon Ronson, *So You've Been Publicly Shamed* (New York: Riverhead Books, 2015), as a stark example of how social media has ushered in a new form of public shaming.

30. Hunter adds, "The sense of injury is the key. Over time, the perceived injustice becomes central to the person's and the group's identity. Understanding themselves to be victimized is not a passive acknowledgement but a belief that can be cultivated. Accounts of atrocity become a crucial subplot of the narrative, evidence that reinforces the sense that they have been or will be wronged or victimized. Cultivating the fear of further injury becomes a strategy for generating solidarity within the group and mobilizing the group to action. It is often useful at such times to exaggerate or magnify the threat. The injury or threat thereof is so central to the identity and dynamics of the group that to give it up is to give up a critical part of whom they understand themselves to be. Thus, instead of letting go, the sense of injury continues to get deeper." *To Change the World*, 108.

we live in a world where a fifteen-year-old can assume that he has fans (and haters—those who dislike his brand[31] and therefore recognize him negatively) shows how deep the operations of recognition go in our culture. In contrast to the fast times, the slowdown of dating and first kisses happens, in major part, because of the democratization of celebrity. The tools for recognition can take anyone global—pics and videos do the trick. Who needs to risk the battlefield of romance when social media allows for all the recognition you need? Why risk the battlefield of love, on top of dealing with all the haters out there?

Against this backdrop, it's no wonder that youth ministry has taken a hit. Who has time to participate in youth group when you need to curate your image and seek constant recognition?[32] And even if you fail to get to one hundred thousand Instagram followers, your more conventional *thing* (basketball, piano, jujitsu) can provide some stage for recognition. But because you're driven by recognition, you have to work really hard at it. If you don't play your sport all summer and go to the right camps, no coach, scout, or even friend will recognize you as good at your thing. Their evaluation provides the communicative feedback you need to secure your identity. You might *feel* like a star athlete, but at some point you need someone to recognize this feel or you need to find a new thing and therefore a new identity.

So the pull of romance, which once fed the youth group, has been eclipsed by the more frantic and sophisticated games of identity construction through recognition. And even if certain young people aren't interested in being mini-celebrities, all sense that their identity necessitates recognition at some level.[33] And in turn they detect that their future is contingent on at least playing the recognition game enough to get into college. The pseudoromantic ethos of the youth group no longer has pull, because in the slowdown direct romance has been delayed for the sake of the ever-open new media avenues of recognition. And church youth groups have no (or very, very little) currency in the pursuit of recognition.

Yet, sensing this, many youth workers allow recognition to be an overall strategy for relating the youth ministry to the church. Both liberal and evangelical youth workers have had their own sense of *ressentiment*, living out a

31. Every kid with a profile on any social media site has a brand.

32. See Donna Freitas, *The Happiness Effect: How Social Media Is Driving a Generation to Appear Perfect at Any Cost* (New York: Oxford University Press, 2017), for a social science take on this very phenomenon.

33. "Celebrity culture plunges us into a moral void. No one has any worth beyond his or her appearance, usefulness, or ability to succeed. The highest achievements in a celebrity culture are wealth, sexual conquest, and fame." Chris Hedges, *Empire of Illusion: The End of Literacy and the Triumph of Spectacle* (New York: Nation Books, 2009), 32.

narrative of injury. This narrative claims that the church as a whole has over-looked, and therefore not given recognition to, young people—leading many youth workers to animosity and the odd expectation that church should be a perfect place. Inside this narrative, not only can youth workers easily feel victimized by the church, but also they can make the soul of their ministry overly ecclesial, seeing youth ministry as primarily for getting an institution and its denomination to recognize youth.[34] Recognition itself becomes the point. "See the youth" becomes the purpose of youth ministry. Inside this struggle for recognition, which so quickly breeds *ressentiment*, attention to divine action and the calling of Jesus can be lost. As we'll see, a heavy focus on recognition, which breeds *ressentiment*, can also have a significant negative impact on the humanity of the youth worker.

The End of Mercy

This talk of *ressentiment* takes us back to young people and culture as a whole. Intense focus on recognition for the sake of identity quickly breeds *ressentiment*. People's attention on someone else quickly moves me from heated competition to seeking revenge. Losing out on recognition threatens my identity. I feel injured because I lack the recognition I had hoped for. Revenge is something you seek when you feel someone else has directly wronged you. In this loop between identity and recognition, to lose out on recognition is to feel harmed and therefore justified in revenge—again it is bound in *ressentiment*, a narrative of injury.[35]

And if you can actually find a wrong done by your recognition competitor (an insensitive comment, a rude post, anything he's done to violate the ethic

34. See the Youth Ministry Alternatives series by Pilgrim Press for an example of this, and the book *Growing Young: Six Essential Strategies to Help Young People Discover and Love Your Church* (Grand Rapids: Baker Books, 2016), by Kara Powell, Jake Mulder, and Brad Griffin, for an evangelical version. At the core, both of these projects are very helpful, but they teeter on this line of making ecclesial recognition more of a central driver than divine action or obedience to discerning and following the living Jesus. What ultimately mobilizes their mutual initiatives is church recognition—which they believe will win retention.

35. Melissa Orlie provides an alternative to the politics of recognition that I affirm: "A politics of the good does not begin and end with questions about 'who I am' or 'who we are,' as the politics of recognition does. Rather, as I develop the notion here, a politics of the good presses us to say what our visions of the good are, to say what we consider it good to do and to become. To say what our vision of the good is, is at the same time to say something about who we are: To say what we believe is good is to say what we stand for, which no doubt is related in some ways to where we stand and, thus, to what we and others have taken our identity to be." "Taylor and Feminism: Recognition of Identity to a Politics of the Good," in Abbey, *Charles Taylor*, 140.

of authenticity, seeming intolerant), then you have the angle to use against him, mercilessly calling for revenge and public shaming. We demand tolerance; James and Holly Dahl call it an essential good they're trying to instill in their daughters. Tolerance is helpful on the front end of the identity-to-recognition process. Tolerance allows everyone the freedom to define for themselves what it means to be human, protecting the ethic of authenticity.[36] This is very good! But when it comes to the need for recognition, tolerance is a virtue that often *cannot* stand alone.[37] It crumbles quickly in the battles for recognition, leading competing individuals and groups to run to narratives of injury, producing *ressentiment*. In the heavy recognition game, tolerance is used as an offensive weapon to justify revenge: "I have to publicly expose this person because they're so intolerant and closed-minded; we need transparency." Tolerance, without linking it to a Christian virtue like humility or mercy, can become a bloody dagger in the grappling for recognition.

When the need for recognition, then, gets bathed in *ressentiment*, both the revenge seeker and the spectators can quickly become addicted to *Schadenfreude*, finding happiness when others with more recognition crash and fail. It oddly helps you feel better about your *self* to watch others lose positive recognition. It's great not only to receive positive recognition but also to watch your enemy (and she's perceived and called "enemy" because she rivals you for recognition) receiving hate (negative recognition)!

It's assumed that you're justified in seeking this revenge because your lack of recognition is embedded within *ressentiment* within this narrative of injury, and exposing your competitor's comment proves to you and the world that this rival is a bad person, a violator of the ethic of authenticity. Therefore, her true identity is fake, and she deserves to have recognition turn on her, exposing her for who she really is (what her true identity is).

36. Twenge observes that "many iGen'ers (and younger Millennials)" experience even simple disagreements as traumatic and respond in a "deeply emotional" way. She concludes they might better respond to these disagreements by ignoring them, discussing them, or developing logical arguments against them. After all, she claims even "opinions that are racist, sexist, homophobic, or transphobic" can be refuted with "logical arguments." *iGen*, 306.

37. "This is the dark side of tolerance; it begins with the good intentions of including everyone and not offending anyone but ends (at best) with a reluctance to explore deep issues and (at worst) with careers destroyed by a comment someone found offensive and the silencing of all alternative viewpoints. . . . This shows the two sides of campus tolerance: on the positive side, a kind inclusiveness, but on the negative side, a quick and brutal judgment of anyone who makes a comment deemed offensive, even if it's misinterpreted or meant as a joke." Twenge, *iGen*, 251, 254. Joustra and Wilkinson add, "Politically correct language is about recognizing people in ways that do not harm or distort them. And being denied this form of recognition is seen as oppression, Taylor says. When I recognize you, then, I authenticate you. I impart dignity to you." *How to Survive the Apocalypse*, 111.

All the Way Back to Demi Lovato

This takes us all the way back to Maisy's ten-year-old dance party. Before "This Is Me" came around on the playlist, "Sorry Not Sorry," Demi's biggest hit, was blaring. This song is a hit because it is an anthem to revenge seeking that's so common in this identity-to-recognition loop. Demi didn't get the recognition she deserved, but now she has the ammunition to go on the offensive. She's looking good enough to win recognition; she's "looking like revenge." Empowered by *ressentiment*, she says, "It'd be nice of me to take it easy on ya, but nah!" Not in this game of recognition, not with these social media tools and always watching eyes. Nah, not with me now holding the higher ground. It'd be nice, but because I have a narrative of injury to my identity, I'm sorry, I'm not sorry, I owe you no mercy, for the recognition tables have turned. And "being this bad"—getting my revenge—"has got me feelin' so good," because "I'm showing you up," stealing your recognition, "like I knew I would," like my internal feel of my identity wanted. I'm completely justified—again, "Sorry Not Sorry"—because I now finally have this recognition my identity deserves. And therefore, she tells us, she's happy. It is recognition that produces happiness!

But this happiness through the battle for recognition also runs the danger of evacuating mercy and humility. Who can be humble when you're always on the prowl for recognition? And who can show mercy when so many narratives about haters are in play? And for you not to get your revenge makes you at worst weak and at best wasting an opportunity. In the 2017 Netflix hit series *13 Reasons Why*, a show that captivated millions of young people, Hannah commits suicide, leaving a tape for every reason—really, for every person—that led to her violent act. Each episode picks up on one reason. Every kid who has some responsibility for Hannah's act hides the way he or she participated in the tragic loss, because they ultimately sense that there is zero mercy in the culture. They have no sense that you could confess your wrong and be held accountable but not destroyed for your culpability. Rather, in an age when recognition is king, it's better to never admit you're wrong, to hold your ground, to deny even reality, than it is to say you're sorry and have what feels like the whole of your school or the internet say, "Sorry, but we're not sorry!"

❖

I woke up the morning after the Demi Lovato dance party hungover on pizza. At first I assumed it was just too many slices too quickly. I imagined Joey Chestnut patting me on the shoulder and telling me to leave even the imaginary competitive eating to the professionals. But I couldn't shake it. By midmorning it was clear that this was no pizza hangover after all. It was the full-on flu.

Eight

Happiness, Part 1

Powerball, Endgames, and Sheryl Crow versus Taylor Swift

FROM WINTER TO SPRING BREAK

Things got worse as the day went on. I tried to sleep it off, but sleep gave no rest. My dreams attacked me with a haunted reel of Demi Lovato mixed with the Minneapolis neighborhood and all the words of the three sets of parents. In one dream Demi was even married to James, who then turned into Joe Jonas but was also Prince, but they lived in José and Linda's house, which was really located in the Bahamas, though they were readying the yard for a snowy winter. The fever was clearly cooking my brain. Eventually, enough Tylenol lowered the heat in my head, exorcising the haunting, and sleep finally brought rest.

Yet even days later, now mended, both the thought of pizza and my journey to discover what youth ministry was for brought back stabs of disgust. I'm not sure which was more tragic—the icky wave that came over me thinking about pizza (poor, poor pizza!) or the confused fatigue that hit me when contemplating my journey. I decided a sabbatical from both was a good idea.

Plus, I had no traction on this search to discover what youth ministry is for. I had left the interviews of the three parents in the dark, and the opaqueness had lingered. I'd come far enough to know that Graham was right about the centrality of goods and our overall fear of wasting our lives. And I'd been able to spot what some of these goods were when it came to most middle-class parents. I could see that these parents worked really hard (because it is a high good) to help their kids find their *thing*, ultimately wanting them to be happy by avoiding negative recognition, receiving positive recognition, and therefore feeling good about who they are. A content identity that leads to happiness was a hypergood they sought. Yet to receive this content identity doesn't happen by inertia but happens through intentional, and at times intense, pursuits toward some horizon. We find our identity by questing for something.[1]

And it seemed Wes was right: parents assumed that youth ministry, if it had any value, was to provide an additional tool for each individual kid to use in finding and maintaining happiness in their quest for *this is me*. But the more I tried to discern what this meant for youth ministry, the more it was jumbled.

So I allowed Thanksgiving, disappointing Vikings losses, Black Friday, snow, Christmas, New Year's Day, and bone-chilling cold to come and pass, with my search on hold. Well, all but the snow and cold came and passed. The first week of March, we barely made it out of the Minneapolis–St. Paul airport before a snowstorm dumped over nine inches. Kara, the kids, and I were off to Orlando—a spring break pilgrimage equally divided between Disney World, Universal Studios, and the resort pool.

Maybe my mind was finally clearing up thanks to the central Florida sun, but the words of the three sets of parents started returning to my consciousness. Their comments haunted me again, but this time without the fever. Maybe their desperate longing for their children to be happy came to mind because I was entering The Happiest Place on Earth. It didn't take much reflection to realize I'm just like them, as Mr. Walt Disney and his happiness attractions reached deep into my pocket, relentlessly snatching up my spending money ($25 for a small Coke and burger!). All of us parents wandering around Disney World, racking up credit card debt, are willing to do so for the sake of happiness. Some things are more important (are "gooder") than money and other resources. And Disney World reveals that happiness is indeed one. Maybe number one. To not waste our lives and to be good parents we

---

1. This extends my argument in *The Pastor in a Secular Age: Ministry to People Who No Longer Need a God* (Grand Rapids: Baker Academic, 2019). There I argued that identity is built around the events with which we identify. I still hold to this. This quest to make sense of our core events is central to identity. I think one of the issues with our late modern conception of identity is that too often we believe we individually construct an identity outside of history and narrative. I think it's more theologically rich to think about identity as the events that we identify our being with through narration. This takes us closer to a more theological conception of identity, because events (the historical happenings) of Jesus's life, death, and resurrection become our own events. Our identity is in Christ, because this is the event with which we find, through the Spirit, our being identifying. And the story of this event narrates our own experience.

need to seek happiness; we need our kids to be happy. And since the 1950s, when a consumer society started and we sat on the precipice of the dawning age of authenticity, Mr. Disney has provided us a place—a direct locale—that promises an experience of happiness.

As we entered the tram for day two, we were shoulder to shoulder like Tokyo commuters, though we were all supposedly on vacation. It's hard not to overhear conversations in body-touching-body proximity. I could pick up a few couples in quiet but intense passive-aggressive conflicts. I know these from experience. And being a spectator is like watching my own private reality TV show. But mostly I overheard parents pumping up their kids, readying them for the amazingly happy time they were about to experience.

In our tram car there were dozens of parents with children under four. Many were holding their children in their arms, giving them pep talks on how *fun* this was going to be. After the expense of day one, I was aware that each of these families with children under four would spend hundreds, even a thousand dollars or more, that day, on top of the entrance ticket, airfare, and hotel. And yet, more than likely, their child would have no direct memory of this trip to Disney.[2] Yet as I looked around the tram car, it was clear this didn't matter. This is what a *good* parent does; she takes her daughter to The Happiest Place on Earth—why wouldn't you?! Mom and dad do this not only because it is fun (they could have had fun in much cheaper ways) but, more so, because at the core of being a good parent is the deep longing for your child to be happy. Disney World and Universal Studios are cathedrals to our highest good: the pursuit of happiness. Watching these parents, I thought of Wes and wondered what youth ministry could be if this kind of happiness was our highest aim.

This isn't the first slowdown, though this might be the first slowdown since the modern creation of adolescence. But young people have been slowed down in growing up before. Before modernity, in the late fifteenth and early sixteenth century, a time with very different cultural conditions than our own, people were calling for a slowdown.

Let me paint this historical picture as a way of leading us into examining why happiness has become such an important aim for us. My brushstrokes will need to be broad. The history I'll unfold in this chapter and chapter 10 will err toward generalization, but for the purpose of making larger cultural points about happiness.

2. For a more in-depth philosophical discussion of Disney, see Vincent J. Miller, *Consuming Religion: Christian Faith and Practice in a Consumer Culture* (New York: Continuum, 2003).

In the late fifteenth century, just before the time of Luther, it was common for families to hold back their children—more precisely, their sons—keeping them from jumping into adulthood. Like today, marriage, family life, and a profession were delayed. And though no one called these young people teenagers (or adolescents—you need psychology for that), they mirrored some of those stereotypical behaviors. These boys over fifteen, who in other times, or with less means, would be fighting as knights, apprenticing trades, or married and working fields, were instead free to goof around and run pranks while attending the budding European universities. These university boys' behavior disturbed priests and the other guardians of society. Many were *Animal House* long before *Animal House*—a kind of Jim Belushi or Seth Rogen meets Jaime Lannister, *Superbad* meets *Game of Thrones*.

While this shows a kind of continuity between medieval young people and our contemporary conception of the teenager (though it's somewhat odd to make adult annoyance and goofing around something more than a tangential similarity), the reason for the slowdown reveals a glaring difference.[3] The medieval slowdown occurred because parents hoped to give their children more chances to enter into a holy vocation (especially for younger children who wouldn't inherit the family estate). Holding them off from marriage and the conspicuous tangles of trade workers or knights kept their ecclesial options open. It's hard for us to imagine now, but a church vocation was as desired then as working for Google or Apple or attending an Ivy League school is today.

Parents and family patriarchs slowed *some* young people down, not so they could win recognition and be happy but so the family would have someone who attended to the holy and could partake in heaven (it's like having a doctor in the family today). This, too, had the result of producing moments of happiness. But this happiness came *not* from the construction of your identity bound in the recognition you received in your ordinary life. Rather, happiness was a transcendent reality, something far beyond our ordinary lives, bound in heaven itself.

While everyone else was attending to the profane realm of the everyday, changing diapers, milking cows, plowing fields, and drinking ale, with some time at the university you'd be led into a church vocation. In that vocation you'd attend to matters of the sacred realm. Even if you weren't a priest, being

---

3. My critique of Crystal Kirgiss's book revolves around this point. There is no doubt some historical precedence for tangential similarities between today's and yesteryear's conceptions of young people, but Kirgiss gives no attention to the radically different conditions of those cultures. Without attention to these deeper, philosophical, named conditions, what is very divergent can seem connected; the tangential overplayed as proof of a continuity that simply can't be. See Kirgiss, *In Search of Adolescence: A New Look at an Old Idea* (San Diego: Youth Cartel, 2015).

a secretary for a bishop would connect you deeply with the most important institution in the Western world. And this institution's business (though it is a crass projection of our own time to call it "business") was salvation. The things (and actions) of the church possessed a charge of heaven. To handle church affairs was to be in the realm of the eternal.[4]

Thinking about Happiness

Happiness wasn't absent from people's imagination. Because they thought of heaven, they could imagine happiness and even at times experience it. But unlike for the three sets of parents I interviewed, and all those on the crowded tram car into Disney World, happiness was far from an essential pursuit, and not at all dependable. Unlike today, happiness wasn't a high good and therefore wasn't planted at the center of the moral imagination. Happiness might come, but it was assumed to be episodic, not something that stuck around, surely not something to build your life on. Happiness wasn't something to pursue as the very point of life, and therefore not something to make into a hypergood. Few people were on an out-and-out quest to acquire it, and no one would stop themselves like we do today and ask, "Am I happy?" assuming that if the answer was the negative, they'd be in an identity crisis. No one imagined that happiness could be a constant in life.

In late modernity and our age of authenticity, however, we assume that happiness can indeed be the steady state of a person's life.[5] People are always battling to get back to this supposed natural steady state of happiness. And because happiness is assumed to be a natural state, everyone, not just those with holy vocations, can pursue and achieve it. Happiness is no longer a transcendent echo coming from eternity but a natural feeling we believe can be somehow uninterrupted. Happiness since the Enlightenment is "less an ideal of godlike perfection than a self-evident truth, to be pursued and obtained in the here and now."[6] Procuring this steady state of contented happiness becomes our deepest longing, the horizon of our highest moral good.

4. See Keith Thomas, *Religion and the Decline of Magic* (New York: Penguin Books, 1991), for more on this.

5. By "steady state" I mean the following: "In systems theory, a system or a process is in a steady state if the variables . . . which define the behavior of the system or the process are unchanging in time." See Wikipedia, s.v. "Steady state," last modified February 4, 2019, https://en.wikipedia.org/wiki/Steady_state. However, I'm also thinking of the cosmological theory of the universe as steady state, as opposed to the view now, post-Hubble, that the universe is anything but in a steady state and is continually expanding.

6. Darrin M. McMahon, *Happiness: A History* (New York: Grove Press, 2006), 13.

Parenting practices today center on protection, not necessarily because children are fragile, but rather because a steady state of happiness is the aim. Avoidance of emotional injury is a hypergood because not only do emotional wounds upend the contentment of identity but, as a result, they puncture the natural steady state of happiness, which is the ultimate measure of a good life. Parents like the Rodriguez-Eriksons, Tuckers, and Dahls must carry the heavy burden of protecting their child from all wounds, pain, and sadness so they can be happy. Of course, though this steady state is the aim, it's very difficult to achieve, making even young children feel stuck as they manage negative feelings next to cultural pursuits of a steady state of happiness.

Enter the Christian prophet Mr. Rogers. In the 1960s he encouraged children to accept feelings of frustration or anger, to embrace the reality that happiness is no locked-down steady state free from negative emotions. Mr. Rogers told them it was OK; such feelings wouldn't destroy them by upending the cultural pursuit of locked-down happiness. Daniel Tiger (and the show *Daniel Tiger's Neighborhood*) has kept Mr. Rogers's prophetic and counter-cultural proclamations going for the next generation.

Mr. Rogers has been so prophetic because it's assumed that to have happiness as a steady state, you need to eliminate and barricade all pain, suffering, and even sadness. If you follow this logic, missing what Mr. Rogers wanted to teach parents as much as children, then parenting will be very challenging in late modernity, because you're responsible to protect your child not only from suffering and loss—such as disease, violence, homelessness, and hunger—but also from all forms of negative emotion. When happiness is assumed to be a natural steady state sanitized from all forms of suffering, and when this steady state of happiness is the measure of a good life, then parents must take on an incredibly difficult task. It's the parents' job to make sure their children are happy by insulating them from all negativity (something nearly impossible in the *ressentiment*-soaked realm of broadcasting your identity for the sake of recognition).

Parents, then, have to work doubly hard to provide the possibility of a steady state of happiness, because, oddly, we assume that those who miss out on happiness do so because of their own fault—it is a natural state, after all. It's presumed that every modern person controls, in some way, the means to happiness, as long as they have the right attitude and some protection to feel safe. We suppose that happiness is a kind of natural state that, if not distracted or corrupted by emotional injury in childhood, is ubiquitous.[7]

7. McMahon traces the history of how happiness began to be seen as a natural state. It starts after the Enlightenment. He explains some of the context: "In the eighteenth century, news of Captain Cook's 'discovery' of Tahiti and Hawaii inspired paeans to the pristine happiness

If It Makes You Happy

As Sheryl Crow sang in "If It Makes You Happy" back in the 1990s (I know, a Pat Benatar reference and now Sheryl Crow), if you're happy, "It can't be that bad." Similarly, she asks you to consider that if you're happy, "then why the hell are you so sad?" Crow's chorus is irking, snagging our imagination, because she passionately—truthfully, even—sings about an incongruence we assume is impossible. We imagine that happiness is a force field, a steady state to our being that keeps all sadness out. To be happy is to be absent sadness; it is to live in a steady state beyond suffering, loss, and pain. While we assume that happiness is a natural state, we fail to see that asking happiness to be a force field that keeps out all sadness is a biological impossibility. Death reminds us that happiness cannot do the work we ask of it. Happiness, no matter how full, cannot evict all sadness, loss, and suffering. We can only assume that happiness can do this if we ignore death, which is just what our culture has done.[8]

Therefore, in our cultural imaginary, to say I'm happy and yet sad is like somehow saying that a room filled with light is somehow dark. Light means, by definition, the absence of darkness. In a similar vein, we tend to imagine that happiness means the absence of sadness; happiness is the light that casts out all gloom. Parents want their kids to be happy, more so because they're frightened of them being sad. The sense is that if you can just pursue, procure, and perpetuate a state of happiness, then sadness and all other negative emotions can have no place in your life.[9] But here is Crow, in one of the lasting

---

of unspoiled oases, adding details to the reveries of earlier Enlightened dreamers like Philipp Balthasar Sinold von Schütz, the German author of *Dieglückseligste Insul'auf'der ganzen Welt*, *The Happiest Island in All the World*. Ever since, travelers on holidays have reenacted this venerable myth, flocking to once deserted isles to restore—and hopefully to find—themselves." *Happiness*, 235. He continues, "For if happiness was truly a natural condition, a law of our nature and the way we were intended to be, then how to account for the continued existence of misery? And if earthly happiness was treated primarily as a function of good feeling, the balance of pleasure over pain, then what of the age-old links tying happiness to higher things: to God, virtue, or the right ordering of the soul? Was feeling good the same as being good? Was being good feeling good? Was happiness a reward for simply living, or a reward for living well?" (201–2). And he says further, "And what, until then, had been only a guarded thought was proclaimed openly: If happiness was a natural state, why could it not be attained entirely by natural means, without divine guidance at all?" (196).

8. For discussions on this, see Ernest Becker, *The Denial of Death* (New York: Free Press, 1973), and J. J. Valberg, *Dream, Death, and the Self* (Princeton: Princeton University Press, 2007). And for a more popular take, see Atul Gawande, *Being Mortal* (New York: Metropolitan Books, 2014).

9. A cinema example of this is *Garden State*. Writer and director Zach Braff's cult classic revolves around his character Andrew Largeman's quest to overcome his father's need for him to always be happy, going to such a height as to medicate him so he'd feel no sadness. The movie

hits of the 1990s, saying that this conception of happiness as the firewall to sadness is not right. Here she is happy and yet sad.

Crow revealed in an interview that this famous chorus was inspired by conversations with people when they learned that she wrestled with despondency.[10] Just as Crow was achieving recognition, and therefore a solid identity as a successful musician (just as she was receiving notoriety for her *thing*), she was hit with depression. Her friends echoed the disbelief of the culture: If it makes you happy to be known for your *thing*, to have an identity recognized, then why the hell are you so sad? This is a seeming incongruity! Like we said, you can't be sad if you're happy, and particularly if you've successfully moved through the identity-to-recognition loop. Yet Crow is both content with her recognition (stating directly that she is happy) and yet has a deep sense of unease—maybe because she has now received the recognition she always desired. She has achieved a sought-after horizon, only to find it doesn't save. This song is haunting because it reveals that something isn't quite right in our cultural imagination. Contented identity won by high recognition through your thing is supposed to secure a steady, constant state of happiness, blocking out all sadness. Each of the three sets of very different parents I interviewed believed this. And yet Crow reveals that while recognition for her thing does give her pleasure, nevertheless her being doesn't slide into a natural steady state where happiness is uninterrupted.

Crow's friends and management are flabbergasted because Sheryl continues to claim that she's content with her identity/recognition as musician. She's satisfied to be known this way—it's good. And yet she's not buffered by happiness, protected from the penetration of discontent. Her friends and the listener are left to shake their heads and think, *If I were on the radio, if I were on the cover of Rolling Stone, I'd be happy, because finally I'd have the recognition I need to be content with my identity, to feel good about who I am and claim my natural happiness.*[11]

---

is about awakening, through Andrew's falling in love with Sam, discovering that true love is not free from pain and sadness but bearing that reality. At the end of the film Andrew is still quite sad but filled with joy, for Sam has shared in his humanity through his loss, and in their union both are transformed and ready to live.

10. For more on the experience behind this song and album, see Fred Schruers, "Sheryl Crow: She Only Wants to Be with You," *Rolling Stone*, November 14, 1996, https://www.rollingstone .com/music/music-news/sheryl-crow-she-only-wants-to-be-with-you-177839.

11. In some sense alternative rock of the early and mid-1990s was all about the lies of happiness won through recognition. Nirvana, Pearl Jam, and the other grunge groups from Seattle highlight this perspective in their lyrics, stripped-down composition, and ethos. But even in pop artists this discontentedness can be heard. Not only is Sheryl Crow an example, but maybe the height of this discontent is found in Counting Crows. Their first album, *August and Everything After*, is about Adam Duritz's longing for recognition. It was a hit. Yet the

The only answer for Crow's sadness is that she isn't completely content with who she is, not able to live from the natural state of happiness. But Crow reiterates twice in the chorus, which repeats five times, that she is indeed happy—at least contented with this identity—and yet she is sad. A content identity is supposed to produce the hypergood of a steady state of happiness, but it hasn't. And this, I believe, is because we've asked happiness to do something it inherently can't.

Sheryl Crow's 1990s hit warns us that there is something else lurking, something the ancients knew but we've buried. Crow's chorus points to the fact that happiness is never a continuous steady state; to assume it is, is to ask happiness to be something it isn't. Happiness is a feeling, and therefore to demand it be a constant state of being is like asking the sun to keep shining and the night to never come. Happiness has no power to serve as a force field to keep out the sad, and Crow's hit witnesses to this reality.

The Happiness Gamble

The ancestors of our intellectual history never assumed that happiness could function as all of us Disney tram riders tacitly believe. Back in the late medieval slowdown, happiness wasn't conceived in any way as a steady state or an always available reality, given the right attitude. Rather, happiness was a game of chance, and a pious person often didn't believe it was something that could or should be pursued. We're quite different than our ancestors in seeing happiness as a hypergood. As a matter of fact, Mary Clark Moschella, drawing on Darrin McMahon, says, "The root *hap*, related to *happenstance*, suggests good luck. As . . . McMahon puts it, 'Happiness has deep roots in the soil of chance.'" Moschella continues, "We are happy when things go our way, when we laugh and have fun, or when we have experience ourselves as fortunate."[12] Happiness, our forefathers and foremothers assumed, was for

---

second album, *Recovering the Satellites*, is all about how this achieved recognition failed to provide the happiness it promised. Novelist David Foster Wallace picked up many of these themes. The 1990s were a time when we realized that the good of recognition couldn't deliver happiness, and that happiness itself wasn't a good worth building our lives around. Yet instead of seeking deeper forms of meaning and listening to our young adults, we just slowed down the next generation, thinking that more direct parental involvement, organization, and assistance would pave over the problems that the Seattle scene and Adam Duritz sang about. McMahon wonders something similar, saying, "Might not the search for happiness entail its own undoing? Does not our modern commandment to be happy produce its own forms of discontent?" *Happiness*, 15.

12. Mary Clark Moschella, "Calling and Compassion: Elements of Joy in Lived Practices of Care," in *Joy and Human Flourishing: Essays on Theology, Culture, and the Good Life*, ed. Miroslav Volf and Justin E. Crisp (Minneapolis: Fortress, 2015), 100.

the lucky, not necessarily the holy. And in the medieval slowdown, holiness, not happiness, was a much higher good.

A life wasted, then, wasn't a life absent happiness, as we'd assume today. No parent in medieval Europe assumed that the highest good was to make sure your child was happy. Building your life around and for happiness would have been foolish. To our intellectual ancestors, saying the point of life is to be happy would have sounded to them like someone today saying the point of life is to win the Powerball. It's a wonderful happenstance if you can turn twenty dollars into two hundred million. But the odds are so slim. Therefore, it's not good—it's a waste of time, resources, and, if it goes too far, a very lifetime—to build your existence around winning the lottery.

Happiness, then, was anything but a steady state, and therefore not something to shape your life around. And for our ancestors, it was a truism that happiness and sadness could intermingle. They didn't have our sense that you could secure your being in a way that made happiness your constant reality. Yet today people often say (almost as a concession that means "I really don't want much"), "All I want is to be happy." Or parents might say about their child applying for college, "In the end it doesn't matter if she doesn't get in. All we really care about is that she's happy." This shows that happiness is a very high good and also that we assume happiness is a natural state. In the end it's (modestly) all we want! Now that we're trapped in ambition or overwhelmed with our need for recognition, we tell ourselves that all we really want is to be happy, to get back to some innocent, natural state. Our ancestors would do a double take. To them our proclamation of wanting to *just be happy* would sound like, "Oh, I don't want much. I just want to experience nothing but perfect luck my whole life. Is that so much to ask?"

Happiness: "I Want to Be Your End Game"

To escape my retro reflection on 1990s music and Sheryl Crow and return to some very small semblance of being cool, let's get back to Taylor Swift. Her biggest hit in 2018 was "End Game" (this is the song we discussed in the previous chapter, in which she sings about drama loving her). It's a song of high romance interlaced with *ressentiment*. Swift wants her lover to make her his endgame—the love he'll commit to and spend his life with. She even sings, "(I don't wanna be) Just another ex-love / (I don't wanna miss you) / Like the other girls do." In the game of romance, which means maneuvering around all the rivals and haters, she wants this guy to see her as his last move.

Darrin McMahon, in his book on the history of happiness, explains that for the ancient Greeks like the Stoics, happiness was not a goal, a crowning move, or an endgame.[13] Because life was filled with tragedy and sadness—an emotion not to fear but embrace—the point of life was never to pursue happiness; it was to live well.[14] Happiness was a surprising and welcome ending to a life well lived. And the only way Greek philosophers like the Stoics knew to live well was to pursue not happiness but virtue.[15]

Because happiness was contingent on a virtuous life, you couldn't reach happiness until the very end of your life. It wasn't something you secured by the sixth grade. Happiness came at the end of life because it took a whole lifetime of practicing virtues to mold your life in a certain direction. Then, and only then, could you come into happiness. And then you died![16] Happiness was predicated on a whole life lived well, not just particular moments, and for sure not the dream that life itself could be a string of happy moments without interruption. You lived life well not by seeking happiness at all but by aiming for virtue in direct confrontation with tragedy, suffering, and sadness. "Cicero goes so far as to argue that the man of perfect virtue will be happy even under torture, even on the rack."[17]

13. Ellen T. Charry adds, "The ancients agreed that happiness is enjoying oneself in living morally and productively, and it is an external judgment on how one is faring at life. It is a judgment on how one orders one's life as a whole, and it is the enjoyment of that life's positive results. Both the enjoyment and the judgment are inspired by a pattern that identifies a life that is going well enough to be called a fine life—we might even say, a beautiful life. Overall, well-being comes from using oneself consistently, intentionally, and effectively, and hence it is a moral undertaking. Flourishing reflects the moral quality of one's ultimate purpose or organizing principle." *God and the Art of Happiness* (Grand Rapids: Eerdmans, 2010), 4.

14. Nicholas Wolterstorff adds, "Happiness does not belong to the content of the good life; it *characterizes* the good life. The good life is constituted of activities; and what characterizes those activities is that together they make one's life a well-lived life." "God's Power and Human Flourishing" (unpublished consultation paper, Yale Center for Faith and Culture, 2014), 5–6, http://faith .yale.edu/sites/default/files/nicholas_wolterstorff_-_gods_power_and_human_flourishing _0_0.pdf.

15. See Plato's *Five Dialogues* (Indianapolis: Hackett, 1981). In it he reports Socrates's discussion about the point of life as he faces his execution. Socrates and his friends can see only virtue as the point of life. And Socrates is willing to die for the ideal of his virtues rather than to escape and live and die happily though having turned from virtue.

16. McMahon goes back to Herodotus to make this point: "In the understanding of Herodotus and his contemporaries, then, happiness is not a feeling, nor any subjective state, a point highlighted by the irony that Croesus originally thinks that he is happy, only to be shown otherwise. Happiness, rather, is a characterization of an entire life that can be reckoned only at death. To believe oneself happy in the meantime is premature, and probably an illusion, for the world is cruel and unpredictable, governed by forces beyond our control. A whim of the gods, the gift of good fortune, the determination of fate: Happiness at the dawn of Western history was largely a matter of chance." *Happiness*, 7.

17. McMahon, *Happiness*, 55.

The ancient philosophers who believed this followed what's called the *eudaimonic tradition*.[18] Their aim, focus, or highest good (*summum bonum*) wasn't happiness but a flourishing well-lived life, which came through virtue. Virtue was their focus; character their aim. They contended that you couldn't really get to happiness by aiming for it. You had to aim for something deeper than moments of pleasure and contentment. Virtues such as prudence, temperance, courage, and justice were what you aimed for by taking on certain habits and practices.[19] So in this sense, happiness wasn't really an endgame at all. The moves you set up, and the overall game you were trying to win, revolved around virtue itself. Happiness was a welcome but auxiliary experience.

For those in the eudaimonic tradition, then, happiness simply happens. You pursue virtue; happiness just occurs. Like the saying "Stuff happens," it was the same for these ancient Greeks. If you aimed your life toward virtue, maybe at the end of it all, or in fleeting moments you shouldn't try hard to hold onto, you'd find yourself happy. I can see the bumper stickers on Plato's chariot now: "Happiness Happens" is right under "Honk If You're Stuck in an Allegorical Cave."

Hedonistic Bad Blood

Yet, like Taylor Swift and her frenemies, the eudaimonics had their rivals. There were others, like the philosopher Epicurus, who thought it wasn't virtue that was the *summum bonum*. For Epicurus and his followers, happiness was the endgame. Happiness wasn't an auxiliary happening but a direct goal. The aim of life wasn't virtue but pleasure.[20] This pursuit of pleasure that stood in opposition to the eudaimonic way was called *hedonism*.[21]

We tend to hear this word pejoratively. In our minds, hedonism has the connotations of 1970s swingers' parties with naked, coked-up people swinging from chandeliers. Few of us would call this an image of a good life. This

---

18. Here I'm crossing boundaries a bit, moving this ancient conversation onto the ground of positive psychology. Positive psychology and its discussions of happiness have tended to place a eudaimonic approach in contrast to a hedonistic approach.

19. Here I'm referencing Aristotle.

20. Immanuel Kant explains, "The Stoics maintained that the virtue was the *whole summum bonum*, and happiness only the consciousness of possessing [virtue], as making part of the state of the subject. The Epicurean maintained that happiness was the *whole summum bonum*, and virtue only the form of the maxim for its pursuit." *The Critique of Pure Reason* (Chicago: University of Chicago, Encyclopedia Britannica, 1952), 339.

21. The relation between Epicurus and hedonism is more complicated than I have space (or the reader has patience) to explore here.

sense of hedonism seems like a clear picture of waste and sin. None of the parents I interviewed would name hedonism as the inspiration for their parenting style. The slowdown in growing up in the early 2000s happens to protect from these kinds of fast times. It would be quite hard to claim even the non-church-connected Dahls were hedonistic in this popular usage. They were actually quite disciplined, even conservative, ordering their lives around the basketball schedule.

But wild parties and fast times were not what Epicurus and the other ancient Greek hedonists had in mind. As a matter of fact, Epicurus was anything but a party animal; he believed the epitome of pleasure was soft bread, a shady tree, and conversation with some friends. Hedonism, in contrast to eudaimonia, made the happiness of pleasure the highest pursuit. The point was (and still is) to avoid, extract, and firewall off sadness and pain, for the sake of increasing pleasure. Hedonism makes happiness now, today, the aim, the very thing worth pursuing. Every human being—as we've argued throughout—is pursuing something. You can't be a human being without (directly or indirectly) pursuing something you call good. Team eudaimonia claims that the best pursuit is virtue, which may (or may not) in the end deliver happiness. But while happiness is hoped for, it is inconsequential because what matters is living well. And it's the virtues that promise this well-lived flourishing life. Team hedonism moves happiness from the periphery and makes it the center. The very thing worth pursuing most passionately is happiness itself.

Seen this way, Disney World, not Amsterdam's red-light district, may be the true hotbed of hedonism, for it makes everything in its tight and invisible walls about the pursuit of pleasure. Disney invites you not into a moment of erotic escape but into elaborate, narrative-based ways of life where happiness is the highest pursued good, and what is most important in life is feeling good, not living well. Of course, it could be silly to assume a straight line from Epicurus to Walt Disney. This shift to hedonism has a long zigzagging history, showing up in the thought, for example, of Thomas More and Jeremy Bentham, among others. Yet when it comes to distribution of this sense that life is about happiness, Walt is the true twentieth-century hedonist sage, exchanging a toga and a shady tree for an animation table. He shifted the nascent consumer society of the 1950s onto the tracks of Epicurus and the hedonists.[22] Walt, like Epicurus, sees virtue's value not in

22. Even to trace the evolution of happiness in its more contemporary history would take way more space then I have here. However, I think a case can be made that the Bohemian/Romantic-inspired age of authenticity was the hinge that shifted at least American culture toward a hedonistic focus. Yet I believe this started not in the late 1960s but in the early 1950s

fashioning a well-lived life but only in its relative ability to get to pleasure. We tell the truth, care for our friend, and fight the bad guy so we might live happily ever after—happiness as a natural state is the aim. It's the pursuit of happiness, not an ideal like justice or self-sacrifice, that moves us to action. We act so that happiness might be a steady state, never interrupted by pain, sadness, and sacrifice. Nearly every classic Disney movie moves in the three acts of (1) happiness interrupted, (2) unpleasantness and unhappiness fought, and (3) happiness returned ever after. Hedonism, then, most often comes rated G.

While none of the parents I talked with were hedonistic in the swinging from the chandelier way, they all conceded that happiness was their *summum bonum*; it was their highest good. For instance, all three sets justified their full schedules not in the pursuit of virtue but in the pursuit of happiness. Their deepest wish wasn't that their children would be virtuous but that they would be happy. On a continuum, they all slid hard toward the hedonistic pole rather than the eudaimonic. Youth ministry could only be an add-on because each of these families moved on hedonistic tracks, making happiness their end. They all hoped their children had character, but again, not as an end but as means of being (always) happy.

Values, of course, had their place, and youth ministry could help at this level. The parents mentioned tolerance, commitment, hard work, and even kindness as important. But as with the Epicureans and hedonists, these virtues are present simply for the sake of achieving happiness. Tolerance and kindness shape an environment for identity to be broadcast, void of bullying, so children can be happy with their *this is me* statements. Commitment and hard work produce success at your *thing*, which gives young people the recognition they need to be happy. And when the foundation of happiness is a recognized identity, then even virtues that can produce character must be subordinate to feeling happy. If virtue makes me feel bad about myself, upending my natural steady state of happiness, then for the sake of happiness virtue must be opposed or ignored. It seems that the three sets of parents assumed that with enough parental investment and protection the natural steady state of happiness can be protected, and maybe even added to. For all three sets of parents, happiness was the endgame. And watching my kids running around the happy streets of Disney World, I knew it was for me as well.

---

with the arrival of a mass consumer society. It would take almost twenty years for consumer drive to throw off and kill the more eudaimonic focus on duty and obligation for the pursuits of pleasure. For more on this, see part 1 of my *Faith Formation in a Secular Age: Responding to the Church's Obsession with Youthfulness* (Grand Rapids: Baker Academic, 2017).

Conclusion

As the sun set on day two of our Disney adventure, we started to shift our minds to Harry Potter and Universal Studios the next day. But before returning to the tram to meet again our fellow Disney pilgrims—now sapped of energy and money, all the happiness soaking us with a drowsy fatigue—we took in the Main Street parade. It must have been my sunburn, but in the jubilance of the parade I noticed something I hadn't before. I watched as a handful of medieval Disney characters danced past me: Snow White, Prince Charming, Elsa from *Frozen*, and the princess from *Tangled*. As these medieval characters passed, I noticed that though they kept the medieval castle behind them, their pursuit was Main Street and the pull of Americana. Actually, from just right of the castle, sitting on a little hill, you can see straight into Disney World's version of early twentieth-century America, that (imaginary!) nostalgic time in which we naively believed the steady state of happiness was easy to come by. As those medieval characters danced in front of the malt shops to the beats of Miami Sound Machine, I was taken by the strange juxtaposition. Somehow Disney had been able to remix old tales of virtue, honor, courage, and suffering with a very different *summum bonum*: the steady state of happiness. So completely had they done this that even the medieval had shifted from passionately and anxiously seeking holiness and immortality to seeking happiness ever after. Disney melted the medieval into Americana folklore of a land of never-ending (steady-state) happiness.

As I watched everyone do the conga, wondering if we had aloe back at the resort, I pondered why there isn't a Disney version of Luther. He's the father of the modern age, after all—more responsible than that weird Hunchback of Notre Dame for the birth of this modern world where Disney World is possible. (Yes, I realized just as I thought it that Luther's whole *Anfechtungen*— the dark despondent state that would leave him locked in his room for days— probably isn't brand appropriate for Disney.) Yet even realizing this, as I felt "the rhythm of the music getting stronga," I decided, indeed, Luther is to blame.

Nine

When Goods
Become the Good

LATE MARCH

J oy is a description of our experience of transformation!" I soak my
mind in J's words. I feel in the middle of one of those odd sensations.
It's almost hypnotic. I feel warm and weak, like my mind is bobbing in a
warm bath. I wonder if the last rays of the late-March sun hitting my face
through the window before disappearing adds to this sensation. I do worry
for a beat that the sun will irritate my freshly healed neck; my Florida sunburn is no longer noticeable anywhere but my memory. But this thought
comes and goes, unable to interrupt the moment. I'm aware that in my state
of relaxation, things seem enticingly strange, like when you repeat your
own name enough that you can feel a kind of separation from it, standing
beyond it to experience it as weird. That's how joy feels as J talks about
it. Like something I know so well, like my name, but now alluring and
unexpected.

Eventually it feels right to push the conversation forward. Interrupting
the near-hypnotic moment, I ask, "But aren't happiness and joy basically
the same thing? Hasn't the lead counselor of fun just shifted things by a
degree or two, using a more biblical word?" My question in some ways goes
against what I'm feeling, but I hope it helps me understand more what this

familiar but now strange word *joy* could mean—particularly what it means to J and Lorena.

Sticking to the pattern she has used throughout our conversation, J doesn't answer my question directly but instead takes me back into earlier experiences. When I asked her why she wasn't doing youth group but rather this intergenerational storytelling night, she told me about nearly being fired. Now, in response to my question about whether happiness and joy aren't basically the same thing, she takes me back to the day she found out that Lorena was sick.

"I remember when Lorena's mom called and told me she was in the hospital. Lorena had been sick for over a week and a half. Her mom was keeping me up to date because this big, fun youth group outing was coming up. I'll never forget that, because I was so stressed about the buses and just making sure everything was fun. I felt like that event would make or break me at the church. If kids had fun, I'd keep my job. But then, after that phone call, I just didn't care anymore."

"We just thought it was flu or something," Lorena adds. "I could barely even walk into the doctor's office. I just felt so dizzy and weak. When I got in there and the nurse took me back, she did, like, that blood pressure thingy and then darted out of the room. Next thing I knew, the two doctors were there. They did some other stuff to me. Stopped and whispered to each other, and then did some more stuff to me. And whispered again. I could totally tell something wasn't good, because it was, like, an anxious whisper. Finally, the tall doctor got all calm and matter-of-fact and said, 'OK, Mrs. Martinez, we're going to have an ambulance take your daughter to Children's Hospital; we need to go very quickly.' That was all they said. I was too weak to react, but my mom freaked out. They didn't tell her anything else. She didn't know what else to do, so she called J."

Jumping in, J says, "I met them at the hospital. I'd never done anything like this. I was hired to be the lead counselor of fun, to get kids to like coming to church and build a youth group. I had an event planned that would make kids and parents happy. Now I'm in a hospital waiting with a confused and scared mom who couldn't care less about her kid being happy; she just wants her to be OK. Finally, the doctors came out to give us an update. They said they hoped they caught the infection just in time, but they wouldn't be sure for the next few days. They'd need to keep Lorena unconscious to see how she reacted and allow her body the ability to respond to the meds. And it could be as much as a week or so before they knew if Lorena would recover."

We sit in silence, the fellowship hall now nearly dark.

J continues, "What I'll never forget is Lorena's mom repeating back to the doctors, 'If? If? If she recovers?' The doctors told us even if things took a positive turn, it would be months until she was well enough to go back to school. We were now stuck waiting. Lorena's mom was kind of furiously defiant; she sat down and said she wouldn't leave the hospital until Lorena did."

"My mom's crazy," Lorena says with a loving laugh.

"And that's when I stopped doing youth group," J adds.

I'm moved by the story, and it gives me important perspective, but I really can't see how it shifts things from happiness and fun to joy and transformation. So I ask, "How is this all connected to joy?"

"Maybe it was the stress of the moment or all the Diet Coke I was drinking," J says, "but I started to notice how often people were referring to 'good.' The doctors and nurses used the word many times: 'It's not a good situation,' 'It's good we caught it now,' 'We'll see what her blood tests show; then we'll know how good our chances are.' Lorena's mom just sat in a chair holding my hand for the first hour, repeating, 'This isn't good.' And when we finally did get to see Lorena through the window, unconscious and all covered up and hooked up to machines, I found myself saying, 'This isn't good.' When I said that, all these Bible verses started coming to my mind. 'And God called it Good,' 'It isn't Good for the human to be alone,' 'For every Good and perfect gift comes from above,' and Jesus saying, 'Why do you call me Good?'"

"That's the text you used tonight," I insert.

"It is," J says. "Focusing on the Good has become central to our ministry. I'd actually say that youth ministry is for joy, because youth ministry invites young people to focus on the Good, and only God is Good.[1] *Joy is when you find the Good as an end*.[2] When we attend to the Good—seek it and receive it—we find joy, because we find something that comes straight from God. I noticed sitting in the waiting room that what I yearned for was the gift of

---

1. "As an emotion, joy is always *over* something (perceived) as good, and it presumes proper relation to some (perceived) good—which means that *true* joy presumes proper relation to some *actual* good." Miroslav Volf, "The Crown of the Good Life: A Hypothesis," in *Joy and Human Flourishing: Essays on Theology, Culture, and the Good Life*, ed. Miroslav Volf and Justin E. Crisp (Minneapolis: Fortress, 2015), 135.

2. "Goodness is the cause of joy, and the greatest possible joy is found in possessing the greatest possible good. Thus, Christian morality is not a set of theories and ideas, but an initiation into a way of life that itself constitutes happiness because it unites us to the most perfect and perfecting good." Paul J. Wadell, *Happiness and the Christian Moral Life: An Introduction to Christian Ethics* (Lanham, MD: Rowman & Littlefield, 2008), 5.

God's Goodness, not happiness or fun.[3] I decided right then that I was finished being the lead counselor of fun."[4]

Throughout this journey I've been aware of how near goods are to people's actions. In the ranking of goods, youth ministry slides. Youth ministry doesn't slide because parents no longer think youth ministry has value or see it as a complete waste. Rather, it slides because in the pursuit of a good life that finds its end in being happy, youth ministry is ranked below handfuls of other activities.

Back in September, Kathryn, the youth ministry major, reminded me that parents always want what's good for their kids, but in early March on my Disney vacation, I started to recognize how much of what we imagine is good is framed by the aim for happiness seen as a natural steady state. I'd thought

3. I'm drawing a contrast between joy and happiness that others don't. I'm only doing this to free joy or even happiness from the consumeristic reductions it now has. Above I'm asking joy to serve the same function that Ellen Charry ascribes to happiness. With her I'm trying to have J echo Augustine. Charry says about Augustine, "Here is the foundation of Augustine's doctrine of happiness, indeed, his theology *in nuce*. Happiness is knowing, loving, and enjoying God securely. For that, one must both seek and find God, and this seeking proceeds by cultivating wisdom. It is the highest end of humanity. Wisdom requires virtue but is not itself virtue, for wisdom resides in God revealed in Christ. . . . For Augustine, happiness is the spiritual benefit of knowing, loving, and enjoying God, and loving self and others in pursuit of that goal. It is being at rest in God, as he so famously said: 'Our hearts are restless until they rest in you.'" *God and the Art of Happiness* (Grand Rapids: Eerdmans, 2010), 29, 57. One can see the connection with goodness here: "True happiness is the realization that only one 'substance' is self-sufficient, powerful, honorable, famous, and even pleasurable. The good that people seek piecemeal in so many different temporal goods is, it turns out, one simple 'substance': goodness itself. Those who seek happiness in wealth, office, reputation, and bodily pleasure are grasping at pieces of goodness, for wanting them is to desire the good. Seeking the good in objects rather than in activities is misplaced. Happiness can never be attained in this way because it is not to be had when enjoying any of these goods. The seeker who looks there confuses the pleasure these objects bring with genuine happiness that is enjoying goodness itself even when that brings no external reward and even misfortune" (77).

4. Jürgen Moltmann adds, "Here the distinction between *joy* and *fun* is helpful. Today in the wealthier societies and the rising middle classes, we are living in a 'fun society' (*Spaßgesellschaft*). I want to have a good time, say those young people who can afford it, and go to parties, preferring discos that are so noisy one can't hear oneself speak—but then, it isn't intended for one to speak and listen there. The sole idea is to be 'beside oneself' in the dancing throng. Once one has had one's fun, one is not satisfied but is still hungry for more of it, pining for more, as if, in Shakespeare's words, the appetite had grown from what it fed upon. Life is expected to be a party without end. The older rich people have their cocktail parties, where they exchange courtesies and niceties or watch each other suspiciously. They no longer know how to celebrate a feast. They don't even try. They instead engage entertainers, event managers, and animateurs. They let themselves be entertained because they can't entertain themselves." "Christianity: A Religion of Joy," in Volf and Crisp, *Joy and Human Flourishing*, 11.

a lot about how, in pursuit of a good life, parents rank youth ministry below so many other activities because youth ministry seems to have a blurrier route to happiness through the identity-to-recognition loop than most of the other activities. Even the church-committed parents I interviewed seemed to rank youth ministry below hockey and family time, because it seemed like the right thing to do as they pursued the aim of keeping their kids happy. The slowdown in growing up shows how much parents are investing in their children's happiness, and with this investment, youth ministry's purpose is now unclear.

But J's sense of the Good has a different aim. The Good (here with a capital G) is an end in itself.[5] This Good is even more personal.[6] Seeking the Good is the aim and only measure of a good life.[7] Unknowingly, J was moving

5. Here I'm drawing specifically on Iris Murdoch and her conception of the Good. She says, "I think it is more than a verbal point to say that what should be aimed at is goodness, and not freedom or right action, although that action, and freedom in the sense of humility, are the natural products of attention to the Good." *The Sovereignty of Good* (London: Routledge, 2013), 69. Melissa Orlie explains the connection between Charles Taylor and Murdoch: "If we compare Taylor's concept of the good with that of Iris Murdoch, whom he cites often and approvingly, we can see more clearly what is at stake in the tension between different conceptions of the good within Taylor's thought. For Murdoch, there is something profoundly delusional about the claim to the incomparability of one's good or group. Such claims are delusional precisely because the good is not finally definable. If I read him correctly, sometimes Taylor's understanding of the good accords with Murdoch's and, like her, he stresses the ways the good is always beyond us, is something that we can never fully articulate. This sense of the undefinable good is especially strong in Taylor's discussion of personal identity and the good in the early sections of *Sources of the Self*, in his discussions of the arts and, more recently, in his work *A Catholic Modernity?* At other moments, however, Taylor treats the good as something common, as the sort of thing to which a group can lay claim in saying who they are. This more substantial sense of the good appears especially when he reflects on group identity in 'The Politics of Recognition,' but also at some moments in *Sources of the Self*." "Taylor and Feminism: From Recognition of Identity to a Politics of the Good," in *Charles Taylor*, ed. Ruth Abbey (New York: Cambridge University Press, 2004), 150.

6. Fergus Kerr explains Taylor's perspective on Good with a capital G: "There are two moves here, both of which Taylor generously notes as being anticipated by Murdoch. The first is the move beyond the question of what we ought to do, to the question of what it is good for human beings to be. The second is the move beyond the question of what a good life for human beings might be, to the consideration of 'a good which would be beyond life, in the sense that its goodness cannot be entirely or exhaustively explained in terms of its contributing to a fuller, better, richer, more satisfying human life.' Taylor goes on at once to say that it is 'a good that we might sometimes more appropriately respond to in suffering and death, rather than in fullness and life'—and he allows that this takes us into 'the domain, as usually understood, of religion.'" "The Self and the Good: Taylor's Moral Ontology," in Abbey, *Charles Taylor*, 91.

7. I'm echoing Mary Clark Moschella's point here—but pushing it even further—when she says, "Joy also signifies a broader and more transcendent sense of goodness, one that links not just to personal well-being, but also to the larger reality, and to a vision of broader human flourishing." "Elements of Joy in Lived Practices of Care," in Volf and Crisp, *Joy and Human Flourishing*, 100.

back into eudaimonia, taking direct steps away from hedonism. Instead of trying, explicitly or implicitly, to make a case for how youth ministry can add to the goods of pursuing a happy life, J, sitting in the waiting room, saw the Good as an end. As she sat with Lorena's mom, with Lorena hooked up to machines, the aim of happiness quickly evaporated, and the Good as an end was the only aim for which they yearned.

Getting back to J's words, I respond, "That's a big move, to decide right there in the waiting room that you're done being the lead counselor of fun." I'm so intrigued by that moment of transformation that I ask J to say more.

She reflects for a few seconds and then says, "When I was supposed to make things fun, I felt like parents were asking me to play a small part in keeping their kids happy. But what I learned from Lorena's experience is that things are really different when you aim for the Good as opposed to the fun. I mean, that's my point about hearing all the 'it's not good' or 'it will be good' at the hospital. I started to realize that all I wanted for Lorena, all her mom wanted—I mean, her mom would have even died—was the Good for Lorena. Not happiness, but Good. I just got captivated by the thought. I realized I didn't want to be a successful youth pastor; I wanted to be a youth pastor who sought the Good. I didn't want our kids to think church was just a place to have fun and be happy but a place to look for, even participate in, the Good. Again, that's why it's joy. Because joy is the experience—the emotion, I guess—of encountering the Good."

"And only God is Good," I jump in, repeating the text from the night. "Only God is the fullness of Goodness. So joy is the experience of the Good. The Good has its source in God, in the love of the Father for the Son in and through the Spirit," I say, embarrassingly getting a little too theological.[8] But I can't help myself, and I find myself adding, "That means to feel joy is to touch something that is bound within God. It is a gift that transforms, because it's the inner feel of God's trinitarian life.[9] It transforms because it gives us

8. Charles Mathewes echoes this point further: "We are called to become participants in the endless joyful round of love that is the Trinity, and though in this dispensation that round has been splintered into a fugal structure, it has not been severed from that end; and so our lives here are a matter of learning to receive rightly the proleptic gifts of eschatological joy today." "Toward a Theology of Joy," in Volf and Crisp, *Joy and Human Flourishing*, 65.

9. Mathewes takes this deeper: "Joy seems less a general mood and more a responsive state prompted by some discrete object or action. Joy is a responsive act of exaltation and thankfulness, implicating one in an extra-subjective relationship. In contrast to the (necessarily unselfconscious) immanence of happiness, joy speaks immediately of transcendence, of what is outside." "Toward a Theology of Joy," 66.

a new aim and direction to our lives. We seek the Good. And when we seek the Good, we experience joy."

Youth ministry is to help kids not waste their lives. Making youth ministry about God helps them aim their lives toward the Good. Seeking a living God means not just committing to some ideas (or even ideology) but encountering God in our lives. God is there, not to keep us happy,[10] but to be an encounter of the Good. To encounter God in our lives means living a life that is taken up and drawn into the Good. A life that encounters the Good is never wasted, because a life that is aimed toward the Good is opened toward a transcendent horizon, toward encounters with the living God. No one is against happiness. But a full life, a truly well-lived life, is not simply a happy life. It's a life that encounters the Good.[11]

A life aimed toward happiness as its *summum bonum* still seeks goods, as we've described above. But these goods are locked on the track of hedonism. In the end this makes my aim myself: the recognition of my own identity, the fun of my own moments, the keeping of my own steady state of happiness.

And this is what J teaches me.

Youth ministry is for the Good. For youth ministry to be about God, it must be about seeking and following the Good. Youth ministry's aim is not just a good life—every basketball camp, debate club, and computer club claims to deliver this. This kind of good life offers—and sometimes provides—happiness, identity, and recognition. Yet what youth ministry aims for is a Good life. It seeks to give young people *visions* and *practices* in which the point of life is to encounter and participate in the Good. It aims for the Good as an end, and it seeks an encounter with God as the source of the Good.

When Dietrich Bonhoeffer defined discipleship, he said boldly, "When Jesus Christ calls a person He calls him or her to come and die."[12] This is a

10. Which is one of the key assumptions of moralistic therapeutic deism.

11. Sociologist Mihaly Csikszentmihalyi discusses the difference between happiness and joy by pointing to the good: "Thus it is essential to cultivate enjoyment because it is one of the most powerful means to experiment with alternatives to the trap of routine. Pleasure does not lead into new territory because the means to it may change but the goal itself does not grow. Enjoyment, on the other hand, consists in satisfying goals themselves capable of cultivation. The 'good life' is not a life of pleasure seeking, but it does involve the pleasurable experience of enjoyment. We derive enjoyment from the use of our own skills or the skills of others: from superior performance in athletics, music, work, or social interaction. Enjoyment, which leads into the future, must be tended to survive; otherwise, it turns into mere pleasure." Mihaly Csikszentmihalyi and Eugene Rochberg-Halton, *The Meaning of Things: Domestic Symbols and the Self* (Cambridge: Cambridge University Press, 1981), 245.

12. Bonhoeffer, *The Cost of Discipleship* (New York: Touchstone, 1995), 89.

vision of a Good life that has something very different than happiness as its aim. Bonhoeffer's discipleship seeks the Good, and this Good that is bound in God's very self is found in a hidden place. This Good is found where it shouldn't be: in dying. In dying to the self's aims for happiness, what the disciple finds isn't nihilism but Goodness.[13] She finds the very being of God bringing new life out of death. She finds a new identity that rests not on the flimsy foundation of her own happiness or achieved recognition but on the solid ground of the Good. As a gift she's given a new identity called Christ: "She no longer lives but Christ lives in her, and the life she lives in the body is Good, for she lives by faith" (paraphrase of Gal. 2:20). She experiences the ultimate Good through faith—the overcoming of death. And this overcoming is the feeling of joy. Joy is the experience of the Good, which comes upon us when we receive the gift of new life out of death, by faith.

I think Bonhoeffer has this sense of the Good in mind. Jesus calls us to seek for the Good, which we find by following him. In his book *Discipleship*, Bonhoeffer actually uses the same text J does. The rich young ruler is good. He's even kept all the commandments since his youth—since he was in youth ministry. And yet he lacks one thing. He must go and sell everything and *follow* Jesus (he must *Nachfolge*, as Bonhoeffer shouts). He must surrender the goods of a happy life and seek only the Goodness of God. But the rich young ruler cannot do this by furiously working hard to accumulate goods or even by taking on the activity of asceticism as his *thing*—he must seek the Goodness of God by following the person of Jesus. He must give up all pursuits of happiness—*not* for the sake of being a martyr but for the sake of the full personification of Goodness, Jesus himself.

The rich young ruler must find his life in Jesus, who is the fullness of the Goodness of God. The rich young ruler must do one thing: he must abandon his goods. In our day the rich young ruler would be asked to let go of his pursuit of happiness, which he had been trying to obtain through the performance of an identity for the sake of recognition. Happiness is no evil; if it comes, it's welcomed, even celebrated. But it's nothing worth aiming for,

---

13. Mathewes beautifully furthers this point: "So joy is excess, and an excess beyond the self. This leads to the second thing to say about joy, which is that, because it is so supremely intimate to oneself yet also intimately related to an other, joy is a reality best understood in the 'middle voice'—that is, a reality that is not purely passive, happening to us, nor simply active, something we do; but partaking of both receptivity and dynamism. Other, equally significant phenomena in Christian life are also framed in the middle voice; the Koine word for feeling compassion is *splagchnizomai*, which is another crucial 'action' that is in the middle voice; and a similar thing can be said of *elthon* ('to arrive' or 'to come,') which is used for the prodigal son's recognition, amid the swine, of the reality to which his life has come (of longing for the quality of life of pigs)." "Toward a Theology of Joy," 67.

no sought-after horizon for a well-lived life. Rather, the rich young ruler is told to seek the gift of the Goodness of God, which comes in the hidden and opposite places. This Goodness is revealed and given in the suffering of the cross.[14] We find the Good by following Jesus, who calls us to come and die, to come to places where God is delivering the ultimate Good to creation, consuming death with such a ministry of love that new life breaks through it.[15] When following this Jesus to the cross—into death—we'll have the joy of living in and for the Goodness of God, by being transformed, being in Jesus, who is the fullness of the joy of God.

Thinking about Bonhoeffer reminds me of Luther. The Goodness of God is found in a place that appears as the stark opposite of happiness, which to any eyes but those of faith looks like anything but Good. Yet Luther reminds us it's in the opposite of what is good, on the cross, that we find the Goodness of God.

I've been thinking a lot about Luther. On my last day at Disney World, I decided to blame Luther for the modern happiness extravaganza. After our first day at Universal Studios, I was thinking about where I'd nail my ninety-five theses.

14. Iris Murdoch, though not seeking to espouse anything like a *theologia crucis*, points in the direction of death and the cross and explores how this draws us toward virtues of humility (which will be the focus of forthcoming chapters): "Goodness is connected with the acceptance of real death and real chance and real transience and only against the background of this acceptance, which is psychologically so difficult, can we understand the full extent of what virtue is like. The acceptance of death is an acceptance of our own nothingness which is an automatic spur to our concern with what is not ourselves. The good man is humble." Murdoch, *The Sovereignty of Good* (New York: Schocken, 1971), 103, quoted in Robert Roberts, *Spiritual Emotions: A Psychology of Christian Virtues* (Grand Rapids: Eerdmans, 2007), 73.

15. Stephen E. Fowl draws out Paul's understanding of joy and the suffering of the cross, which we'll develop more fully in the chapters to come: "This is, in fact, the only way to account for Paul's joy and his call to the Philippians to rejoice with him. Death is not a cause for joy. As Paul notes, death is an enemy who will be defeated (1 Cor 15:54–58). Fidelity in the face of death or any other enemy is a cause for joy. Thus, Paul concludes this section by expressing his own joy and calling the Philippians to participate in his rejoicing. The great temptation for believers here is to reduce joy to happiness. When believers manifest lives worthy of the gospel of Christ, it is an occasion for joy. Such lives, however, may well entail pain, hardship, and deprivation. These can frustrate one's sense of well-being, but must not frustrate one's ability to rejoice." *Philippians*, Two Horizons New Testament Commentary (Grand Rapids: Eerdmans, 2005), 129.

Ten

Happiness, Part 2

Holiness, Virtue, and Luther's Freak-Out

THE END OF SPRING BREAK

I suppose nailing my own ninety-five theses to something wouldn't work. I'd somehow have to hack my way into the huge ESPN Zone video screen, rolling my own theses across it, scrambling *Pardon the Interruption* with my own interruption.

We were seated out on the patio of The Chocolate Emporium restaurant, waiting for our burgers and shakes after a long day in the world of Hogwarts. My kids were two of at least a hundred, just in the restaurant, draped in black robes, right hands clenched around a sixty-dollar piece of plasticky wood that represented a magical wand.

From our place on the patio we could see the whole of Universal City Walk. It was quite an impressive sight. Lights flashed from restaurants and shops constantly. The structures of these restaurants and shops were elaborate. No detail had been overlooked. And people were everywhere, seemingly coming from every direction: high school kids with T-shirts from Baton Rouge, a table away from us a family from Vancouver, and a whole school of twelve-year-olds from Spain sitting on the steps by the Bubba Gump Shrimp Company.

I had ended the previous day at Disney World thinking about Luther. Watching the parade, I wondered why he didn't have a place next to the Hunchback of Notre Dame. Now, halfway through my burger at Universal City Walk, I wondered what Luther would think if—in the style of *Bill and*

Ted's Excellent Adventure—he fell out of a time machine in front of the Hot Dog Hall of Fame.

I was sure rage would be his reaction, chased by sausage with mustard. *Idolatry!* would be the gist of his spitting diatribe. It wouldn't take long for him to see our societal soul. Human beings are animals who build material things, which are inescapably intertwined with symbolic meaning. Our architecture always tells a story. And when city bonds are spent and state debt incurred for amusement parks and sports stadiums, the message is clear: Our moral horizon is the immanent pursuit of pleasure and happiness. We are a whole society moving on the track of hedonism.

In 1511 Luther made a very different kind of pilgrimage than those at Universal City Walk. As a spiritual journey not for pleasure but for pain, Luther walked fourteen hundred miles to Rome. What he saw in Rome laid some of the earliest seeds for the nailing of his Ninety-Five Theses to the Wittenberg church in 1517. Luther witnessed sacred sites in disarray, their holy reverence tarnished by neglect and misuse. He began to wonder if the Holy City's neglect was a sign of papal inner rot. Looking out over Universal City Walk, I recognized that we have our own—very different—cathedrals and revered places. Ours are interlaced with consumerism, leisure, and ultimately the pursuit of happiness in our everyday lives. People come from everywhere, spending money they may or may not have, to get not to St. Peter's Basilica but to Harry Potter's Hogwarts. Just as very different kinds of people gathered in sixteenth-century Rome for the sake of holiness, so, too, do very different kinds of people from very different kinds of places gather at Universal Studios for the sake of pleasure and to pursue happiness.

❖

When Wes said parents assume that youth ministry is for tools and that these tools are connected to happiness, I think this is what he sensed. When a slowdown occurs in a hedonistic age—when life feels so fast that we take steps to slow down our kids from growing up, and parents become more involved in pursuing their children's happiness—youth ministry will inevitably be pushed to the edges. In contrast, in a hedonistic age of fast times, youth ministry will become youth group.[1] The group's mission is clear: keep young people from growing up too quickly. But what youth ministry is for in a hedonistic-age slowdown becomes unclear. It can be helpful in providing some further tools—some assets in achieving the aim of happiness. But if this

1. One could sketch out a much longer history here. For instance, I think it's plausible to argue that modern youth ministry can only come to be at all inside a hedonistic age.

pursuit of happiness can be found in other activities more directly connected to finding and expressing your identity and more interlaced with your *thing*, all the better.

As we said at the beginning of chapter 8, there have been other slowdowns. We mentioned particularly the medieval slowdown right before the time of Luther. While this slowdown produced university hijinks and perturbed elders, it nevertheless ran on a very different track than our own late modern slowdown.

For instance—again, to paint a history in broad strokes—the medieval slowdown had its impetus in allowing male children every opportunity to find a highly valued church vocation. The direct value of a church vocation wasn't necessarily in pearls and gold, or even happiness and leisure, but in heavenly treasures. Parents and family patriarchs hoped a child could quite literally work for heaven by attending to the sacred realm. The church was the storehouse of holiness, after all. It didn't provide stock options, a company car, and six weeks of vacation to pursue happiness, but, better, the church possessed the power to give heavenly holiness and earthly prestige. Slow them down, because with a little university education and attention to holy virtue, you could qualify to work for the hub of holiness.

So the medieval slowdown, unlike our own slowdown, moved on a eudaimonic track (the pursuit of virtue), not a hedonistic one. Admittedly, it's reductionist to assume just two tracks; things are always more complicated. For instance, there were many different ways to ride these two tracks. But here we'll stick with just the two for the purpose of showing how happiness has become so central and the problems this creates. To simplify it, we can say that the highest good people pursued during the medieval slowdown was not happiness but holiness. Even when things became deeply problematic—or in hindsight even evil, like in the selling of indulgences—the point was holiness. There was a market for indulgences because people's aim and sense of living a good life wasn't happiness but holiness—and this aim was exploited.

As it had been for the Stoics, happiness for medieval Christians was an auxiliary that, if nowhere else, happened at the end, though this time that meant in heaven! You might get a little taste of it before death, especially if you worked for the church, but ultimately happiness wasn't your aim. It was holiness you sought. And holiness was achieved by taking on the virtues that the holy church sanctioned as the means of receiving (achieving) salvation. Things were moving so squarely on the eudaimonic track that it made sense to slow young people down. A young Luther so deeply believed that he needed to pursue holiness through virtue that it nearly cracked him.

Luther's Freak-Out and the Shifting of Virtue

As we pointed to above, in the first two decades of the sixteenth century, right in the midst of the medieval eudaimonic slowdown, things got severely off-kilter. The pursuit of virtue for the sake of heaven became so weighty and all-encompassing that it was being dislodged from the grace of God. The supposedly most virtuous people were also the most corrupt. Soon the supposedly virtuous were selling forgiveness—the indulgences. The church gave out tokens of holiness, and you could hold heaven in your hand.[2]

Aware of hypocrisy throughout the church hierarchy, Luther could see that human virtuous action was far from producing holiness.[3] In a technical sense this experience made Luther an anti-eudaimonic; he even called Aristotle "that devilish fellow." But in another sense Luther's protest wasn't necessarily against the eudaimonic track, just an Aristotelian version of it.[4] For instance, in no way was Luther intending to pull the switch that would shift things from the eudaimonic to a hedonistic track. (Nevertheless, he is partly to blame—as we'll see.) Instead, what Luther hoped to show was that human action, even human-sought virtue, was stuck in impossibility. Luther saw that human action, cut off from the gift of God's act and being, could never reach the aim of holiness.

Luther called Aristotle "that devilish fellow" because the great philosopher held that human action aimed toward virtue through perpetuation of practice could achieve its sought-after end. Yet Luther saw something very different. Without the direct act of God, without the gift of God's grace, human virtue possesses no intrinsic capacity to achieve the holiness it seeks. Luther wasn't

2. Yet even before this, Western Christendom had been moving in and out of the pushes and pulls for reforms for most of its history. This reforming spirit of the West had much to do with the impact of this eudaimonic tradition (especially of Aristotle through Aquinas). The East could focus more on glorification, the mysterious inner life, the essences and energies of the Trinity, and hesychasm. The West, on the other hand, was more inclined to attend directly to human flourishing and manifestation of the virtues. How the human agent lived, what the human agent lived for, was always an anxious concern for those in Western Christendom.

3. "For Luther, in contrast, such an effort to put on virtue will only be a 'put-on,' and putting on Christ is instead properly understood as assuming a mask. The attempt to act virtuously in order to become virtuous is seen as essentially hypocritical." Jennifer A. Herdt, *Putting on Virtue: The Legacy of the Splendid Vices* (Chicago: University of Chicago Press, 2008), 2. We can only put on Christ and truly *be in* Christ by dying and being resurrected.

4. I think that Luther could affirm this base understanding of the eudaimonist. When Jennifer Herdt says that Luther is anti-eudaimonist (see *Putting on Virtue*, 188), she means in an Aristotelian way. I believe he could affirm Nicholas Wolterstorff here, and that's how I'm using it above. "The eudaimonist holds that the ultimate and comprehensive goal of each of us is (or should be) that we live our lives as well as possible, the well-lived life being, by definition, . . . the *eudaimōn* life." Wolterstorff, "God's Power and Human Flourishing" (unpublished consultation paper, Yale Center for Faith and Culture, 2014), 5, http://faith.yale.edu/sites/default/files /nicholas_wolterstorff_-_gods_power_and_human_flourishing_0_0.pdf.

opposing virtue necessarily;[5] he was simply, but profoundly, questioning the human capacity to reach the level of virtue that could actually deliver holiness. Of course, this questioning shifted things.

If Epicurus and the hedonists made pleasure the aim, and the Stoics, Aristotle, and the Roman Church's goal was virtue, Luther's *summum bonum* was faith. And faith wasn't an idea, but *the very person of Jesus Christ*. Christ and him crucified was the aim. But to say it again, Luther's redirected *summum bonum* wasn't necessarily to end virtue and the eudaimonic way in toto, but to make it possible by acknowledging that Jesus Christ alone possessed the virtue to be holy. Luther *did* shift the virtues from the center of focus (choosing to imagine his theological project somewhere else), but never to eliminate the eudaimonic sense of a well-lived life through the growth of faith. Yet eudaimonia was now radically reimagined outside of Aristotle and the Greek philosophers.

A well-lived life was now constituted only through the life, death, and resurrection of Jesus Christ, through the dialectic of cross and resurrection. To live well was first to find your own actions rendered powerless, and then to have them transformed into something new. Looking at the virtues through the *summum bonum* of Jesus Christ changed them, making them appear anything but glorious. The virtues were no longer a staircase to heavenly holiness or human-achieved balance but ways to perceive the mystery of faith in and through the mystery that the God of heavenly holiness comes in ways opposite from what we'd except (in a manger and on a cross).

Now the ways of living that produce a good life were transformed. Virtue was no longer needed to lead you to holiness, for only Jesus Christ was the holy one. And Christ was found not in achieved excellence or individually won flourishing—not even in happy recognition—but solely on the cross.

It's not that the cross is the only thing that this Jesus is doing, somehow so nailed up that he can't do anything else; or that the Christian life and all theological reflection are only about Jesus's generic presence in suffering. Rather, the resurrected Christ continues to act. He is alive, bringing forth a kingdom of healing and new life. But because Christ has borne sin and death on the cross, it has become a core mark of his identity. The cross is the core event with which not only Jesus but also his Father identifies.[6] This makes the cross of Christ the hermeneutic, the lens through which to see, know, and encounter the fullness of God. Luther is often considered one of the founding

---

5. Though he chose to attend more to the negative element of deadly sins than to virtue per se.

6. This is to echo Eberhard Jüngel's assertion that God identifies with the perishing Jesus, so that perishing now becomes part of God's own identity. See *Death: The Riddle and the Mystery* (Philadelphia: Westminster, 1974), 95–115.

fathers of the modern identity.[7] The *summum bonum* of faith as the person of Jesus Christ on the cross makes identity important.[8] There would be no Demi Lovato and Taylor Swift songs without this shift in *summum bonum* (though it would take many more shifts and turns to get to the kind of identity quest they're singing about).

For Luther, the cross is the determining event of Jesus's identity. The life-giving God identifies so deeply with the dead Jesus that death is overcome. God acts to raise Jesus because the Father so identifies with the event of the Son's crucifixion that death itself cannot hold Jesus down.[9] Death is overcome not because the Father abracadabras it away but because, in the deepest love and compassion, the Father identifies with the event of Jesus's death, making it forever part of God's own identity.

Incidentally, seeing identity through the cross gives us a way to affirm the need for recognition without conceding recognition to a performative, competitive battle. Recognition in itself isn't bad; it only becomes poisonous when individually achieved happiness becomes our moral horizon. The gospel actually demands that we recognize the events that shape people and forge their identities. For instance, the gospel demands we recognize the events of bigotry and dehumanization others have experienced. Recognition becomes problematic when it is directed not toward lived events that make our identity but toward ideologies, demanding that others recognize my identity as an ideological position as a way for me to win esteem. This is the issue with the misconception that identity is only an internal quest and not a discourse that seeks to make sense of events we encounter. The problem is that ideological conflicts often have zero-sum winners and losers. And this is what happens in the identity-to-recognition loop, which eliminates virtues like mercy, compassion, and forgiveness. I demand that you recognize my identity, not by sharing events that make me who I am so we can find communion, but so that I can win ground and possess the power of recognition itself.

The *summum bonum*, for Luther, is faith, which is the person of Jesus Christ. And this person of Jesus Christ is found not in excellence or holiness

7. See Charles Taylor, *Sources of the Self: The Making of Modern Identity* (Cambridge, MA: Harvard University Press, 1989), 218–56.

8. This is a much more complicated assertion than I have room here to develop. But my point is that the focus on faith leads to a sense of self and self-responsibility. Asking "Who am I?"—I think—is made possible by asking "Who is Jesus Christ in and through the event given to us in the biblical text?" Luther makes the identity of Jesus central to our salvation, which allows such questions about our own selves to be center.

9. This is to echo—in different ways—the thought of Eberhard Jüngel (*God as the Mystery of the World* [Grand Rapids: Eerdmans, 1983], 226–314) and Robert W. Jenson (*A Theology in Outline: Can These Bones Live?* [Oxford: Oxford University Press, 2016], 13–51).

or even balance (sorry, Yoda) but in the event of the cross. Because faith is the aim, the objective is not to somehow work ourselves into holiness but to be found in Christ. We, too, are called to identify our own being with the event of the cross, to seek the cross not as a masochistic work but as the event that reveals God's being.

This event of the cross transforms virtue by putting it to death and resurrecting it as something new. Moving through the dialectic of cross and resurrection, not only are virtue and the eudaimonic unhooked from being the means of salvation and the road to holiness, but there is also a shift in what is considered virtuous. Virtues must now be seen through the event of the cross itself. Conditioned by the cross, which reveals Jesus Christ as the object of faith, the virtues play a supporting role in helping us rise above all the other pleas for identity and its recognition.

But this is what's profound about these virtues transformed by the aim of faith. These transformed virtues are actually no help in rising above or balancing anything. Rather, they form us in ways to remember, retell, reenact, and reembody the event of the cross itself. So, through the cross, humility, gratitude, obedience, friendship, compassion, and sacrifice are the true virtues, for they take us low (kenotically) to direct us to the object of faith, Christ and him crucified.[10]

In a shifted (non-Aristotelian) but nevertheless eudaimonic way,[11] Luther asserted that the aim remains holiness (growth in faith). The point is to flourish in living well, and flourishing still has holiness as central. But holiness is not something we achieve by collecting virtues, like scout badges, until we have

10. Here is Luther in his own voice; these comments show that Luther still has a place for something like virtue or direct attention to the living of the Christian life, though it is radically transformed: "We do not, therefore, reject good works; on the contrary, we cherish and teach them as much as possible. We do not condemn them for their own sake but on account of this godless addition to them and the perverse idea that righteousness is to be sought through them; for that makes them appear good outwardly, when in truth they are not good. They deceive men and lead them to deceive one another like ravening wolves in sheep's clothing [Matt. 7:15]. . . . So a Christian, like Christ his head, is filled and made rich by faith and should be content with this form of God which he has obtained by faith; only, as I have said, he should increase this faith until it is made perfect. For this faith is his life, his righteousness, and his salvation: it saves him and makes him acceptable, and bestows upon him all things that are Christ's, as has been said above, and as Paul asserts in Gal. 2 [v. 20] when he says, 'And the life I now live in the flesh I live by faith in the Son of God.' Though the Christian is thus free from all works, he ought in this liberty to empty himself, take upon himself the form of a servant, be made in the likeness of men, be found in human form, and to serve, help, and in every way deal with his neighbor as he sees that God through Christ has dealt and still deals with him. This he should do freely, having regard for nothing but divine approval." Luther, *The Freedom of a Christian Man* (1520), in Hans Hillerbrand, *The Protestant Reformation* (New York: Harper Torchbooks, 1968), 19, 21.

11. Eudaimonic in the sense of seeking a life lived well that is not hedonistic in the Epicurean sense.

enough. Rather, human beings can only receive holiness as a gift, for we are far too stuck in the thick mud of sin and impossibility for our own actions to move us into holy virtue.[12] We must die to sin—and virtue, too, must die as idolatry. Sin will always upend virtue, unless virtue comes under the sign of the cross. Virtue must be negated and resurrected and transformed now in the image of the cross itself. So the virtues that ready us for this gift appear personified in their opposite. Jesus is the truly virtuous one, though he dies as a criminal. Jesus is holy and glorified, though he is bleeding and suffering. Jesus is the fullness of God, true God of all-powerful true God, though he is lying vulnerable and weak as a baby in a manger.

For Luther, virtue bears one name: Jesus Christ. And holiness is one thing, to be found in this Christ.[13] The aim or pursuit of the good life, then, is Jesus Christ himself.[14] He is the *summum bonum*. And his Father is the Good (Luke 18:19). We flourish only when we are found in him, swept up into the divine being. But Luther reminds us that we can only be swept up into the divine being by being in Christ, and this Christ is found in one place—on the cross, dying a death absent of virtue to negate and transform virtue itself. The divine being comes in its opposite, so that we might share in it. But to say it again, this doesn't mean ending the eudaimonic, but rather giving the pursuit of a well-lived life both a deeper christological aim and a more realistic anthropology.[15]

Youth Ministry and a Move toward Virtue

Graham and I were actually on the same page more than I knew back in September. He told me that youth ministry was for *helping young people not*

12. See Risto Saarinen, *God and the Gift: An Ecumenical Theology of Giving* (Collegeville, MN: Liturgical Press, 2005), for more on Luther and gift.

13. Admittedly here I'm leaning heavily on the Finnish interpretation of Luther, particularly the work of Tuomo Mannermaa. See his *Christ Present in Faith: Luther's View of Justification* (Minneapolis: Fortress, 2005) and *Two Kinds of Love: Martin Luther's Religious World* (Minneapolis: Fortress, 2010). For more on holiness in a similar vein, see John Webster, *Holiness* (Grand Rapids: Eerdmans, 2003).

14. "Luther does not trust that the aspirant to virtue can progress gradually from acting for the sake of external goods to acting for the sake of internal goods, caring for the neighbor for her own sake, since preoccupations with oneself and one's own efforts stand in the way. Luther argues that the student of virtue cannot avoid thinking about how the virtuous perceive her actions, how actions are shaping her character, whether she is acting in a way worthy of her own approval, and ultimately whether she is acting in a way that will win God's praise. This is for Luther such a severe problem that it can be resolved only by making the indwelling Christ the agent of human virtue." Herdt, *Putting on Virtue*, 184.

15. Two things Luther thinks the devilish Aristotle cannot do.

waste their lives. When he asked me what I thought youth ministry was for, I awkwardly said, "God."

If Luther had stumbled into our conversation, holding a tall, cold Hefeweizen in his hand, trying to find his way back to Bill and Ted's time machine, he would have said, "Youth ministry is for Jesus Christ." He'd have pointed to Graham and said, "He's right; we are moved by goods. All human beings seek some implicit or explicit *summum bonum*. We are desperate to not waste our lives." And looking at me, he'd have continued, "And it is true that to avoid this waste we should seek to live well by attending to the holiness of God. God's holiness, as the Good, must be our pursuit. Peace with God must shape our imagination."

But gulping down the dregs of his beer, Luther would have cleared his throat and leaned in closer. "While we should affirm that virtue is the way into holiness, the only way to keep virtue from turning on us like a family dog gone mad—once the embodiment of home, now leaping for our neck in bloodlust—is for the *summum bonum* to be Jesus Christ alone.[16] It is to seek only Christ and him crucified (1 Cor. 2:2) as our deepest longing. This is what youth ministry is for—to seek Christ and him crucified."

Jesus Christ is the sole holy one, completely virtuous. It is only through his person that we can be taken into the holiness of the Father's heavenly glory. But to experience this holiness we must find it in lowliness (1 Cor. 1). Christ and him crucified recasts virtue. Now humility, gratitude, friendship, compassion, and sacrifice become the way to holiness.[17] Not because these virtues can save. But because in practicing humility, gratitude, friendship, and compassion we're taken to the cross, to call our situation of sin and impossibility what it is. Following Luther's *theologia crucis*, the virtue of naming death—peering at the cross—becomes central, because it is the place where God acts, doing God's Good work of bringing life out of death.

Pausing for a moment, Luther would have then added, "Youth ministry prepares the young not necessarily for virtues themselves but for love and service for our neighbor. These transformed virtues of humility, gratitude, friendship, compassion, and sacrifice don't necessarily produce holiness, but they lead us to love and minister to our neighbor. It's here that we find holiness, for we encounter the real presence of Jesus."

16. One can see now how close Bonhoeffer's *Cost of Discipleship* is to Luther.

17. One of the important transformations of virtue here is that this cruciform disposition of virtue allows the supposed "least of these" to partake. This list of lowly virtues is not dependent on cognitive ability. Those with disabilities, for instance, are deeply invited into these practices. Ben Conner shows just this in his youth ministry book, *Amplifying Our Witness: Giving Voice to Adolescents with Developmental Disabilities* (Grand Rapids: Eerdmans, 2012).

To go somewhat beyond Luther, then, we might say that virtue remains, not for the sake of climbing a staircase to heaven but rather to take us to hell, to the cross, preparing us for the encounter of revelation that comes in and through serving our neighbor. The transformed virtues are to lead us to love our neighbor as the place of encounter with Christ.

The Steep Downhill

Luther came of age during a eudaimonic slowdown. But his Reformation, and particularly the Calvinist one that followed, would end it. The years after the Reformation were fast times. While there are very loose parallels between Martin Luther and Jeff Spicoli, and John Calvin and Brad Hamilton[18] (which are mainly just fun caricatures), the fast times after the Reformation were very different than those in the last decades of the twentieth century, as we said earlier.[19]

The fast times right after Luther occurred because ordinary life now possessed new importance. Luther made the peasant's home as holy a domain as the cathedral, and the milking of cows and changing of diapers became sacred vocations.[20] Before Luther, elders were slowing down the university boys for the sake of calibrating the lucky few for the speed of a holy vocation. After Luther, the multiple speed limits became one.[21] Now all vocations and all parts of ordinary life bore the significance of salvation. Because virtue was recast to take us to the cross of Christ, and faith alone became the *summum bonum*, any lowly activity done in obedience to Christ was a holy act. Luther and Calvin freed virtue from the apparatus of the cathedral and the cultic operations of the priest.[22] This was for the sake of making every min-

18. Brad Hamilton is Stacy's older, fragile but responsible brother played by Judge Reinhold in *Fast Times at Ridgemont High*.

19. However, it must be said, without the new fast times after the Reformation, the late twentieth-century fast times that birthed the era of the youth group would not have been.

20. Discussing Luther's conception of vocation, Miroslav Volf gives us context: "To be a husband, wife, child, or servant means to be called by God to a particular kind of activity, it means to have a vocation. When God's spiritual call through the proclamation of the gospel reaches a person in her station or profession, it transforms these into a vocation. The duties of the station become commandments of God to her. In this way, Luther links the daily work of every Christian inseparably with the center of Christian faith: for a Christian, work in every profession, and not only in ecclesiastical professions, rests on a divine calling." *Work in the Spirit: Toward a Theology of Work* (Eugene, OR: Wipf & Stock, 1991), 106.

21. Charles Taylor discusses the change in speed in *A Secular Age* (Cambridge, MA: Belknap, 2007), 62–72.

22. In turn, they provided the early conditions that would allow for the disenchantment of Western society as a whole.

ute of every part of their ordinary lives the locale for living out their faith. In practical terms, this meant that carnival—a sanctioned time when it was OK to let off steam and be bad by being unvirtuous—was over. And a new attention to manners and politeness across society was necessary, even for children and the ignoble.[23]

With this new affirmation of ordinary life in place, boys and girls needed to grow up quickly, for no longer was the monastery or nunnery a higher vocation than the farm. It was at the speed of ordinary life—marrying, having children, working a trade, and making money in the new capitalist societies—that, in faith, they encountered the living God. And even small children needed to learn manners, speaking appropriately and dressing properly as a sign that they were saved by faith. The virtues of faith were to conform them to the presence of God in the opposite, to witness the Good in the lowly and ordinary. Therefore, people now needed to attend diligently to their ordinary lives, examining them constantly, critiquing them continually. They had to make sure that in their ordinary ways faith was indeed their aim, for it was only in following Jesus Christ in faith that they lived well.

This didn't end the eudaimonic way, but rather, particularly for Calvinist societies, had the opposite effect. It ran the eudaimonic track steeply downhill. These post-Reformation fast times meant heightened responsibility for each individual. Everyone now needed to take responsibility to live up to the high bar of the priest, even in the ordinary tasks of selling buttons and making beds or just being a child. And it was the parents' job to protect their children from hell by reminding them of their deep responsibility in ordinary life to work hard, pray constantly, and not waste a minute of their time in impious frivolity.[24] These were fast times, but ones far removed from the parties and pot smoke of the hedonistic, late twentieth-century fast times. These fast times ran squarely on eudaimonic tracks, secured by religious commitment. Young people were encouraged (prodded) to grow up quickly and take responsibility for the working out of their own salvation.

23. Taylor traces this history in the first part of *A Secular Age*. He calls this the rise of the polite society.

24. Ruth Abbey explains Taylor's perspective: "Protestantism rejected the belief that some sorts of activities are qualitatively superior than others and proposed instead that all activities are potentially worthy; what matters is how they are conducted. The accent shifted from what one does to how one does it. What mattered was that one carry out one's deeds worshipfully, to the glory of God. From this perspective, even the most menial activity could become sanctified, if practiced with the appropriate attitude. One way of expressing this transition is to say that the object of strong evaluation changed. Previously activities themselves had been deemed noble or base, whereas now it was one's way of participating in them that became admirable or degenerate." *Charles Taylor* (Princeton: Princeton University Press, 2000), 89.

Jumping Tracks

This affirmation of ordinary life is why I decided to blame Luther for theme parks on our spring break. Luther, with genius, made faith the *summum bonum*.[25] Yet, even with this genius, Luther (or better, Protestantism) deserves some blame—or if you're the Disney Corporation, some laud—for making The Happiest Place on Earth a possibility. I thought Luther deserved an animated character alongside the Hunchback of Notre Dame because if not for the Reformation's affirmation of ordinary life, our obsession with the individual being happy would not be possible. Luther and Calvin's strict call to constantly and continually review and reexamine our lives, to assess whether our most ordinary moments are faithful, shifted the human focus.[26] Thanks to the Protestant attention to faith in ordinary life, people were led to see identity as an essential pursuit, and recognition as the necessary affirmation of this sought-after identity. Identity and recognition are part of the legacy of Protestantism (they just become very different, self-enclosed, and idolatrous realities, as we'll see, when happiness, as opposed to faith or cruciform virtue, became our aim).

Protestantism's affirmation of ordinary life ran tracks downhill, picking up intensity as people now constantly needed to review and reexamine every part of their lives. Shifting into fast times meant growing up faster. Through a eudaimonic lens, that meant growing up faster with the focus of living well. This demanded that each individual focus on her own inner life, searching it for sin and disobedience, examining whether her soul was content before God and, in turn, whether her house (marriage, children, business) was in order. These tracks were unequivocally eudaimonic. The aim was faith, received by living a life of humility, gratitude, and self-sacrifice.

Yet, as Protestantism rode these eudaimonic tracks, hidden hedonistic tracks appeared alongside.[27] They appeared as an accident. The focus on

25. We'll follow this intention, trying to recover faith as the *summum bonum* of youth ministry, below. But like files on a failed hard drive, it will indeed have to be recovered. To focus on faith without freeing ourselves from the *summum bonum* of happiness—which too many youth ministry resources have failed to do for fear of being too rigidly old-school Calvinist, for instance—keeps faith, despite our best efforts, as only an accessory to the quest for a good life achieved by all sort of other activities and *things* that achieve happiness. This will make it nearly impossible to imagine flourishing beyond the identity-to-recognition loop.

26. Jennifer Herdt explains this practice and how it pushed into deep forms of *self-reflection*: "Part of the impulse behind Puritan autobiographical writing is the hope that if we cannot achieve a full self-understanding, full grasp of the ways of God with us, as we live our lives, perhaps we can do so in retrospect. Perhaps the narration of one's life can achieve that elusive honesty, can penetrate the momentary successes of self-deception." *Putting on Virtue*, 208.

27. Taylor (*Sources of the Self*, 206–16) discusses at great length the impact of the rise of the compassionate marriage. I've avoided the temptation to discuss it above, but this, along

the inner life of contentment before God, and the social concern for an ordered, well-run ordinary life, allowed happiness (as opposed to faith) to sneak in as a legitimate aim. These modern hedonistic tracks were, ironically, formed out of the shifted concerns of Protestant faith itself and the new modern moral horizon it gave them.[28] The eventual move from eudaimonia to hedonism happened not because of a loss of devotion to faith but, ironically, because of Protestantism's high commitment to faith as the *summum bonum*. It is this new commitment to feeling close to God in ordinary life that allows for happiness to outstrip faith, character, and virtue.

Through the nineteenth century, these hedonistic tracks were mostly covered in dust; only a few people were brave enough to use the momentum of the ride on the Protestant eudaimonic tracks to jump to hedonistic ones (people like those in the enclaves of the Bohemian Romantics that inspired the age of authenticity).[29] But in the twentieth century, as the consumeristic impulses of the mass society dawned after World War II,[30] the switch was thrown with almost no one noticing. Darrin McMahon says, "If advertising can be said to be the business of selling dreams"—and I would interject, if our dreams are fused with our moral horizons of the good—"the dream now is often a variation on the theme of happiness—at all times, in all places, in all things. Have a Coke and a smile. Indulge in 'happy hour,' savor 'genuine satisfaction.'"[31]

---

with the other phenomena that I mention, allows for what I've highlighted above. Like Taylor, I'm contending that it is Protestantism's deep belief in God—through the *summum bonum* of faith—that allows for the condition of unbelief.

28. I'm resisting the temptation to provide a long discussion of the modern moral order. But this shift is essential to allowing the hedonistic tracks to appear. The modern moral order comes to be when we shift from honor to dignity, and what is seen as "moral" is shifted to focus on society being organized for mutual benefit, particularly in the economic sphere. Because of the attention to ordinary life, concern for moneymaking becomes connected to one's attention to faithful living in the ordinary. Therefore, society must work to allow everyone the mutual benefit of commerce. We need this new modern moral order to eventually get to the kind of consumerism that allows for these hedonistic tracks to be laid.

29. To give a direct example, and maybe a time frame on this track-jumping, look at the differences between the pastoral perspective and preaching of Jonathan Edwards in the eighteenth century and Henry Ward Beecher in the nineteenth. Both came from Puritanism. Beecher took a very different track than even his own father, Lyman, a disciple of Edwards. Edwards was clearly and forcefully on the eudaimonic track, and Beecher followed this track as a boy but then jumped it with a Jesus of love and happiness. Edwards's preaching was long, erudite, and challenging. Beecher's preaching was entertaining, funny, and left its listener never condemned but feeling good. Edwards preached for discipline, Beecher for pleasure. The train had jumped the tracks without anyone really noticing.

30. For more on this, see part 1 of my *Faith Formation in a Secular Age: Responding to the Church's Obsession with Youthfulness* (Grand Rapids: Baker Academic, 2017).

31. Darrin M. McMahon, *Happiness: A History* (New York: Grove Press, 2006), 465.

By the second half of the twentieth century, Protestant America was no longer on the eudaimonic tracks. It had shifted to the hedonistic ones.[32] The shift has been so complete that twenty-first-century parents like the Rodriguez-Eriksons and the Tuckers can make a hypergood of their kids' happiness, feeling it as *the* moral horizon. For even these devout, churchgoing parents, all else is periphery to happiness.

And this is the conundrum that youth ministry now faces.

Youth Ministry and the Track Switch

Youth ministry can have a clear purpose even when the culture is running on hedonistic tracks. It will no longer be about the discipline of education for the sake of ordinary life, like it was in the British Sunday school movement. Nor will youth ministry be about constantly examining, and then publicly pledging, your commitment, like it was in Christian Endeavor. Youth ministry can't have these purposes because the unthought cultural tracks it inherited de facto are no longer eudaimonic. Therefore, the Sunday school and pledging societies are mostly dead. Yet, as I just said, even now on hedonistic tracks, where the aim is happiness, youth ministry can have a clear purpose. But only during fast times.

Youth ministry got a sweeping makeover after World War II, and more particularly after the late 1960s counterculture. When the whole culture shifted onto hedonistic tracks and we entered the age of authenticity, we did so with momentum, and we did so in fast times. (It was the fast times of post-Reformation affirmation of ordinary life that allowed the velocity to jump tracks.) Parachurch organizations like Young Life and Youth for Christ, and congregation-based youth ministries with youth groups, became the exact right response to the fast times of the new hedonistic age in which pleasure and happiness was the aim.

Youth ministry's purpose was clear in the fast times on the hedonistic track—decelerate young people's growing up so they don't derail and crash. Give them religious socialization through peer groups of wholesome fun. Use the youth group as a way of translating religious institutional commitment into the language and dispositions of aims for happiness. Show how Jesus can make you happy.[33] It's not surprising, then, that in 1988 a surprise Top 40 hit was Bobby

32. By the last years of the twentieth century and first decades of the twenty-first century, Protestant America was over.

33. This works so powerfully because it happens at the same time as (or even because of) what Taylor (*Secular Age*, 299–313) calls the nova effect. All sorts of third options and new

McFerrin's "Don't Worry, Be Happy." It's a song now epically linked with the 1980s, as Sheryl Crow's song "If It Makes You Happy" is with the 1990s. The simple but catchy song not only spilled from boom boxes and Walkmans but also was a youth ministry sing-along "hymn" at nearly every Young Life club and youth group gathering.

Recognizing how youth ministry responded to, and silently affirmed, this shift, it makes sense that the masters of this youth ministry makeover in the fast times of the hedonistic *summum bonum* would become founders of the megachurch movement. Connecting the lessons learned in the youth group for mixing religious institutional commitment with the pursuit of happiness, they started churches like Willow Creek and Saddleback, to name just two of the most famous.

From Fast Times to Slowdown

But now that the fast times have ended, what is youth ministry for? It's very hard to say. Happiness is no longer sought through parties, older boys, and fast cars, but instead through SAT tutors, constant parental oversight, and risk aversion. What's the purpose of youth ministry now that the whole culture is slowing young people down and they're growing up not too quickly but too slowly?

The slowdown is in effect, as we've said throughout, not because the *summum bonum* has shifted from happiness but because we've doubled down on it. It's now too risky; the hypergood of happiness could potentially be lost if we allow children to grow up too fast. We must shift from free adolescent space and time to constant oversight. Those who grew up in the fast times have wagered that their own children will be happier through future accomplishments and avoidance of emotional injury than by having loads of free time and space to do what they want. With the slowdown in effect on the hedonistic tracks and happiness assumed to be best achieved through parental oversight, it's hard to know what youth ministry is for.[34]

---

spiritualities appear, untethered to organized religion, that are free to assist people in being happy and finding pleasure. The nova effect can happen in major part because no spirituality or religion need serve my pursuit of a happy identity. Spirituality can give some meaning and even weight to the light, fluffy moral horizon of happiness, but it is not essential.

34. I want to be clear—because it will relate directly to the forthcoming vol. 3 of the Ministry in a Secular Age series—that this slowdown is in effect because of the overall speeding up of modernity and the fear of its alienation. In my mind, slowing down kids' growing up has everything to do with the sense that things just keep going faster and faster. And we all sense that embedded in this speed is the risk of alienation. Parents don't want their kids to experience alienation, and yet want them to be ready to live at the high speed of modernity, so they slow

The hedonistic slowdown, which has rendered youth ministry aimless, causes us to look back at the mid-century youth ministry makeover. Even in those supposed glory days, there was an inherent problem we still confront. Now that the blur of the fast times is over, we can see more clearly that youth ministry has had an inherent misaim since its makeover. We couldn't see this until the slowdown because the fast times gave youth ministry a purpose (slow them down!), even if it was self-defeating. If we now look closely, we can recognize that this mid-century youth ministry makeover conceded the moral horizon of happiness itself. It never really asked whether youth ministry was for more than slowing young people down for the sake of happiness. Happiness is not something to oppose, but neither should it be the highest good pursued. Youth ministry never broadly asked if its purpose was, rather, to invite young people (and their families) to aim for the Good, providing visions and practices to live well and flourish by aiming for something much deeper than happiness.[35]

Meaningless Happiness

We must be careful here. As I said above, no one should be against happiness. Happiness is never the enemy. It's wonderful to feel happy; it's a welcome emotion. But as the ancients reminded us, it's not something worth pursuing

them down. Again, this is not for the sake of slowing down life, but to make them ready to live at the high speeds of modernity. I'm indebted to and convinced by Hartmut Rosa's position in *Social Acceleration: A New Theory of Modernity* (New York: Columbia University Press, 2015). In vol. 3, I'll construct a whole ecclesiology with Rosa's theory as the central interpretative lens.

35. In the early 2000s, right when the slowdown was taking effect, people like Mark Yaconelli, David White, Kenda Creasy Dean, and Mike King reflected extensively on youth ministry. I believe that in their own ways and from their own communities, each of them was seeking to correct the errors of the mid-century youth ministry makeover. They were trying to shift youth ministry away from its focus on happiness and onto a eudaimonic track. In various ways, each was successful, and all four (and more not mentioned) should be lauded for this revolutionary shift. However, I believe they all missed (or didn't develop) what Luther might offer through the dialectic of the cross and resurrection. These virtues and practices, as I will elaborate on below, need to be transformed, taking a cruciform shape that none of these important voices offered. They intuited what was problematic in Protestantism and therefore called for a return to practices and virtue, but in my respectful opinion, they overlooked the genius of Protestantism and how faith through the cross can provide a fullness to life and in turn give us virtues of humility, gratitude, and sacrifice. This is what I will reveal through the story of J and her claim that youth ministry is for joy. Yet, to conclude this long note, it is important to recognize that other youth ministry projects such as Fuller's Sticky Faith and Growing Young have been unable to directly free themselves from the hedonistic track or even challenge it. They continue to want to talk about forming faith, but in those conversations faith can look like institutional commitment that adds layers of happiness and protection. They, too, have failed to see the dialectical dynamics of the Protestant perspective on faith.

as our highest good. It is not a good that can deliver us to the Good. Happiness, ancient wisdom tells us, is not a wide enough moral horizon to give our lives meaning. The firmer we place ourselves on the hedonistic track—slowing ourselves down so that we and our children never derail—the more we are struck with a sense of meaninglessness. The slower we go, the more we find that meaning is hauntingly hard to find. This ironically makes us all the more invested in finding it through the moral horizon of happiness itself.[36]

This is why people living on the hedonistic tracks sometimes become obsessed with an individual expressive identity and demand to be recognized. Identity becomes *the* task because it is *the* way to give this moral horizon of happiness meaning. Happiness as a moral horizon is like an indulgent uncle who tells us that its worthiness is in its freedom. Happiness as a moral horizon imposes few outside demands or strictures on us; it asks us to listen to what gives us pleasure. But while seeming fun and free, like after spending a long week with that uncle, we quickly discover that this supposed freedom is vapid and hollow. We feel rudderless, disoriented by the freedom to eat candy for breakfast. We are free from all outside demands, invited to attend to inner pleasure, but we soon discover that there is little meaning in this pursuit. So the indulgent uncle tells us to find some, to look deeper within the good of the self's inner pleasures. We are to forge an identity, a free self-definition, that delivers the meaning we seek. Happiness has no intrinsic meaning but does deliver the freedom for us to look inside the self and find our own meaning in and through what makes us happy.

The slower we go toward the goal of happiness, the more the identity options become both exponential and furiously fought for. The more committed we are to happiness as our moral horizon, the slower we go, which in turn makes the malaise of meaning more staggering. This leads us to all sorts of

36. Douglas John Hall provides insight into the vapidness and meaninglessness of an age in which happiness is the end. It is particularly insightful because of his discussion of Donald Trump, who at the time Hall was writing was thirty years from being president. Hall says, "When Howard Hughes died at the biblical age of seventy, he was reputed to be 'worth' more than 2.5 billion dollars, and had become a complete recluse. *Time* magazine wrote of him: 'In his latter years, Hughes had become the epitome of the 20th century tragedy, a man so preoccupied with gadgets and power that he severed the bond with his fellow men.' Of another and later multimillionaire, Donald Trump, a recent edition of the same magazine, in which Mr. Trump was the feature presentation, ended with these words: 'One man who knows Trump well does see a rhyme and reason. Trump is a brilliant dealmaker with almost no sense of his own emotions or his own identity, this man says. He is a kind of black hole in space, which cannot be filled no matter what Trump does. Looking toward the future, this associate foresees Trump building bigger and bigger projects in his attempts to fill the hole but finally ending, like Howard Hughes, a multibillionaire living all alone in one room." *The Steward: A Biblical Symbol Come of Age* (Grand Rapids: Eerdmans, 1990), 88.

new creative identities we need in the desert of meaning. And in turn, these new identities can lead us to new enemies who don't recognize these identities we need in order to not choke on meaninglessness. So instead of getting off the hedonistic tracks, we just imagine that if we can express our identity and, just as importantly, win recognition for that constructed identity, we'll have the meaning we need to make happiness less hollow. This would give us a sense of fullness that seems surprisingly absent against the moral horizon of happiness.

An Encore for Sheryl Crow

This sense of hollowness is why Sheryl Crow's song is irking. Her song is not just about the journey for happiness through identity and won recognition but also about the arrival. It's about making it to the summit of happiness and finding it indelibly infused with discontent. The 1990s were a transitional period between fast and slow times, and that made it easier to spot the meaninglessness of the moral horizon of happiness. Most of the lasting cultural articulations of the decade, like Pearl Jam, Nirvana, and David Foster Wallace, point it out. Decades later we find it much harder, because the core strategy to avoid the meaninglessness of the moral horizon of happiness has been to escalate the identity options and fight them out on social media. Crow's song reveals that though she is happy, she is depressed—sad—and this is because happiness in itself cannot deliver the meaning for which the human spirit longs. Happiness is no natural steady state, for it has no ability in itself to deliver a meaning that matches the depth of the human spirit.

Crow arrives at her aim, now possessing the good of happiness confirmed by recognition of her chosen identity. And yet she is sad, because the moral horizon of happiness could not bring her to the Good. She did what the moral horizon of happiness asked; she constructed her own identity. But getting to her goal, she realizes it is meaningless; it produces no horizon beyond the insatiable thirst for more and more recognition, sending her deeper into herself.[37] She is sad because she now senses that happiness *achieved* produces only the options of narcissism or depression.

This is why celebrities are the sages of happiness in our age. And though we know that few of them escape narcissism or depression—only those who

---

37. And this way of living stands in opposition to how we are created—as the theological anthropologies of Wolfhart Pannenberg (*Anthropology in Theological Perspective* [Philadelphia: Westminster, 1985]) and David H. Kelsey (*Eccentric Existence: A Theology Anthropology* [Louisville: Westminster John Knox, 2009]) state, showing how the eccentric is central.

find a higher moral horizon like the truth of art or family or religion—we still make them our role models. They are the models of those living a good life; they've reached the moral horizon of happiness. Reaching the good of being happy usually makes us bad people, but we still wish to be like these celebrities because *they are happy*, winning global recognition for the unique identities they constructed. Celebrities themselves are dying in the acrid reality that happiness through identity and won recognition provides no meaning. But we can't help but wish to be them, finding our own meaning in seeking a global level of recognition for our own identity.

If there is a lesson from the sage celebrities of happiness—one that too often we ignore—it's that it's better to never arrive at the horizon of happiness, better to be always reaching for it, anticipating and longing for it. This is the only way it can have meaning. The search for happiness, won through the recognition of our identity, is always better than its fulfillment (see, for instance, Bradley Cooper's character Jack in *A Star Is Born*). Happiness is too flimsy to get to the Good. No wonder, then, Sheryl finds herself depressed. While happiness, as a moral horizon, frees us with one hand to be happily whoever we want, it nevertheless enslaves us with the other. For in this supposed freedom to be happy, we have no meaning other than that which we create from within ourselves. There is no ecstatic or transcendent horizon to pull us out of ourselves and give us meaning.[38]

When Happiness Becomes Mean

If we fail to recognize that happiness, as our highest good, cannot deliver meaning, we are thrust into identity wars. Identity politics becomes our way of being in a hedonistic time of slowdown, because we fail to recognize that the cultural aim for happiness is too lightweight to provide the meaning the human spirit needs.[39]

The moral horizon of happiness lies to us, telling us we can all get along because we all just want to be happy. Everyone is imagined to be free to find their own happiness and their own meaning through discovering their own

38. It's not that people don't try. Tourism, yoga, rock concerts, etc. are sought for their ability to take us out of ourselves and connect us with something bigger. But these often are only episodic, for they never free us from the hedonistic track. They only give us some meaning while we seek happiness as our *summum bonum*.

39. In fast times on the hedonistic track, a neo-Nietzschean hero ethic is more prominent. The fast times allow the dark edges of a nihilistic time to come to the surface. Hence, the 1970s and 1980s was an epic period of heavy metal music; Metallica's *The Black Album* was released in 1991 as the height of the art form.

this is me. But the problem is that human beings are not just independent receptors of emotions of delight. There really is no such thing as "you do you" without your doing affecting my "doing me."[40] The moral horizon of happiness seems to assume that you can forge your own meaning through your identity alone inside some bubble. But this is not how the human spirit is constituted. The human being is fundamentally a language animal. To find and possess meaning we must communicate it and have others hear, see, and respond. To have an identity we must discover it in and through some kind of discourse. For identity to deliver meaning it must, in some way, be found outside ourselves.

So this happiness-imposed freedom to be whoever we want compels us to express the meaning our identity gives us. To get to happiness, then, the free identity we've constructed must win recognition. In order for me to be happy, you must recognize my identity. For while happiness allows me the freedom to be whoever I want, I have no meaning unless you recognize me. So if you refuse—or even overlook or dismiss—my expressions of my identity, you are assumed to have violently stripped me of meaning. You've left my moral horizon of sought happiness hollow, and that makes you an enemy who must be exposed and destroyed. Your inability (or unwillingness) to recognize my identity startlingly reveals—like the end of an M. Night Shyamalan movie—that the moral horizon of happiness is shockingly flat. Ironically, then, the moral horizon of happiness has an inherent nihilism to it; that's why it seems to be able to produce only narcissism or depression. The more we make happiness our aim, the more we risk falling into a nihilist pit of meaninglessness, *ressentiment*, and revenge seeking.

Again, to be clear, happiness *isn't* evil. We should welcome it. But when it becomes our moral horizon, it becomes a kind of gremlin. The ancients in wisdom knew we must aim for something else, something more transcendent and mysterious than happiness alone can possess, something weightier, even if that weightier aim chafes at times and even keeps us from immediate pleasure. But this kind of moral horizon gives us meaning by moving us outside ourselves (not deeper within ourselves, to boomerang out and demand that others recognize our identity). For the Greeks this was virtue. For medieval Christendom it was holiness through ecclesially sanctioned virtue. And for

---

40. "In general, relationships conflict with the individualistic notion that 'you don't need someone else to make you happy—you should make yourself happy!' That is the message iGen'ers grew up hearing, the received wisdom whispered in their ears by the cultural milieu." Jean Twenge, *iGen: Why Today's Super-Connected Kids Are Growing Up Less Rebellious, More Tolerant, Less Happy—and Completely Unprepared for Adulthood* (New York: Atria Books, 2017), 214.

Luther, and my construction from him, it is transformed virtue through faith in the crucified Christ. They all spotted, to paraphrase Jesus's words, that "people cannot live on happiness alone." And yet this has been exactly the project of the consumer society of late modernity, which youth ministry, in its visions of formation, has not challenged.

When Faith Is for Happiness

The recent refocusing on faith formation in youth ministry shows that indeed we sense something is wrong. With the fast times over, almost all youth workers are ready to assert that youth ministry is about cultivating faith, not just about fun and games. But even in giving this attention to faith formation, we've too often acceded to the *summum bonum* of happiness; even our renewed emphasis on youth ministry has unintentionally allowed faith to be imagined as an asset (not an aim). Faith is reduced to a frame of mind that can serve a young person well on the tracks toward happiness; faith is an important part of self-constructed identity. We've lost the *sola fides* Luther gave us, contending instead that faith is to help us to be happy, rather than it being the *summum bonum* itself. When we represent faith as an asset that moves us toward the moral horizon of happiness, rather than the true moral horizon itself, faith is impotent in leading us to the Good.

We remain, then, Protestants in name (and in our affirmation of our ordinary life) but not in substance. For to truly be (theologically) Protestant is to see faith as the only means of salvation and therefore the only route to the Good and Holy. Youth ministry, along with most other aspects of contemporary Protestantism, hasn't recognized that faith cannot be formed on the hedonistic track. Faith will always come out as moralistic therapeutic deism when happiness is the highest aim of our moral horizon. Not until youth ministry itself challenges the happiness *summum bonum* can it form faith that is reflective of how Bonhoeffer, Luther, and Paul imagined it—as a transformation that "conforms us to Christ" (Bonhoeffer), that "turn us into little Christs" (Luther), that puts us to death so that "I no longer live, but Christ lives in me" (Paul in Gal. 2:20).

On first read, most everyone would agree that faith must be our *summum bonum*; happiness has its limits. But what we miss, because of our own trappings on the hedonistic track, is that unless faith bears the mark of the cross, which Luther taught us—putting us to death, to resurrect us anew—"faith" will be overtaken by the hedonist and serve the pursuit of happiness. Yet it makes many of us squirm to even say that faith must bear the cruciform mark of putting us to death. We feel it is almost immoral to express that, which shows how completely the happiness *summum bonum* possesses us. Yet our faith formation will be no match for the *summum bonum* of happiness until it is cruciform. We can only really make youth ministry about faith if we remember that faith is the *summum bonum*, possessing within itself the negation, summation, and transformation of virtue itself.

Faith is a way of life and therefore must include the eudaimonia. But this way of life, because of its connection to virtue, puts us to death, taking us to the cross. When faith is not confused as religious commitment or spiritual protection, faith derails us, pushing us off the hedonistic track. It crucifies. It does this because faith's true object is the person of Jesus Christ, the true human being of virtue. And this Jesus is found on the cross, transforming virtue, making us holy in and through his own obedience.

The centrality of faith will not stand for happiness being our moral horizon. Faith is interconnected with the cross. It reminds us that we are sinful and always vulnerable; indeed, sadness is part of the depth of the human condition. As Luther colorfully says (as only he can), "A Christian should and could be gay [happy], but then the devil craps on him."[41] There is no getting to the Good simply by bracketing out sadness and suffering.

Rather, faith is to find the Good—the living person of Jesus—in and through suffering, not only happiness. This faith produces the ecstatic experience of joy. For what our being longs for most is not satisfaction but salvation, not contentment but transformation, not resuscitation but new life. And it is only through the cross that happiness is shown to be a moral idol. And virtue is reborn in the womb of grace.

Conclusion

When we returned from our spring break, the snow that had rudely pushed us from home was gone. It was no match for the climbing temps and more intense spring sunshine. Spring was being birthed, but it came with stops and starts. Once we landed home in muddy Minnesota, we slid quickly into Holy Week. On Easter Sunday, Maisy got us up early, the anticipation of her Easter basket stronger than a triple-shot espresso. Wrapped in pajamas and topped with bed head, Maisy searched for her basket. She was now too old for us to hide it in any way that wasn't lame; it took her just seconds to find.

41. Martin Luther, *Tischreden, 1531–46*, vol. 2, Kritische Gesamtausgabe (Weimar: Hermann Böhlau), 522 (no. 1490), quoted in Erik Erikson, *Young Man Luther: A Study in Psychoanalysis and History* (New York: Norton, 1993), 245 (modified slightly).

When she carried the basket back to our living room to explore its contents, it was spilling over with candy. The basket couldn't hold all the candy because important real estate was being taken up by a shiny Harry Potter book and two POPs (big-headed action figures) of *Stranger Things* characters. Maisy spent this Easter morning, before the most sacred hour of our faith, in the mythology of Harry Potter and *Stranger Things*.

The Tuesday after Easter, during a coffee catch-up, my friend asked, "So how was Easter?" Too tired for any deep intellectual conversation, and yet not able to shake the Easter basket scene for the last two days, I found myself saying, "Fine, I guess. I mean, besides my kids being more captivated by the mythology of Harry Potter than the narrative of cross and resurrection. Harry just has a whole infrastructure—like amusement parks and toys—that delivers happiness."

Once it came out, I regretted saying it. It wasn't the kind of regret that signaled a violation of some unspoken code of conversation. I just realized it was an odd thing to say. I love Harry Potter, after all. It just seemed to take our nice coffee time into a whole other direction for which I wasn't sure I had the energy.

I followed up, trying to redirect the conversation but only getting myself deeper. "It just feels like the loss of the cross. And I don't mean that as doctrinal statement. I'm just wondering how cross and resurrection become stories—or better, experiences—that form peoples' lives. It feels like youth ministers have a hard time embodying it."

"Most do," my friend responded, "but I know one who doesn't. It's actually an amazing story."

"What do you mean?" I asked.

"The leader's name is J. I met her when I used to do some training for denominational camps."

"I don't know her," I responded.

"I'm not sure why you would," my friend said. "And honestly, when I met her, she was so forgettable, not someone I'd pick to end up doing this amazing stuff."

Now intrigued, and thankful the conversation had turned from my Harry Potter–addicted kids, I asked, "What happened?"

"I really can't explain it," he said. Knowing I had interviewed some parents and had been journeying to figure out what youth ministry was for, he said, "You'll have to go talk to her."

Eleven

Joy and the Custodian

What Youth Ministry Is For

LATE MARCH

'm not sure why I felt so compelled to reach out to J. I'm told about exemplary youth workers all the time. And too often, especially when put on the spot by some podcaster or question-asker after a presentation, I can almost never recall anyone specifically. Maybe that's why I so quickly emailed. Right before meeting my friend for coffee, I had recorded a podcast. The host and I had a rich conversation about youth ministry. I still didn't have a direct answer to what youth ministry is for. But I discussed the identity-to-recognition loop and the impact of happiness as our *summum bonum*. And, hitting my sweet spot, I drew out how important the impact of theological thinking is to youth ministry.

"That's awesome," the podcaster said, "and I know we didn't talk about this before recording, so I'm putting you on the spot, but can you tell us about a few youth ministries that you think are doing this? What do they look like?"

My mind went blank, but not inert. I couldn't think of anyone, making my brain fire with embarrassment, the suffocating air of my office filling with a plume of imposter syndrome. I was breathing it in deeply as I sought something to say. The embarrassment was making my sunburned neck sting. I just said names that came to mind, hoping that only those living on the moon would have access to download the podcast.

So, still feeling a dull echo of a total absence of recall, my friend's suggestion to reach out to J made good sense. Returning from coffee, I emailed her.

❖

Two weeks later I find myself in that nondescript fellowship hall. The sun has now set, and we're sitting in the dark. But it's no metaphor for what I'm experiencing. The outside dusk that leaves the room in darkness has a tint of mystery that makes the dimness feel warm and welcoming, almost like a candlelight service. *One of us should get up and turn on the light or suggest that we finish and pick up the conversation at another time.* But I'm feeling on the edge of a breakthrough, or at least in the middle of an engaging story. I worry that suggesting artificial light will chase away the mystery of the moment.

As we sit in silence, thinking about the experience of Lorena's illness and how it shifted J to aim anew for the Good, my mind can't shake how joy is the experience of the Good. Luther may have waggled the Christian life free from an Aristotelian virtue, but in so doing he saw the cross as recasting the direction of a flourishing life that receives the gift of the Good—just as the cross of Lorena's illness seems to have shaken J free from believing youth ministry is just about fun and happiness. The cross is the concrete historical event of the Good, as J seems to be witnessing. The event of the cross plants the Good as deeply as possible within the world.

Yet this can't be. Lorena is sick. And this is not Good.

At first glance the cross appears to be only the end of the life of a good man, an unjust political and religious act; the cross seems to be only the victory of death and the insatiable reach of destruction. But when we peer closer, we see the opposite. We see death being subsumed and suffered, so that three days later it might be finally and fully overcome in the very body of this Jesus who is dying but will be made alive.

In words J read to the intergenerational storytelling group an hour earlier, Jesus tells the rich young ruler that only God is Good. For only God can be beyond nothingness and death. Only God can be outside contingency. Only God is without the need or necessity of something other. Only God can be God's own moral horizon. And yet this noncontingent God, who lacks nothing and therefore is solely the Good, chooses in freedom to be Father to the Son. The Father sends the Son into the world to face nothingness and death. The God who is the Good enters the most contingent of relationships (parent to child),[1]

---

1. By "contingent" I mean that it needs a moral horizon outside of it. Like Karl Barth's opposition to natural theology, I'm claiming that there is no enclosed moral horizon within creation itself. It is only in encountering the Creator, not the creation alone, that the moral horizon that delivers the Good can be witnessed. Again, only God is Good, for only God in Godself can be a moral horizon.

sending this Son into a world that God creates good but contingent, to suffer and die.[2]

The God who is Good is now inextricably the Father who bears the loss of the Son. The resurrection is the union of love between the Father and the Son, in and through the power of the Spirit. The trinitarian life of God, even before creation, is constituted in the perichoretic joy of union. Joy is the experience of the inner being of the triune God. Just as every household has its own smell, which seems to be a kind of invisible hint of the family's lived experience—Apartment 3 smells like Tide and oranges, Apartment 8 like chipotle and garlic, Apartment 14 like wet dog and Febreze—so dare we say the tangible feel of the inner life of the triune God, if we can imagine it, is joy. It is the emotive aura of shared life.[3] God is a communion of joy in and through the constant communion of discourse between the Father, the Son, and the Spirit.[4] The cross plants the Good into the world, because it offers all humanity participation in this very union of joy, to be indwelled by the Spirit and therefore taken through the humanity of Christ into communion with the Father.[5] By the Father identifying so fully with the death of the Son, the God who alone is Good opens God's life of discourse to all humanity. The cross and resurrection are the events that open the trinitarian life to us all.[6]

The rich young ruler is good; he has kept all the commands. He's lived a virtuous life in every way *he* can. If he were to ask Aristotle what he must do,

2. This is a central fact that even the natural sciences affirm: all of the created realm is contingent.

3. I'm following Charles Mathewes here in asserting that joy is a kind of sacramental state. He says, "Thus understood as an excessive rapture, catching us up into a reality in the 'middle voice,' joy is a sort of sacramental state: in creation yet prompted ultimately by something beyond and before creation, a reality simultaneously speaking of immediacy and transcendence, something done to you yet something you manifest, express, realize, and participate in. Here and there, now and not yet, you and another, creation and Creator—joy can serve as a synecdoche of the Christian life as a whole. And that is how I propose to understand it here." "Toward a Theology of Joy," in *Joy and Human Flourishing: Essays on Theology, Culture, and the Good Life*, ed. Miroslav Volf and Justin E. Crisp (Minneapolis: Fortress, 2015), 67.

4. This is to echo Robert W. Jenson's articulation of the God of Israel as a speaking God. See *Systematic Theology: The Triune God* (Oxford: Oxford University Press, 1997), 1:63–90.

5. Matthew Croasmun and Ryan McAnnally-Linz point to this perspective of indwelling: "Human beings are created to be indwelled by God—that is, for God to be in them and to work through them—and in a different sense by one another. To be human is to be created for this indwelling. Openness to God is not an optional add-on to human life, the human equivalent to a car's power sunroof. It is simply what it means to be human." "Introduction: Miroslav Volf and Theology of the Good Life," in *Envisioning the Good Life: Essays on God, Christ, and Human Flourishing*, ed. Matthew Croasmun, Zoran Grozdanov, and Ryan McAnnally-Linz (Eugene, OR: Cascade, 2017), 4.

6. This is why Robert W. Jenson claims that God is roomy. See Jenson, *Systematic Theology*, 1:47–60, for a further discussion on this point.

the philosopher might say, *Just keep doing what you're doing, keep practicing the virtues and keep the commands*. Yet Jesus tells him that even with all his good virtuous practice, he still lacks the Good—reminding him that he is no self-constituting god. So Jesus tells him to follow him to the cross, to sell all he has in order to enter death. Only then will he find the Good. Jesus tells him he must enter death to find the Good and flourish, and that he must do so not through his effort but through a communion. The rich young ruler is commanded to follow not an idea, or plan, or program, or even a doctrine, but Jesus's very person.[7] He is to leave all behind and follow Jesus. He's to die to himself. But Jesus promises a new communion where this self that has died is resurrected and forever lives. Jesus will lead him into death to experience the Good as new life born out of nothingness, giving him a union he couldn't imagine.

The rich young ruler goes away as depressed as Sheryl Crow, for he refuses to follow Jesus through a death experience that promises to deliver a union of new life that can only be described as joy, for it comes only from the Goodness of God.[8] It is easier for a camel to go through the eye of a needle than for a rich man to enter eternal life. The rich man has made himself happy; he must give this up to enter suffering in order to find himself in a communion of joy.[9] Marianne Meye Thompson says, "'Joy' is not a coping mechanism for dealing with difficulty, but the way one lives with others and before God."[10] The rich young ruler chooses to be happy with all his *things* rather than encounter the joy of union with the Father, Son, and Spirit in and through a death experience.

Joy, then, is the communal experience of life coming out of death, which produces union with God and neighbor. It can be an individual experience, but it always takes us into something beyond us. Paradoxically and profoundly,

7. This is to directly echo Bonhoeffer's contrast of cheap and costly grace in *The Cost of Discipleship*.

8. When I say "death experience," I mean something like Stephen E. Fowl does in relation to Paul: "Conforming to Christ's death is not really about the manner of Paul's death or ours. Instead, this sort of fellowship in Christ's sufferings provides a way of ordering Paul's life and our lives so that we seek the benefit of others in willed self-emptying and obedience to God. Rather than describing a manner of death, the phrases 'sharing in Christ's sufferings' and 'being conformed to his death' work as a shorthand expression of a standard of fidelity." *Philippians*, Two Horizons New Testament Commentary (Grand Rapids: Eerdmans, 2005), 157.

9. "Joy is best experienced in community. Joy seeks company ('come and rejoice with me') and the company of those who rejoice feeds the joy of each. Feasts and celebrations both express and nourish joy." Miroslav Volf, "The Crown of the Good Life: A Hypothesis," in Volf and Crisp, *Joy and Human Flourishing*, 133.

10. Marianne Meye Thompson, "Reflections on Joy in the Bible," in Volf and Crisp, *Joy and Human Flourishing*, 34.

J is witnessing to how joy is interlaced with the cross. Because God reveals God's being through the act of identifying fully with Jesus on the cross, the cross itself becomes the experience that brings humanity into union with God. And to feel this union is to tangibly feel it as joy. Joy is bound, then, in the being of God. Luther's *theologia crucis* may make revelation and suffering interconnected, but because it does, it reveals that this God who comes to us in the suffering Christ is a minister of life out of death. The only feeling to describe a union that stretches so deep that it can turn death into new life is joy. Happiness—as we've described it above—has a moral horizon that sends us not out of our selves but deeper into them. God's own inner life is one of joy, for God's triune nature is revealed to us in the incarnation, crucifixion, resurrection, and ascension. These events reveal God's being as eccentric (following Wolfhart Pannenberg's meaning as to come out of one's self, to be moved out of the center). God's being is in becoming—moved being, constituted in a shared life. Joy is the experience of being in communion through acts of love, mercy, friendship, gratitude, and compassion. Happiness cannot produce eccentric experiences of joy, because joy is born from within the gift of receiving something new from beyond you, sharing in a union that includes you but is more than you.[11]

The disciple lives a life of joy, for she was dead and yet is now alive. And now alive, she is free to live in joy, going and sharing in the life of her neighbor as an experience of joy. Now alive, she has only one aim: to seek the Good and flourish by taking on the actions of God, by entering into death experiences of her neighbor to participation in the birthing of new life. Made alive, she seeks to flourish by continuing to participate in the being of this God who acts to bring life out of death, by following this God to the cross, as the very hidden but tangible place where the Good is revealed in the trinitarian life. The suffering of the cross, which delivers the real presence of God, produces not melancholy or dourness but joy, for it invites us to participate—to be found in—the very life of God.

The Custodian

As I think about joy as the communal experience of life coming out of death, I ask Lorena, "So, how long were you unconscious?"

---

11. I'm seeking to highlight Volf's point here: "I trust that by the time our somewhat arduous lab work is done, you will be persuaded that joy is much richer than the feeling of happiness, even great happiness, and that the authentic joy, though not itself the good life, is the emotional substance and manifestation of the good life." "Crown of the Good Life," 129.

"Too long!" she says.

"Oh, sorry, I didn't think anyone was still in the building," interrupts a squat man who looks to be in his late fifties. J introduces Bernard, the half-time church custodian. He apologizes and quickly leaves, flipping the light switch on as he goes.

J then says, with a whisper of reverence rather than secrecy, "If it wasn't for him, I'm not sure any of this change in me and our youth ministry would have happened."

Twelve

Borne Burdens

Youth Ministry and Stories of Joy

LATE MARCH

I tilt and slowly shake my head in confusion, like a dog hearing a strange noise, not understanding this plot twist, unsure of how to make sense of this attention to the church custodian. It leaves me with too many imaginative loose ends, and I lose the thread of our conversation. When the silent pause becomes too much, Lorena interjects, "Six days. They woke me up after six days. But I was pretty out of it for another three or four."

"Did your mom really not leave the hospital for that whole time?" I ask, finding my bearings.

"She did leave," J says. "She didn't quite keep her promise to not leave until Lorena did. We finally convinced her to take a break after Lorena woke up. But she only did because we now had six people at the hospital at all times."

J explains that after quitting being the lead counselor of fun, she canceled the big, fun event she had planned, the one she imagined the future of her job rested on. She figured they'd fire her; there was at least seven hundred dollars in nonrefundable deposits that they'd lose. "I just had this overwhelming sense that the hospital was where God was calling me. If they fired me, then fine. I was over trying to save my job."

At the hospital, she wrote an email to all the parents, called her youth ministry board, and sent a group text to all the kids. With Lorena's mom's permission, she informed them of what Lorena was facing, asked for their prayers, and said if they needed her, she'd be where God had called her, sitting next to Lorena's mom.

There is something captivating about a person claiming, in fragile confidence, that God has called her to a particular place and time—giving up all else to seek the Good, doing what the rich young ruler couldn't. It was so captivating that within an hour Lorena's two closest friends and their moms showed up. When they arrived, J explained the situation and asked them all to simply sit with Lorena's mom and pray silently. They did so for a few hours. Then, after getting Lorena's mom some food, they left, only to be replaced by others. By the next day, every young person who'd signed up for the big, fun event—and more who hadn't—made it down to the hospital to sit and pray, feeling the pull of the Good to be together. But what was even more amazing is that not only did the high school kids show up but other people from the congregation did as well. Kids and adults were now sitting together in the waiting room, praying and talking. Together they were following Jesus to the cross, seeking the Good by sharing in the ministry of God, who comes near in a death experience, calling us into communion through it.

To J's surprise, on the afternoon of day two, Bernard showed up. When he arrived, his body communicated that he was feeling out of place and yet determined to be present. As a matter of fact, over the next week Bernard was as present as anyone. It was beautiful but weird. He was officially a member of the church. That's how he found out about the custodian job. But besides making it to worship once in a while, he wasn't around the community much. J would only learn later that he was a faithful member of a Tuesday morning Bible study and a committed participant in the church's AA group. However, none of the young people except Tannon really knew him.

Tannon was a senior who worked five to eight hours a week at the church, helping Bernard move tables and prepare the Sunday school rooms on Sunday afternoons for the coming week of preschool. Tannon was a good but direct kid. He had no problem asking difficult questions and pointing out things he found odd or misdirected.

When Tannon made it to the hospital, Bernard was in the middle of his second six-hour stint. He hadn't said much but just quietly sat across from Lorena's mom, listening in as kids and other church members talked and prayed. He'd become the soda runner those first few days, intent on keeping Lorena's mom and J fueled on Diet Coke. J would be lying if she didn't admit that she'd wondered more than a dozen times why Bernard was there.

But soon that all became clear. And when it did, it changed everything for the next few days at the hospital, and from that point on, for the whole church. When Tannon arrived and saw Bernard, he sat down next to him and respectfully but loudly asked, "Why are you here?" Tannon and Bernard had spent enough time together for Bernard to not take offense. The two had built their relationship around direct talk. More than a few times Bernard had pushed Tannon to work harder and take more responsibility, even calling him back to church twice after 10:00 p.m. to redo his inadequate work from earlier in the afternoon.

Nevertheless, when Tannon asked Bernard why he was at the hospital, it sounded confrontational. Everyone seemed to freeze, holding their breath, not sure what would happen next.

Bernard looked at Tannon and said, "Twenty years ago, my baby girl died of something like this. And I wasn't there. I was high."

The vacuum created by Tannon's question was now filled with something else. Already frozen people froze stiffer, not knowing how to react.

Then Lorena's mom, who had been in a kind of dazed state, snapped back into the moment, looked directly at Bernard, and said, "What happened?"

And so Bernard told the story—all of it. When he finished, something remarkable occurred. For the next two hours different people, mainly adults, shared stories of loss, regret, forgiveness, and hope that most of the young people had never heard. People cried and people laughed; young people hung on every word. Tannon's direct question created an opening that was now filled with a spirit of communion, in and through the confession of the cross.

J tells me she remembers vividly thinking to herself, *Now, this is Good.* "It wasn't good, like, *Oh, good, this will distract people!* or *It will be good to get some happiness and fun back in this hospital waiting room!* It was just stand-alone Good. It was Good to be together. It was Good how the stories revealed and connected us. It was just Good." She pauses and then says, "I looked around at everyone's faces while people were telling these stories, kids and adults sharing in each others' lives, experiencing God's work together. I remember this was the first time I thought to myself, *Youth ministry is for joy.*"

Discerning

Because human beings are language animals, words do something to us.[1] These nonmaterial noises can shape actions that forge civilization. Words

1. Even Yuval Noah Harari's reductions point to this truth: "A second theory agrees that our unique language evolved as a means of sharing information about the world. But the most important information that needed to be conveyed was about humans, not about lions and bison. Our language evolved as a way of gossiping. According to this theory *Homo sapiens* are primarily a social animal. Social cooperation is our key for survival and reproduction. It is not enough for individual men and women to know the whereabouts of lions and bison. It's

can break bounds and construct new ways of being. Words move us. *Joy*, as a word, is often experienced as trapped in a bizarre Tim Burton–like craft fair. It hasn't yet been made retro cool by some hipsters in Brooklyn or a new Wes Anderson movie.[2] Rather, *joy* seems tacky and dusty, grossly perfect for a cross-stitched casserole carrier, old Norwegian-American woman's sweater, or mainline hippie-inspired church banners in use since 1978. Joy belongs in some closet that, when opened, has such a heavy stench of mothballs that your eyes water.

But it's only possible to see joy this way if we untie it from our conversations about goods and the Good. If we explore joy against the backdrop of our human necessity for some moral horizon and our propensity to chase false, destructive, or vapid moral horizons, we recognize that joy is anything but tacky and dusty. Rather, joy becomes an essential experience for discerning whether we're living a flourishing, abundant life directed toward the Good.

Sheryl Crow's friends think, "If it makes you happy, it can't be that bad." Crow's friends are asking happiness to do something it can't. They're asking happiness to be a kind of emotive signpost that signals whether Sheryl's aimed-for moral horizon can deliver the meaning and connection for which her spirit longs. Yet happiness can't bear this kind of weight.[3] So in the end her friends can only offer, "If it makes you happy, it can't be that bad." What can't be? The realization that the moral horizon—the goods—of having your identity so recognized that you're now a celebrity is void of meaning and connection? That realization can't be *that bad* if you're happy your songs are on the radio. Sheryl can be happy and yet directed toward a false moral horizon (which is what makes her deeply discontent). Happiness can be experienced outside or beyond the Good. Even the devil, who has no Good in him, can be happy.[4] But he can't have joy, for joy is the fruit of the Spirit; joy belongs

---

much more important for them to know who in their band hates whom, who is sleeping with whom, who is honest, and who is a cheat." *Sapiens: A Brief of History of Humankind* (New York: Harper, 2015), 23.

2. Although Marie Kondo, in her book *Spark Joy* (Berkeley: Ten Speed, 2016), has popularized joy in a much different way from how it's explored here.

3. Again, this is not to demonize happiness but to show that in our consumerist, late modern Western society, we've asked it to do something it simply can't.

4. I'm going in a different direction with joy than Jennifer Herdt does in the quotation below. In essence I agree with her, but following Iris Murdoch, I'm playing with the idea of joy always being directed toward a good that has ontological weight. It doesn't need to be fundamentally Christian or even religious. I'm actually more closely following Miroslav Volf, whom she quotes in her footnote, saying, "Volf therefore differentiates joy from 'true joy': 'true joy presumes proper relation to some actual good.'" I'm trying to save joy for this kind of joy. Here is the context of Herdt's statement: "While joy is always pleasurable, joy is not always good, since one can delight in bad things as well as in good; I might delight in radiant fall splendor or in

to (better, *in*) the Good. Joy is a communal experience, and the devil looks only to divide. Joy can only be experienced when you find yourself pulled toward the Good. This is why many religious perspectives have held that to experience joy is to be connected to the divine, and why I contend that to experience joy is to experience God's own Good inner life.

So joy is different and much more durable than happiness. Joy, unlike happiness, can bear the weight of witnessing your proximity to the Good. To experience joy is to discover that you've moved correctly toward the Good.

To ask, "Does this make me happy?" provides no clear vision that you're following the moral horizon of the Good. Our lives are filled with many moments in which the question of happiness is enough to orient us to our wants, and sometimes even needs. Does this Netflix show make me happy or should I pick another? Am I happy with this meal? In small ways, particularly base consumer ways, happiness can be a helpful means for discernment, but only if that which we're discerning is narrow and assumed to have no real moral horizon.

For instance, there's little at stake morally if I drink 1% or 2% milk. If I ever escape my socialization and find that I actually can decide what milk to drink—not just buying the one my mom did—it's logical for me to intuitively wonder which will make me happier. I might choose 2% because it tastes better, or I like the colors on the carton more, or because I get a quick stab of closeness to my mom for choosing the one she would.

Recognizing the emotion behind the last statement is what revolutionized marketing in the mid-twentieth century, particularly the Madison Avenue, Don Draper–type of ad creation (check out season 6, episode 13, of *Mad Men* for a vivid depiction of this). This new adman wrote this logic into the relatively benign decision around consumer goods and how we measure these products through happiness. The adman pushed this consumer discernment through happiness into the whole of Western life. By the late 1960s, advertisements told us that the products we buy are directly related to living a good life. Therefore, it only makes sense that if we discern products through happiness, then we should in turn use happiness to discern every part of our lives—including nonconsumer spheres like our marriages, vocations, and spiritual involvements. This push of a consumer logic into the whole of society placed the crown of discernment for a good and well-lived life on the head of happiness. Yet happiness's neck is not strong enough to bear the weight of the crown.

seeing a despised colleague taken down a peg. Our joys reveal what we care about, and we tend to care in distorted ways—for the wrong things, or too much, or too little. Assessing joy is thus not a neutral enterprise; we know whether someone else's joy is worth approving and rejoicing in only if we know whether it is indeed delight in the good." "The Lofty Vocation of the Humble" (unpublished consultation paper, Yale Center for Faith and Culture, 2017), 1.

The best happiness can do as a measure of discerning a flourishing life is say with Sheryl Crow, "Well, I guess if it makes you happy, it can't be that bad." This is quite a reduction of human life, but we almost don't notice. And even those who do feel something is wrong nevertheless seem trapped in the logic, claiming that indeed whether we buy 1% or 2% milk matters. They find meaning and moral significance in committing to being a vegan and drinking only almond milk. Or we moralize and fight about whether it is good or bad to reduce natural fats in our diet, giving us a faux sense of meaning and connection as we disparage those who don't hold our position on milk drinking.

Joy and Narrative

To experience joy, on the other hand, reveals that we've encountered the Good. To discern whether we are flourishing, experiencing the abundant life that Jesus promises (John 10:10), is to ask not if we're happy but if we've been "surprised by joy" (to quote a phrase from C. S. Lewis): surprised that so often the birthplace of joy is communion, friendship, and received compassion right in the middle of some kind of death experience (at the cross), surprised that entering this death experience frees us from ourselves to find ourselves living for the Good (participating in resurrection). To feel joy is to receive confirmation that your moral horizon is the Good. It is to feel yourself participating in the Good. So to discern that your moral horizon is the Good is to experience joy.

Yet this can be confusing, because joy and happiness have similar, even overlapping sensations that get us confused. For instance, if we asked two people whether they're experiencing the joy of Christmas, they might both say yes, but witness to two very different moral horizons. One person might say, "Yes, I got everything I asked for," feeling warmly satisfied. The other person might say, "Yes, my son who has been in prison for six years received early release on Christmas Eve. I just can't believe he's out! I feel like I could jump out of my skin, I'm so joyful. I just needed him home, after the sadness of missing five Christmases with him." These responses reveal two very different orientations to the Good.

There is no reason to shame the satisfied present-getter. He's had a happy Christmas; good for him. He's experienced goods, and that's nice. But it doesn't mean he has encountered the Good. As we have said many times, happiness isn't bad; we should all wish for more happiness in our lives— even to get what we want for Christmas. That said, happiness can't bear the weight we've asked it to in a consumer society. Happiness is nice but flimsy. It is unable to give us meaning, purpose, direction, and ultimately flourishing. It can be no help in discerning whether we are aimed toward the moral horizon of the Good.

What ultimately reveals happiness's flimsy inability to deliver a Good life of flourishing is its flat story. To ask the present-getter to narrate his feeling will be very difficult for him. Likely, the more he tries to narrate it, the more both he and the listener will become nauseated. How will he tell the story of his warm satisfaction? He'll say, "Well, I've always wanted to drive a Lexus. We rented one when we were in Jackson Hole for vacation. I felt powerful and important driving it. And I've always been drawn to those Lexus Christmas commercials with the car under a big bow. So I got it. I've now entered the Lexus class. I feel happy and important. Besides that, I don't know, it's just something I've always wanted." This is barely a story. It has little content; it's flat. He can only really talk about his subjective experiences of want. The story is all about him. More than likely, if he's in touch with himself enough to even form this flat narrative, he'll feel embarrassed speaking it. Even a story that has more socially acceptable goods in the narrative ("I wanted an electric car; I haven't had a new car in years; I gave my old car to my mom") will ultimately fall flat.

Actually, the more the present-getter tries to narrate his feel, the more he'll be taken into himself, and soon he'll lose any sense of why he wanted the car in the first place. He no doubt has a story that is tacitly driving him to want that car, but he has a hard time either getting in touch with that story or expressing it. More than likely, when asked why he wanted the Lexus, he'll say, "I don't know, I just did." The story becomes lost in basic arithmetic—"I just wanted to be counted as someone with a Lexus"—flattening the story further.

If he could somehow hold to a narrative and not allow it to disappear into some reptilian wish fulfillment, either the story would become self-referential, making its goods only his own satisfaction and sense of success, or the vapidness of the story would convict him, unmasking that his pursuit of happiness and his sense of flourishing are misdirected. Absent a rich narrative, meaning and purpose disappear even in the moment—which is why we often feel gross even when we get something nice we really wanted.

When we recognize the staleness of our happiness, and decide that it can't be our own fault, we're tempted to move into anger. Experiencing happiness's inability to produce the flourishing of Goodness, we look around for someone to blame. Happiness's lack of a rich narrative that might connect us, giving us communion, turns on us, revealing our deep unhappiness. In the void of this lack of a story that connects us to someone, giving us meaning, we are tempted to take on new stories of injury. If things turn dark enough, we start looking for someone to blame for our lack of happiness, wanting them to pay for us feeling so alone and void of a sense of fullness or flourishing. At this moment, the flat narrative of happiness takes a new shape, in a new story born from the womb of unhappiness. At this moment, this sense of unhappiness can, surprisingly, produce a captivating story.

This new story is no longer primarily about happiness at all, but instead is fueled by *ressentiment*. Happiness's lack of a story reveals that it can't bear the Good. But once happiness fails and turns to *ressentiment*, it provides a weighty story that happiness never could. So the Good, as well as evil, possesses the power of story. The Good is fueled by communion and joy, evil by *ressentiment* and fantasies of revenge.

It is no wonder, then, that an overwhelming majority of rampage shooters in American history have been white males. White males, tragically, more than anyone else in this country, have believed and been promised that happiness produces true flourishing. When it doesn't— because it can't—these men are susceptible to deep forms of *ressentiment*, and some start fantasizing about getting revenge.[5] On whom is unclear, because they want revenge on the whole system that promised them meaning and purpose through happiness, and it invariably failed them. In a consumer culture that peddles happiness as the *summum bonum*, strict gun laws will be a must, but ultimately what is needed is for the narratives of *ressentiment* to be challenged. People will need to be embraced in communions of joy with deeper narratives of the Good (which, ironically, our internet debates can't produce).[6]

But even if it doesn't go this far and our present-getter stays happy enough with his new car, eventually the purpose and meaning behind the happily received new car will be lost—particularly when the warm sensation of the new thing cools (which is a brute fact of consumer possession) and the Lexus is a year old. By next Christmas or even by March, oddly but logically, he won't

5. Mihaly Csikszentmihalyi points to what gives *ressentiment* its teeth. It is the feeling of having meaning taken from you. In that void of meaning, evil grows, allowing for a new story of self-injury to possess you, tempting you into revenge seeking. Csikszentmihalyi says, "The only weapon we have against the deadly power of a terminal materialism is the human ability to create meaning. By attributing meaning to a goal, we can channel psychic energy in practically any direction we choose." *The Meaning of Things: Domestic Symbols and the Self* (Cambridge: Cambridge University Press, 1981), 235.

6. Katherine S. Newman's project on school shootings shows that every white male who committed this crime did so because he had felt pushed from communion, and out of a narrative of *ressentiment* decided he'd get revenge on the whole system that promised happiness but gave him no story to belong to, none of the fulfillment it promised. Spotting that the whole system is a lie, and armed with ammo, easily accessed guns, and *ressentiment*, he kills. See Newman, *Rampage: The Social Roots of School Shootings* (New York: Basic Books, 2004).

like to be reminded of even the flat story of the morning he got the Lexus he always wanted. The lack of a story reveals a disconnect from the Good.

Yet for the mother with the son just out of prison to explain her Christmas joy will only be possible through a rich narrative that takes her deeper into communion. Hearing only the few details of her joy—a son in prison released, the pain of missed Christmases, and the ecstatic feel of his presence—almost demands we hear more. These small details make our spirit thirst for a story. And for her to tell this story, she'll need to give us historical context, which will provide a coherent connection between her sensations ("I could jump out of my skin"), needs ("I just needed him home"), and the events that have affected her, her family, and her boy. In other words, she'll reveal not only historical details, like why he was arrested, but how the event of his arrest had an impact on her own identity.[7] What did his arrest mean for her own sense of being in relation to the Good? How did she feel about being a good mom and raising a good boy now that he had been in prison? And what did his release mean in relation to both of their self-definitions? By taking us into her narration, she'll have to confess the death experience to be able to witness to the profound arrival of the Good, which overtakes her with joy.[8]

Joy's arrival in and through the death experience doesn't simply thrust the mother into storytelling; because joy reveals the Good, it does even more. It ordains her to testify and witness, to become a preacher who cannot but tell her narrative of joy in and through the death experience. (This confession is what breaks *ressentiment*. Telling our stories in the shape of cross and resurrection is a radically different kind of storytelling that unties revenge from recognition.)[9] The present-getter has a story about his Lexus but doesn't want

7. Craig Dykstra adds, "Although stories that reveal character can often be short stories that focus on one or a few important occasions, the full stories of our lives are long and complex. We are historical beings to whom and in whom many things have happened. Life stories pick up many of the details of this history and place them in relation to one another. Such stories are not, however, merely chronicles that become more complete when more items are added. They are interpretations. They pull on the past in ways that give that past some sense and meaning that can be understood in the light of the present and intended future." *Vision and Character: A Christian Educator's Alternative to Kohlberg* (New York: Paulist Press, 1981), 54.

8. "To be a person is to occupy a place within a sequence of events that is not a mere succession, a 'tale told by an idiot,' and therefore could not be reversed: to be a person is to inhabit a world that has a telos. Now it is humankind's general conviction that the world indeed is going somewhere, a conviction not fully eradicated even by religions that seek salvation in bringing the movement to a halt. But almost as general is a sort of metaphysical anxiety, that the world might not get there; where this becomes religiously thematic it is accompanied by an accepted or even willed loss of personhood." Robert W. Jenson, "*Anima Ecclesiastica*," in *God and Human Dignity*, ed. R. Kendall Soulen and Linda Woodhead (Grand Rapids: Eerdmans, 2006), 67.

9. N. T. Wright, in a discussion of Paul, gives us a sense of what the mother experiences: "Paul transposes this into the cosmic context in Rom. 8:18–25, interpreting the groaning of all

to share it. The mother who receives the gift of the Good, and is surprised by joy arriving to bring new possibility out of death, can't help but preach.

Joy, as we've said, is the aura of the union of the inner life of the triune God. God's union as Father, Son, and Holy Spirit is bound in discourse. This is a speaking God, and God speaks to God's self as a manifestation of the joy of God's union.[10] It is out of this union that God reveals God's own being to the world through the act of speaking to Israel, through Jesus being the Word sent into the world.[11] Christoph Schwöbel says, "Taking the understanding of God as conversation seriously, implies that God is eventful, relational, personal, communal. The divine being is understood as freely communicative speaking so that the world's being is freely communicated and dependently communicative speaking."[12] The speaking God invites humanity to share in the joy of God's life.[13]

---

creation as the birth pangs of the new age. This results not in joy *despite* suffering, but in joy *because* of suffering—not in some masochistic sense (Paul is still quite capable of speaking with horror of the pain and anguish he himself has endured, as in 2 Corinthians), but because Paul insists on seeing the suffering in terms of the crucifixion, resurrection, and ascended lordship of Jesus." N. T. Wright, "Joy: Some New Testament Perspective and Questions," in *Joy and Human Flourishing: Essays on Theology, Culture, and the Good Life*, ed. Miroslav Volf and Justin E. Crisp (Minneapolis: Fortress, 2015), 55.

10. "The doctrine of the Trinity can here be understood as an attempt to answer the question: 'Who is God if God is as he speaks, is spoken to and is spoken of in the divine-human conversation recorded and carried out in Scripture and continued in the church?' The trinitarian identification of God, summarised in the invocation of the triune name of Father, Son, and Spirit, is expressed in identity-descriptions and in the proper names of Father, Son, and Spirit. It states that God is really as God says and acts in the conversation with Israel, in addressing the whole of humanity in Jesus and in enabling humanity's response in the Spirit. The important point which has to be noted is that Luther's way of understanding the communicative being of God not only satisfies the criteria of trinitarian dogma but also clarifies it. The hypostatic identity of the three persons (*treis hypostaseis*) is constituted by their conversational relations, just like the unity of the divine essence (*mia ousia*) is constituted in this conversational relation." Christoph Schwöbel, "God as Conversation: Reflections on a Theological Ontology of Communicative Relations," in *Theology and Conversation: Toward a Relational Theology*, ed. Jacques Haers and Peter De Mey (Leuven: Leuven University Press, 2003), 63.

11. Schwöbel adds, "God relates to humanity in the way in which God is eternally in relation. God is in conversation with creation, because God is as conversation." "God as Conversation," 63.

12. Schwöbel, "God as Conversation," 66.

13. Schwöbel connects this to Luther: "Luther also gives a technical explication of the ontological status of relations which corresponds exactly to the way in which he portrays the Trinity as conversation. From a philosophical perspective relations must be understood as external relations between substances, and therefore they have no subsistence of their own. Because of that their ontological status is minimal: '*Relatio in rebus non efficit rem, ut dicunt, relation est minimae entitatis, et not per se subsistens.*' With regard to the Trinity which can only be spoken of within the discourse of faith, the relations between the three divine persons must be understood as internal and constitutive relations: '*In divinis relation est res, id est, hypostasis et subsistentia.*'" "God as Conversation," 64.

To echo the biblical story, the mother becomes like Mary Magdalene at the tomb, the first and true preacher, who from within a death experience witnesses the fullness of the Good in the resurrected body of Jesus.[14] The next move is to immediately narrate this experience, so in joy and fear Mary runs to tell the story to Peter and the others (John 20).

Telling Stories

The arc of the narrative helps us discern whether we're aimed toward the Good, but in telling the story we come to discover joy. Joy and narration are interconnected. Even a baby who can't speak her story is wrapped as much in a narrative as in a blanket. The fact that we name children means we wrap children in a story. Joy and narration's connection doesn't mean that every person in the story must possess the capacity to tell the story (or even be able to speak). But it does mean that the relationship that binds them is a union that can be narrated.

When the mother gets the phone call from the county that her son will be released, she feels numb, confused, washed over by incoherence as the information is reported (remember, we're often surprised by joy). The event horizon of her son's release is too large, too Good to compute at first blush. When she hangs up the phone, she turns to her sister and says in confusion, "That was someone from the county; they said Thomas will be released at 4:00 p.m. today." This short narration, this moment of speaking, unveils her reality, even to herself. Saying these words to her sister brings the overwhelming sensations of elation. She didn't really feel anything until she spoke it and shared it with another. Then joy comes. Joy is often manifest in moments of speaking, because joy is a communal experience of union. Even if the mother were alone, she'd need to hang up the phone, sit down, and tell herself the story of what she just heard in order to recognize that she'd just been overtaken by joy.[15] Once realizing it, she, like Mary, races to tell others.

14. Again, it is in sharing in the death experience that *ressentiment* is broken. This is where the theology of the cross does amazingly important work; it sends us into people's disappointment and felt flatness to share in their humanity as an act of love, giving our relationship of place-sharing as a new context for them to understand themselves and the world. To build communion around death experiences is to invite people into the deepest sense of transformation, but it also is to hold in a communion that protects from the temptation of evil narratives that form from a death experience not shared, from the search for revenge.

15. The mother could have recognized right away that she was in joy, not needing a minute or two to narrate it, but *only* if she'd already been telling herself stories about his coming release, if she'd already been narrating an experience and readying herself to take the new information and experience it immediately.

As she tells the story, not only do the sensations come, but their moral horizon is revealed. The sharing of this narrative with a friend reveals the Good and connects this friend, too, with the experience of joy. Then, hearing the short narration, her sister, too, is overcome by joy, so she now participates in the Good, witnessing the moment of new life coming from death. "It is the privilege of entering into deep communion with one's neighbor that holds the potential for . . . ecstatic joy."[16]

Narration is core to the discernment of the Good through joy because it delivers a communion that is a direct reflection of God's trinitarian life. As Craig Dykstra says, "Part of our task, then, as moral beings is to see well and to interpret truthfully."[17] Unlike the flat pseudonarration of the present-getter, the mother's story transfers joy to another; the story takes another into the experience of joy as they, too, encounter the Good. It is joy if it begets union, for its origin is the union of the triune God. The happy moment of a received Lexus doesn't do this, because its story is too flat, revealing its moral horizon might be good but not the Good. When the present-getter tells his story, the listener must do a lot of work to care and not be thrust into apathy, envy, or jealousy. The flat narrative engenders the opposite of union (again, making it dangerously open to evil temptations of *ressentiment*). Sensing this, the present-getter himself tends to shut down the narrative, embarrassed or braggadocian—both responses resisting the listener. The flat story of his happy possession is not able to produce the communion that reflects the inner life of the triune God who is joyfully Good.

Returning to the mom: with the depth of the moment confirmed in the telling of the story, and the story transferring back and forth an experience of joy, the mother is compelled to tell it further, to let joy reign in and through her narration. Joy begets narration, claiming her as a preacher, reaching out indiscriminately to give joy to others by taking them, too, into the story. The mother is compelled to tell the story, and others are eager to hear it.[18] So she tells everyone she can that Thomas will be home for Christmas. With every new call and retelling, the story gets longer and more detailed, pulling in further the depth of the death experience and ways it has been answered, giving her an all-new footing of flourishing. She says to her neighbor, "I was so broken when he was convicted, so depressed that I didn't get out of bed for three weeks. You remember that, right? It was so awful I couldn't even pray, but I knew you were praying for me, and now I'm so overcome. God has turned my weeping into joy."

16. Mary Clark Moschella, "Elements of Joy in Lived Practices of Care," in Volf and Crisp, *Joy and Human Flourishing*, 102.
17. Dykstra, *Vision and Character*, 60.
18. Unless they are caught up in themselves and tripped up by envy and sin.

The more she narrates her experience of the Good and the joy she feels, the more connections, providence, mysteries, and awe she sees and needs to tell. She says, "I just got off the phone with his lawyer. When he went to Raymond instead of the workhouse, I thought it couldn't get worse, but now I see that it was God's plan. They're only giving early release to people at Raymond."[19] Unlike the present-getter, the more she tells the story of the Good gift of her son's release, the more she has to say, and the more she sees, the more her self is included in something bigger.[20] As she tries to narrate the Good, she increasingly discovers its overwhelming texture, depth, and mystery.

Joy as the experience of the Good takes her out of her self, while more deeply embedding her experience in a larger story. As Darrin McMahon says, "Joy result[s] from our ability to connect with this larger order and force, to stray outside the confines of the self."[21] Joy reveals vividly that self-enclosed pursuits of identity must be opened up, taking us out of our selves to truly find ourselves.

The mother even starts telling the story of Thomas's release in and through the stories of God's Goodness to Israel and to the dead body of Jesus. She doesn't just use but even needs these biblical stories to give her the vision and language to express the joy she now knows with the arrival of God's Goodness, which turns death into life.

Identity Needs a Story

Youth ministry has lost its purpose because the identity options have escalated and in response parents have instituted a slowdown, encouraging a slower roll into adulthood. Recognizing the escalation of identity options and feeling little power to directly influence an identity choice, parents work hard to provide their children with opportunities to find their *thing*. The thing is believed to possess the power to direct, or corral, the identity options. Hockey, violin, swimming, and so much more are believed to gently direct identity choices. Finding your thing is believed to help you find your *self* (or at least not stumble into a negative/dangerous identity). And you can't be happy without knowing who you uniquely are.

19. This is to point to Charles Taylor's assertions about open takes within the immanent frame. See *A Secular Age* (Cambridge, MA: Belknap, 2007), 539–618. Narrating her experience of the Good, and confirming her joy in the Good, leads her to an inevitable open take on reality. The mystery of divine action seems actual.

20. In other words, the more she sees, the more she has an open take on the immanent frame.

21. Darrin M. McMahon, *Happiness: A History* (New York: Grove Press, 2006), 286.

In their own way, each set of parents I interviewed believed this. They contended that finding this *thing* would produce in their child a positive self-definition, believed this positive self-definition would provide goods, and believed that having these goods—confidence, friends, success, grit, experiences—would produce a happy life (absent sadness) now and in the future (getting into a good college and having a successful job).

What this all affirms, as we took pains to show above, is that all people—both parents and kids—are moved by some moral horizon. Every human being constructs an identity by implicitly or explicitly reaching for some good, seeking ways to not waste their lives. It appears that in most middle-class parents' imaginations, youth ministry can be one option on the menu of *things*. But often youth ministry is unceremoniously pushed down the scale of importance when happiness is the highest good or hypergood. Youth ministry hasn't known how to respond. So it has unrealistically demanded young people commit to youth group like they do track practice, or it has turned on the church as a whole and claimed it has failed to recognize young people, living out of a narrative of church-based *ressentiment*.

But this last sentence signals something we've culturally often overlooked, which the church, and youth ministry, shouldn't. Identity is indeed built around moral horizons, but those moral horizons are indelibly related to narrative. There is no way to have a firm identity without a sense of a story.[22] While the middle-class parental strategy is to double down on the *thing*, the thing alone can't give you an identity *without* it providing a narrative that you make essential to your own story. Parents concede that they must provide their child with many opportunities to participate in many different things, hoping one or two will stick. It is costly, but parents know that finding these one or two things comes with more misses than hits. The garage full of discarded tennis racquets, musical instruments, one-time-worn gymnastics outfits, and unused golf clubs witnesses to this reality. As a matter of fact, you could argue that Play It Again Sports' whole business model is dependent on the intensity of middle-class parents' desire to provide their children with their things and yet the reality that most things and the accompanying gear are discarded. Play It Again Sports gives middle-class parents a place to empty out the garage

22. Even young people with cognitive challenges who cannot repeat and retell a narrative are bound within stories. Their person particularly becomes essential to so many people's stories: "Caring for Josh has changed me; the day I met him and spent time with him gave me a new sense of myself." Every parent of a cognitively challenged young person has rich stories that include as central the humanity of this young person. No child with a disability is an island; they're wrapped in story. Even if they can't vocalize these stories, they have their being inside them. See the story of David in Antonio Damasio's *Feeling of What Happens* (New York: Harcourt Brace, 1999); this example shows that story is mystery that reaches deeper than cognitive ability.

of all those artifacts of discarded things, receiving back twenty cents on the dollar for all the once-necessary equipment they purchased.

This graveyard of *things* is massive (enormous enough to stock thirteen Play It Again Sports stores in the Twin Cities alone) because culturally, we overlook how important narrative is to identity. So many things die the death of a trip to Play It Again Sports because the young person can't make that particular thing part of his story; he can't find a story with which to identify within the thing. Doing it may provide positive feelings—"I feel like I can fly when I skate"—but these feelings quickly need to be placed inside a story that the child can identify with and therefore use the thing as a way to state an identity.[23]

The Dahls are a good example. They act as if what matters is activity itself, and of course activity is the core good of their moral horizon. They assume they give no special privilege to basketball. They only offer it as a thing because Holly and James know the game. Holly even says that if one of the girls picked another thing, they'd be fine with it as long as the daughter stayed active. But what they fail to recognize is that in their family, basketball is not equal to any other choice. And this preference for basketball is not simply in the fact that mom and dad know it and seem to like it. It's much deeper. Mom and dad know and like basketball because it's an essential part of a life narrative. Holly and James met and fell in love because of basketball; the girls' grandpa coached basketball for thirty years, retiring with esteem in the community; and basketball helped James deal with a rough home life and an absent father. Basketball meets these girls as a rich narrative. It therefore isn't like picking one thing over another—far from it. This thing, basketball, delivers an important life narrative that moves across generations.

Basketball will become important to the girls too—part of their identity— but not simply because they like zone defense, the feeling of sinking a three, or the sound of squeaking Nikes. They'll love all these things because of the narratives they deliver to them. Zone defense reminds one daughter of Candy, who played at the top of the key. They became such good friends before she moved and had so much fun driving back and forth to games. She remembers how that defense led them back to win the holiday classic tournament, and how Candy had eleven steals. Another daughter remembers how her

23. Nicholas Smith adds, "So for Taylor, just as the self is and must be oriented by a framework which maps a moral space, it must also be located in a narrative which tracks its unfolding in time. As Taylor puts it, 'making sense of one's life as a story is also, like orientation to the good, not an optional extra' [Taylor, *Sources of the Self*, 47]. In order to be able to answer the question of who-identity, the question 'who am I?', one must have recourse not only to strong evaluation but also to narrative." *Charles Taylor: Meaning, Morals and Modernity* (Cambridge: Polity, 2002), 98.

first three-pointer won a home game. The sight of her grandpa jumping up and down was such a thrill, and she remembers saying to herself, *I'll shoot a hundred threes a day to practice*. And still another daughter remembers the day her dad took her to get new shoes, just the two of them on an outing together, sharing in something meaningful to both of them. She remembers the size of those shoes and what she ordered at Applebee's.

In a different but related example, if you ever watch the Columbus Blue Jackets NHL hockey team play, you'll almost invariably hear the story of Seth Jones. Jones is an all-star defenseman and the son of former longtime NBA player Popeye Jones. How the son of Popeye Jones ended up playing hockey and not basketball demands a story, revealing that we intuitively know that all our *things*, if they're to produce an identity, need to be borne within a story. For a thing to stick and to provide an identity, it must provide a narrative that a young person can live within.

Youth Ministry and Identity

This is why it isn't enough for the church to just recognize young people, giving them privileged space for an enclosed youth group. The church as a whole must pass on narratives through their own personhood, which young people can live within. And this attention to narrative reveals an important way forward for youth ministry. In my mind it's a losing proposition to assume that youth ministry can win the status of other *things*, moving itself up the scale of rankings. Youth ministry is assumed to be a thing, but is tacitly ranked far below debate, drama, fencing, and test prep. For a youth pastor to fight the battle of things head-on will only leave him with a bloody forehead. It will be very difficult to make youth ministry the kind of thing that can leapfrog sports, music recitals, and study.

But trying does something worse than just wasting the youth pastor's energy. It concedes to the cultural misconception that identity is forged through self-chosen affiliations, brands, and activities, therefore turning Christianity and the life of the church into one lame version of these. But as we've said, the graveyard of *things* proves that this isn't quite the case. When a thing delivers an identity, the thing itself and the activities it offers get too much credit. No doubt things like sports and music have their appeal as embodied activity, but because we're language animals, those feelings need a narrative or they quickly evaporate, absent the substance to bear the weight of an identity.[24]

24. Ruth Abbey gives some helpful background to this: "This idea that individuals interpret their lives in narrative terms was not originated by Taylor; he cites the work of Alasdair

When the youth pastor fights for youth group to be on par with soccer, he misses that any *thing* only has the power to shape identity because it delivers narratives. It's within these narratives that young people find the vision to state *this is me*. This, then, is the way forward. Youth ministry should forget about competing in the battle of *things* and instead profoundly concern ourselves with *stories*. (This shifts the assessment from quantity of participation to quality of shared life in those times.) This is the powerful inner core of any *thing* anyhow. And unlike packed gymnasiums and pep bands, this is not only something the church can offer but something it has two thousand years of practice doing. The church is a house of stories, and the youth minister's job is to expose young people to as many of these stories as possible. Doing so cuts out the middleman of identity construction, leaving the husk of the thing behind and going straight to the narrative. Identities are constructed only within narratives.

All this is not to say that rituals, practices, and forms of action aren't important. They are essential because they take both our minds and our bodies deeply into narrative.[25] It's at this depth that identity is affected (which is why, in the end, basketball and other things can eventually produce an identity, but often these stories are too flat, leading identity to need constant recognition, making it susceptible to *ressentiment*). To have an identity in Christ is to have, at some very deep level—as we'll explore in the next section—the story of Christ as your own story. This story takes the shape of cross and resurrection, giving identity a place beyond *ressentiment* through shared stories that deliver communions of joy. To have an identity in Christ, then, is to have the story of the living Christ encountering you (or someone in your community), and

---

MacIntyre, Paul Ricoeur and Jerome Bruner as well as Heidegger as influencing his ideas on this topic. However, Taylor's claims about the necessary structure of moral life, that it involves orientation towards strongly valued goods, the desire for their realization and an animating concern with one's place in relation to them, grounds the role of narrative more solidly in moral theory. Of course narratives exist at the wider cultural level too, giving meaning to the histories, present and future of groups. Thus nations tell stories about themselves, and these dominant stories are often contested by different group within the nation's boundaries. Ethnic groups, too, can construe stories about themselves. Religious traditions also develop narratives about their founding and their progress from there. So narratives function at different levels to give layers of meaning in individual lives, and this point illustrates again Taylor's ontological pluralism or recognition of the qualitatively different sorts of goods that exist in people's lives." *Charles Taylor* (Princeton: Princeton University Press, 2000), 38.

25. Here, too, it's important to point to Ben Conner's book *Amplifying Our Witness: Giving Voice to Adolescents with Developmental Disabilities* (Grand Rapids: Eerdmans, 2012). Conner asserts that youth ministry with young people with disabilities should take on practices. Practices invite us to embody narratives. So young people with disabilities still partake in narrative in very rich lived ways in and through practices that they do and that others do with and for them in love.

in turn to have the story of Jesus's own life, death, and resurrection now be the shape of your story.

But we have to remind ourselves again and again that this is a story. Too often youth ministry has tried to forge identities in Christ by offering propositions, statements that young people consent to believe, and give proof of their belief by participating. We've called this faith. But this is not how identity is constructed, and this is not what faith is. Faith is not trust in propositions or commitment to participate, but the identification with personhood in and through stories. Faith is the gift of Jesus Christ, as Luther told us, making faith not data but a person. And a person can only be known and, more importantly, *shared in* through narrative discourse—through prayer, preaching, and confession. Identity is constructed through the hearing and, just as importantly, the telling of stories. Youth ministry should count something, but not how many young people are participating in the activities and believing in the propositions. It should count how many stories young people are hearing, and how many young people are invited to tell their own stories within the life of the congregation.[26]

Propositions can never do the heavy lifting of forging an identity, which makes all our youth ministry efforts fruitless. Propositions can't do this work because they lack a story, and lacking a story reveals that the moral horizon is not the Good. Even the Ten Commandments make little sense, and are ultimately a defeating burden, when the imperative is separated from the indicative, when the rule is divided from the story of Yahweh arriving to claim Yahweh's people and set them free from Egypt. The Ten Commandments start with the narrative, "I am the LORD your God, who brought you out of Egypt. . . . [So] you shall have no other gods before me" (Exod. 20:2–3). This is why narrative unveils whether it is indeed the Good that we're aiming for.[27]

---

26. See Amanda Hontz Drury, *Saying Is Believing: The Necessity of Testimony in Adolescent Spiritual Development* (Downers Grove, IL: IVP Academic, 2015), for a rich articulation of this in youth ministry.

27. Our aim toward happiness on the track of hedonism gives us a blind spot for the centrality of narrative to identity, and may even lead us to fear narrative. Narratives have the power to direct and fuse the human spirit, even over against our happiest intentions. Narrative has the potential to pull us out of ourselves to see that the moral horizon of happiness is vapid. Better to consume comic-book stories, laugh-track sitcoms, and cat videos on YouTube than stories that may challenge and crucify our cultural *summum bonum*. Narrative can also link us to evil, even motivating us into sacrificing for evil. There simply can be no Nazism, ISIS, and more without narratives, particularly of *ressentiment*. Above, I've allowed narrative to unmask vapidness for the sake of the Good. This point stands next to evil. What makes evil so destructive is that it wraps itself in the Good; it deceives us into thinking it is the Good. That's why it has the power to upend and connect. Yet the only way to discover evil masquerading as Good is for us to more fully engage its narrative with other narratives. The Good uses narrative to bring union; evil uses narrative to divide.

Story as Transformation

Story, then, is both the way to discern and the way to direct the human spirit toward the Good. The Good is too large, too transcendent to assume that anyone can master and possess it as if it were a puzzle or a CrossFit workout. The Good is bound in God alone, and God cannot be mastered, even through Aristotelian practices of virtue. We can't direct young people into the Good by telling them to master the Good (any true "master" in any form of spirituality admits she has no possession of the Good; that's the first step). To do so is to flatten the Good under the weight of storyless propositions.

It can't work to just tell young people to commit to church or religion like they do their other *things*. The Good cannot be mastered like tennis or rasgueado guitar strumming. Rather, God's Goodness convicts us and throws us back into impossibility. There are no proficiencies to master, just narratives to embody. As we'll see in the next chapter, this doesn't eliminate the importance of practice. J will invite her young people to become more engaged in practice, but these practices are dialectally bound. They aim to embody the narrative of cross and resurrection, not achieve proficiency. These practices orient the self toward the kenotic, directing us toward this narrative Good.

Like the rich young ruler, we're told that all our good works and achieved goods are no way into the Good. The rich young ruler might as well be a middle-class American mom or dad. He is trying to do good, to accrue goods as a way to be securely happy. But he is missing the Good, because when Jesus convicts him, he leaves sad, unable to bear the death experience.[28] But bearing this death experience is essential, for it not only unveils our reality (giving us that more realistic anthropology) but in so doing gives us a gift, a meaningful story. Jesus never convicts without at the same time giving us the gift of his person as a narrative that ushers us into communion with him. Jesus convicts, telling us that we cannot be our own Good, that all our efforts for happiness have left us void of meaning. But this provides us with the beginnings of a new story that forms us. Through this confession, we find ourselves oriented toward the Good, because we find ourselves deeply within the death experience, at the foot of the cross.

Jesus's words to the rich young ruler remind us that we can never master the Good; we can only narrate our experience of impossibility and God's arrival. And this is the start of a rich narrative because it begins with the

28. David Brooks makes my point here: "When most people think about the future, they dream up ways they might live happier lives. But notice this phenomenon. When people remember the crucial events that formed them, they don't usually talk about happiness. It is usually the ordeals that seem most significant. Most people shoot for happiness but feel formed through suffering." *The Road to Character* (New York: Random House, 2015), 93.

cross and resurrection. It claims that the Good is unveiled where it logically shouldn't be. In the opposite of what is good, in the confession of the death experience, on a cross, we find the fullness of Goodness, taking what is impossible and making it new.

That's what Jesus invites the rich young ruler and his listeners into. After the man departs, unwilling to participate in death for the sake of experiencing the Good, Jesus says to the disciples, "It is easier for a camel to go through the eye of a needle than for someone who is rich to enter the kingdom of God" (Mark 10:25). The disciples are overwhelmed with such a narrative-rich image and respond, "Who then can be saved?" Jesus confesses the shape of the story of God's act and being by saying that for humanity it is impossible, but God who is Good moves from the impossible (Matt. 19:16–26). It takes the gift of faith to trust that such a narrative is so true it could be the story of your life.

But we have to remember: faith is the *summum bonum*. As our ultimate aim, faith is much more than an asset to find a religious self, much more than propositions to consent to. Faith is the person of Jesus Christ; faith is personal (bound in personhood). Faith is the meeting of a person, and it is to place trust in this person to bring life out of death. For faith to direct us into the Good, producing joy as verification, we must share in the person of Jesus in and through our own person. Person-to-person encounters happen in and through discourse, through the sharing of narratives. God is a speaking God of union and joy. Jesus's person comes to our person with the invitation to share in God's being by making the story of Jesus's person our own story.[29]

But to make Jesus's story our own is much deeper than some kind of religious cosplay. It touches all the way down to the level of being, the arrival of joy witnessing that this story penetrates deeper than an epistemological attitude adjustment (affecting our knowing) and instead stretches to the ontological level (to the depth of being). The narrative of Jesus is the shape of his being, for it is fundamentally a story of death and new life through death. The story is about being dead, and being made alive, to live forevermore, flourishing in and through death. So while Jesus convicts us, he does so by giving us his person as a narrative. His life story becomes the shape of our own story. His story as our own not only confirms that we are in the event horizon of the Good, but it does so by transforming us.

---

29. "More broadly, however, sociologists (like psychologists) have increasingly realized that human beings give order to their world through stories. We do not think primarily in concepts or causal chains but in stories that carry those ideas and imply the causes. . . . Stories are important, in part, because they are not merely personal. They exist at the intersection of personal and public." Nancy Tatom Ammerman, *Sacred Stories, Spiritual Tribes: Finding Religion in Everyday Life* (New York: Oxford University Press, 2014), 7–8.

The feeling of that transformation is joy. Joy is fundamentally so much deeper than happiness because happiness stays at the epistemological level, but joy reaches to the ontological. The mother of the released son has joy, for his freedom affects the narrative she has about her own being as a mother to a son.[30] The arrival of a new baby is joy, for the birth of another being redefines your own being in the world. You can never again tell your story and reveal your being (without a major violation) without naming this other. As we share in Jesus's story, in and through our own death experience and rebirth (Gal. 2:20), Jesus's being is transfused into our own being. This narrative transfusion means we no longer live, for human beings can only live with an identity, and identity can only be in and through stories. And our self-referential story is over. But now, through the stories of the community and our own testifying that this story of Jesus born, dead, and raised again is our own story, Jesus is our being.[31]

Passing on Stories

To form and direct young people toward the Good is to provide them with stories that start in the confession of a death experience. That's why Bernard's story changed everything, according to J. The story is squarely set within a death experience: "Twenty years ago, my baby girl died of something like this. And I wasn't there. I was high." This confession yearns for a story. Everyone sitting in the waiting room wants to know more. The confession of the death experience doesn't repel narration but craves it, opening space for a communion, and union through narration itself.

But it takes a brave pastoral act for the confession to move into full narration. J reported that as Bernard confessed, everyone in the room froze. Their bodies signaled that they had moved into fight or flight mode, not the best disposition to encounter a narrative. Yet this was all eased, *not* when the confession was ignored but when Lorena's mom took the brave pastoral

30. It impacts her *Dasein*, to tip my hat to Heidegger.

31. I'm affirming what Christopher Beeley says here: "In patristic theology human flourishing is defined chiefly in terms of the divinization of human beings. Divinization or deification (*theosis, theopoiesis, deificatio*) means the transforming participation of human beings in the very being and life of God, with the result that they become divine or godlike as human beings." Beeley, "Christ and Human Flourishing in Patristic Theology," *Pro Ecclesia* 25, no. 2 (May 2016): 136. He connects this to identity: "For patristic theologians Christ represents and promotes human flourishing not merely through his creating, saving, and consummating work, but, in a more fundamental sense, through his very identity. Christ is himself the archetype and first instance of human flourishing, and other human beings flourish by participating in Christ's divine-human life. We will therefore do best to begin with a summary account of the rudiments of patristic Christology" (129).

step to ask, "What happened?" This framed Bernard's experience within a narrative logic, inviting Bernard to reveal his own personhood.

"It was like she was staring into his story," J says to me. Lorena's mom asked this pastoral question from within her own death experience. She was qualified to reach out to Bernard's person and invite him to narrate his death experience because she, too, was at the cross. She needed his story as much as he needed to tell it. Her pastoral authority to invite him to speak was not in a seminary degree but in the way her own narrative—her own being—was bound in a death experience, seeking for the Good.

And so Bernard told the young people his story. He had been living in a different state, estranged from his daughter's mother. His drug problem had destroyed their relationship. Yet when his daughter became sick, her mother reached out. Bernard scraped together enough money to buy a bus ticket, but before he boarded he decided to get high one more time.

He woke up two days later. His phone lit up with messages, all from his daughter's mom. His baby girl was dead. If he'd gotten on the bus, he could have been with her. The next two years he was more high than not, living between homeless shelters and crack houses. In one of those crack houses, he woke early one morning to a man gently shaking his shoulder. Startled, Bernard pulled himself away, thinking it was a cop.

"The man," Bernard recounted, "knew my name; he called me by name. He said, 'Bernard, your baby girl is with me. Peace be with you.'[32] I covered my face, confused, and the next thing I knew, I looked up and I was alone. I don't know if it was a dream or what, but from that moment I knew I needed to get clean. So I stumbled into our church, looking for a meeting. I got more than that. I got invited to Tuesday morning Bible study. Just me—a junkie— and mainly old women, but I told them my story and they prayed for me. Then a year later Pastor Heather gave me a job. When I heard Lorena was in the hospital, I heard that same voice from the crack house say, 'Go.' So that's why I'm here. I got no other reason."

---

32. This is important context to Bernard's words: "In English translations of the Hebrew Bible/Old Testament, 'shalom' has traditionally been translated as 'peace.' If shalom is what I have just now said it is, 'peace' is obviously a very poor translation. In some recent translations it is translated as 'welfare.' That's better, but still inadequate. 'Welfare' has economic conno- tations; we speak of 'the welfare state.' I think 'flourishing' is the best translation. Shalom is flourishing in all one's relationships: to God, to one's fellows, to oneself, to the natural world, to society and culture. It has both a normative component, being rightly related, and an affective component, finding joy in being so related." Nicholas Wolterstorff, "Human Flourishing and Art That Enhances the Ordinary," in *Envisioning the Good Life: Essays on God, Christ, and Human Flourishing*, ed. Matthew Croasmun, Zoran Grozdanov, and Ryan McAnnally-Linz (Eugene, OR: Cascade, 2017), 164.

Thirteen

Open Takes and Closed Spins

Youth Ministry and Transcendence

LATE MARCH

Wait," said Tannon, "you, like, heard a real voice?"

"Real enough to make me walk into this place. Real enough to get me past my hate for hospitals, to sit in this chair," responded Bernard.

"How do you know it wasn't the drugs?" another young person asked.

"It might have been," Bernard said. "I fried my brain on some nasty stuff. But I've been clean for years. I've had other bad trips and stuff. But these two experiences were just different. But I guess it could be the—"

"I had an experience like that," Kathy interrupted.

Kathy is the mom of Nikki, one of the girls in the youth group. Actually, J tells me that Kathy was her lead critic, expressing most loudly her disappointment in the youth group. It was Kathy who was leading the charge to fire J. The sharp point of her frustration was that Nikki didn't like the youth group and was refusing to go. Kathy kept pleading with J to make it fun, telling her, "When I was growing up, I loved youth group. We had so much fun. I want Nikki to have that experience. So make it fun."

When J asked her what fun looked like, Kathy couldn't provide much, other than to talk about the big Midnight Madness outings her youth group did twenty-five years ago. Kathy had been one of J's advocates when she was interviewing at the church, but when the youth group didn't meet Kathy's expectations for fun, she became a harsh critic.

When J saw her walk into the hospital waiting room, about an hour before Tannon arrived, she worried she was coming with termination papers. The fun event that was canceled was planned in no small part in response to Kathy's frustrations. But to J's relief Kathy just sat down with Nikki and joined the group in their waiting. You couldn't blame J for assuming that Kathy was coming for a direct purpose. Kathy was business from head to toe. J had never seen her in anything other than high heels and a business suit.

So when she interrupted Bernard with her "I had an experience like that," everyone was shocked. Kathy went on to share a story of loss and Jesus's presence in it. Two years before Nikki was born, Kathy had a miscarriage. Rushing to the hospital while working late one night, she tried to save her unborn child. But it was too late. "Crushed, I sat in an empty waiting room not unlike this one, waiting for Nikki's dad to come pick me up. I was overwhelmed, not only because I had lost this baby but also because it was such a struggle for us to get pregnant at all. I was sure it would never happen, and my dream of being a mom was turned into a nightmare."

Everyone was now hanging on Kathy's every word. It was the first time J had ever seen anything close to vulnerability in her. Bernard's story somehow awakened her to share.

Kathy continued, "When that all hit me, for some weird reason I stood up, covered my face, and started sobbing really hard. Next thing I knew, I felt some stranger touch my shoulder and comfort me. It was an old woman. She said, 'Sweetheart, truly, truly, I say to you, you will weep and lament, but the world will rejoice. You will be sorrowful, but your sorrow will turn into joy.' That just made me cry harder, because it was a verse my grandmother used to quote when she talked about my mom being born. She struggled with infertility too. My knees buckled and I almost fell to the ground. I caught myself and sat down. I couldn't believe she quoted that verse. I asked her how she knew I needed to hear that verse, how she knew how precious those words were to my grandmother. She said, 'I don't know, the Holy Spirit just led me. I guess Jesus wanted me here; I thought I had some blood clots, so I came to the hospital, but it looks like Jesus wanted me to be with you.'"

"Whoa!" Tannon said.

Stepping out of the story, J says to me, "I remember feeling so drawn to Kathy's words about joy. 'Sorrow turned to joy.' I realized, sitting in that hard chair, that joy comes from the sharing of sorrow. Joy is this incredible experience of sorrow being shared, leading us into a community of love. That's what I was experiencing, the pure gift of sorrow being shared. I remember thinking to myself, *Yeah, it's true. Youth ministry is for joy because youth ministry is about creating a space for stories and moments of sharing that open us up to something big."*

We sit in silence for a few seconds, and I think about the ramifications of J's words. I then ask, "What happened next with Kathy's story? I'm with Tannon—it's wild that the old woman used that verse."

J continues, "Kathy then told us the old woman sat with her, holding her hand until Kathy's husband showed up. Kathy said, 'We exchanged numbers. I don't know why; it seems weird now. But she started to call me, and then we started to meet to pray together. When I got pregnant again, she was the first person I called, because I was both so happy and so scared. We prayed together every week through the whole pregnancy. I just had this sense that God was leading me through. I'll never forget when Nikki was born, seeing her hold Nikki, crying and praying for her. That's why she's 'Nikki,' because in a waiting room like this God sent me Nichole Hunmurray, to pray for me, to see me through and bless us with our Nichole Marie Mattson."

J tells me that a silence came over everyone. After a minute, Kathy breathed in deep and said, "That's why I came today, why I wanted Nikki to be here. In a very weird way, waiting rooms are holy places to me. I'd somehow gotten myself disconnected from that experience, but when I heard Lorena was in the hospital, I knew I needed to be here." Kathy paused and then said, "I never intended to tell that story until Bernard told his, but I know it's why I'm here."

J says to me, "I thought to myself, *I want my youth ministry to be a waiting room like this one. A place where we share stories and are open to something bigger that ushers us into joy."*

I'm as enthralled by these secondhand stories as I'm sure those in the waiting room were at the time Bernard and Kathy shared their narratives. I'm experiencing the stories connect me to these others I've never met. These stories have particular power because, though J is relaying them, they are part of her own story of a death experience of failing as a youth worker. I feel like I'm sharing in communion with J and Lorena. The narrative has become a kind of sacrament, because it takes us into the Good. It's just Good for my soul to hear these stories, to feel this sense of connection. This sense of the Good that comes in and through these stories is a shared experience that opens us all up to transcendence. Bernard's and Kathy's stories point to an incredible mystery in the world that seeks to encounter us for the sake of the Good.

Yet the Good comes, as these stories testify, in the sharing of a death experience—with a question, "Why are you at the hospital?" that reveals the loss of a daughter and the shame of failure, and then a miscarriage and the shattering of a dream of being a mother. Inside these death experiences Bernard and Kathy encountered a personal force that calls them by name and ministers to them, connecting them to something bigger. The experience of this connection can only be labeled *joy*, for it has no instrumental function, no telos beyond the participation in the Good. The connection communicates that they are not alone but through this death experience can find communion with the triune God through the life and death of Jesus.

Encountering this Jesus in the death experience is joy because it is being alive, having life ("I am the resurrection and life," John 11:25). It is a movement into transformation because it takes us up into something transcendent. It's an experience of transcendence, for this sense of being alive is delivered out of death, far beyond the power of the self to save itself. It can only be described as joy because it is life coming from death as pure gift, casting out the isolation that all death experiences deliver with a new communion stronger than any death, for it has been fashioned by going through death.

I'm so enthralled by the stories that I haven't realized it's almost forty-five minutes past the time we'd set for our conversation. I look at my phone to see a full screen of notifications, all calls and texts from Kara wondering where I am. As we hurry ourselves out of the building, we see Bernard again. He's leaving too, locking the doors behind us. I see him in such a different light now that I know his story. I feel this odd connection to him, a hidden bond of friendship. And yet we haven't even been introduced.

As we walk to our cars, J and I review that we'll meet for lunch Friday, continuing the conversation. I say goodbye to Lorena and wish her the best, thanking her for everything. As I drive home, I'm convinced J is right. Youth ministry is for joy. It is for flourishing. But this kind of flourishing runs counter to our cultural presumptions.

Spins and Takes

In the slowdown all parents are anxious for their children to flourish. They're desperate for their children to live good lives, not wasted. They work hard to protect their children from all sorts of death experiences, believing that too many death experiences will make it impossible to meet the hypergood of happiness. Too many death experiences, they assume, will corrupt the internal search for an identity. Yet, while this blocking out of the death experience *may* allow young people to be happy, free from the risk of any emotional injury, it keeps them from joy. It keeps them from seeing their lives against the backdrop of transcendence, which provides rich visions of purpose and meaning bound to the Good. The hypergood of happiness has a way of reducing our vision to only the immanent, preferring only the natural and material. As we said in chapter 9, we've come to a misguided time when we believe happiness is a *natural* steady state. What is so engaging about Bernard's and Kathy's stories is that they crack open such immanent presumptions.

Because all humans are bound to seek goods through stories, there is no way to be human outside of a history and culture. As much as we tend to ignore it, there is no human life that doesn't appear right in the middle of a history, plopped right in the middle of some culture. No one gets to enter the world and live his or her life from nowhere. The minute we're born, we're somewhere specific, dropped into a moving river of narratives. This specific place that orders our lives, framing our history and setting terms for our culture, is an immanent one.

In the West, our lives are framed by immanence. We presume natural, not supernatural, causes in our world. We all inherit a sense that the world is the way it is because of natural, not supernatural, reasons. We believe this at a cosmological as well as cultural and even political level. It's nearly impossible to escape this immanent frame. Believers as well as skeptics inherit this same immanently ordered society. Yet even within it there are choices.

Charles Taylor gives us two broad ones.[1] We can embrace either a "closed spin" or an "open take," with many different strategies inside these two options. Squarely in the immanent frame, one group of people will spin things closed. This group, coming in many different degrees, will assert that anyone who believes that there are *any* phenomena in the world that are more than, or even outside, the natural and material are deluding themselves. Taylor shows his own cards when he calls this position a "spin."[2] He thinks it actually takes a lot of work, like an exasperated commentator, to spin things closed, requiring us to drown out mystery, beauty, and deep forms of attachment in the human spirit that reach for something more.

Instead of this closed spin, there is the option of an "open take." This Taylor finds more in line with reality and the constituting state of the human spirit—we are, after all, the kind of animals that produce art and write poetry. But Taylor admits it's a "take." There's no foundational view of a phenomenon from outside that phenomenon, no way of evaluating a human life other than within it. It's a take, like your take on why the Vikings can win

---

1. See Taylor, *A Secular Age* (Cambridge, MA: Belknap, 2007), 540–54.
2. Taylor shows not only his Catholic/religious cards here but also his long opposition to rigid naturalism.

the Super Bowl or why Donald Trump was elected president. It's based on reasons, embodied experience, reflection, and more. But even so, it's a take, demanding both commitment and humility.

Bernard is a good example. When the young person asks him if the voice he heard could have been the drugs, he humbly admits that it's possible. But this humility with his open take doesn't negate his deep commitment. He has good reasons to believe it's something more, not the least of these the way the experience transformed his life by drawing him into the Good.

Taylor's point is that in our secular age of immanence, there is no way for our position to be more than a take. But this take can be a deep narrative, meaning that this take can, and indeed does, convert. It unveils the Good, even transforming identity, as we'll see in the next chapter.

Transcendence and Youth Ministry

This take is open to transcendence,[3] open to experiencing the Good, and therefore open to being surprised by joy. This open take is exactly what Bernard and Kathy offer the young people. Youth ministry, then, is for exposing young people to open takes. Youth ministry invites young people to dialogue, doubt, dissect, and ultimately try on the open-take narratives of the people of God who have experienced transcendence inside a death experience, encountering the ministering Jesus.[4] Youth ministry is not just a religious thing among a menu of things, but a secret (in the sense of imaginatively probing mystery, not clandestine) intergenerational group that explores the transcendent in and through the narrative pattern of cross and resurrection.

Exploring open takes through cross and resurrection never shuts us down, pulling us deep within ourselves, but rather moves us out into the world for the

3. Taylor has been criticized for using the word *transcendence*, and he admits it has its problems. Ian Fraser explains, "Taylor is sensitive to this criticism and admits that he is actually uncomfortable with using the term transcendence as it does not quite capture exactly what he wants to say. He recognizes that the term transcendence is both 'abstract' and 'evasive,' but he used the term because he wanted to say something general which could appeal to all people, not just Christians, in indicating how we need to get beyond the narrow focus on the exclusively human." *Dialectics of the Self: Transcending Charles Taylor* (Exeter, UK: Imprint-Academic, 2007), 36.

4. Christoph Schwöbel and Colin Gunton offer a helpful further point, showing that wrestling with a take is not in opposition to God's Good work: "In the Christian tradition the opposite of faith is not unbelief, but sin. This illustrates once more that faith is not to be regarded exclusively as an epistemic attitude, but as a basic orientation of life. As the opposite of faith sin is to be interpreted not primarily as an offence committed against a law, as the transgression of a commandment. It is primarily the violation of a relationship, the relationship between God the creator and his human creatures." *Persons, Divine and Human* (Edinburgh: T&T Clark, 1991), 148.

sake of ministry. Bernard's and Kathy's open takes lead them to the hospital, directing their actions. If not for these experiences, which move them out of their selves to connect their selves to something bigger, Bernard and Kathy would not have gone to the hospital. Their open takes move them to be in the world in a certain way. And because their open takes bear the narrative marks of cross and resurrection, they enter the places of death, open to the possibility of God's arriving.

Youth ministry is for wrestling with open takes of transcendence in and through embodied experiences of ministering to one another in the world. Bernard's and Kathy's own open takes give the young people a sense that entering a death experience can unveil the Good. These open takes can even bring them into encounters with the living Jesus—which is what youth ministry is ultimately for.

It's one of those weeks when I can't believe it's already Friday. The days seemed to vaporize too quickly to keep up with. The speed of the passing days causes me to look broader. Not only do I feel the vertigo of the elapsing week, but I can't believe it's already early April. With spring so fully in bloom in the Upper Midwest, it's hard to remember what it felt like to live in the snow. It's amazing what a handful of days in the seventies will do to your mind, making the foot of snow present only weeks ago feel long past. The temperate temperatures have a merciful way of massaging out the muscle memory of the frigid.

People again are preparing their yards in anticipation of the changing weather, but this time with a welcoming expectancy, planting flowers and spreading mulch. Now that I'm in a T-shirt, those dark, presnowy autumn days talking with the three sets of parents feel like a lifetime ago. And not just because of the passing time and changing seasons, but maybe more so because I now find myself in a different place in my journey.

I'd started this journey trying to get clear on what youth ministry is for. Back in September I felt like I was at the base of a mountain covered by a thick apron of dark clouds. Into the fall and through the winter, I felt like I was making progress, becoming clearer on the cultural challenges youth ministry faced inside middle-class parents' moral horizons. But at the time I still felt foggy on what youth ministry could be for in a slowdown of growing up where identity was strictly self-chosen and happiness the *summum bonum.*

Yet in talking with J and Lorena and experiencing their midweek gathering, it feels like I've ascended above the cloud cover, maybe even spotted the summit. I agree with J that youth ministry is for joy, but only because it is for Jesus Christ. Joy is the felt experience of the Good. Joy is being surprised by the gift of the Good, to feel like your life has been gifted with flourishing. The God who alone is Good (Luke 18:19) gives us the Good gift of Jesus Christ, who meets us in our death experiences, sharing our burdens. Joy is the feeling of a sacramental reality of sharing in something transcendent through these burdens.

Unfortunately, J needs to cancel our Friday lunch, just as I'm sensing that I'm stepping above the cloud cover on my journey. Yet honestly I find it a relief. The end of the spring semester is now within eyeshot, meaning the meetings and thesis defenses are mounting and my inbox is filling up with requests that make me crabby. An extra few hours at the end of the week are welcomed. We reschedule for a few weeks later, which is more the fault of my schedule than J's.

Over those few weeks I find my mind wandering back to the waiting room experience. The more I think about it, the more I'm intrigued by Bernard's and Kathy's stories. I'm thinking a lot about how youth ministry can offer young people open takes through the confession of a death experience. If youth ministry is for joy, and if being surprised by joy is to encounter the Good, then openness to transcendence is essential.

J and I finally meet for a smoothie, now able to sit outside and enjoy the warm sun. Sucking down some reddish blend, I jump right in. "So what happened after Lorena was released from the hospital? How did the experience in the waiting room continue, or did it?"

Unsheathing her straw, J says, "Oh, it continued; it continued by waiting. One of the kids—I can't remember who—actually started calling our midweek gathering the Waiting Room. Actually that's now its official name. That's what you were at a few weeks ago. One of them even made up some T-shirts. Like I said, I stopped doing youth group in the waiting room, but I wanted to continue having young people wait with adults, sharing their burdens with one another as an experience of joy."

"But what were you waiting for?" I find myself asking.

"Well, at the start we were waiting for Lorena. When she left the hospital, she was still pretty much bedridden for the next almost ten weeks. That was super hard for her. She was missing a bunch of school activities and other important stuff. But it was even harder on her mom, who needed to work. She's a single mom, and it just wasn't an option to take more time off. She pushed that as far as she could when Lorena was in the hospital. So we thought of ourselves as gathering together to wait for Lorena to return to us."

Pausing to put her straw into her smoothie, J continues, "But in a crazy way that waiting moved us to do something: the more we were directly waiting for Lorena, thinking about her, the more we felt we had to do something for her. Next thing we knew, kids, parents, and a bunch of other adults from the church were helping Lorena and her mom out. Waiting for her together moved us into action, to do ministry. It was like the waiting ordained so many in our church to share in Lorena and her mom's life by being there for them, by sharing in their burdens. Joy started to spread across our congregation. And that really changed our whole church."

We pause for a second, and J continues, "But the Waiting Room became something else as well, which I guess is what really gave it its name. Right after Lorena went home, we all had this feeling that we'd experienced something important together. We just wanted to be together. But I had no time to plan anything, so I decided we'd just hang out. But the crazy thing is we just kept talking about Bernard's and Kathy's stories."

J's last comment intrigues me. I'm glad to hear that I wasn't the only one who couldn't shake those stories.

"The young people wanted to explore further what the stories could mean," J explains. "We became detectives in mystery.[5] We had these amazing deep discussions about the meaning of life, purpose, and God in and through trying to discern what these stories meant for us, what they said about life. As the weeks passed, I started to read a biblical verse or two, and we'd connect it to these stories. Finally, one of them suggested we keep the Waiting Room going by inviting other people to come and tell their stories. It was like the young people now thirsted for stories, to get inside them and wrestle with them. It was like they needed more stories to figure out what made life worth living, who they could be in this world, and how God was acting. And since then it's now become a whole church thing. So I started inviting other adults from the church to tell their stories. The Waiting Room is now a multigenerational storytelling time when we seek for God together, experiencing something Good together through trying to find meaning and purpose inside our stories."

"Man, that's cool" is all I can muster in response. Pausing, I add, "I bet that has changed your own sense of your job."

5. I'm following Craig Dykstra's helpful discussion of mystery: "I'm using the term in quite a different way, one that is biblical in nature and connects it with the idea of revelation. George Hendry writes that a mystery in the New Testament sense is a mystery 'not because it offers so little to our understanding, but because its superabundant wealth overwhelms our understanding.' Here a mystery is not a problem that goes away once figured out." *Vision and Character: A Christian Educator's Alternative to Kohlberg* (New York: Paulist Press, 1981), 34.

"One hundred eighty degrees," J quickly responds. "It actually felt like an amazing liberation. In the hospital waiting room, I quit being the lead counselor of fun and trying to build a successful youth group. So it's kind of amazing that we now have the Waiting Room every week. It reminds me of what I'm called to, of how God came to me and put one vocation to death, giving me the amazing joy of another. So the waiting room was not only the place where I buried J the lead counselor of fun, but the Waiting Room was also where I was given a new youth ministry life, a new vocation."

"What'd that look like?" I ask.

"I found myself spending more time with adults, coaching them in storytelling. I started learning about storytelling, both its mechanics and its theological importance. I started reading more, looking for stories, aware that the stories that connect us to something bigger often start in loss that's shared, leading to joy. I found myself spending more free time just being with young people, listening more than talking. Rested more than exhausted. I found myself in spiritual direction, being kids' and adults' spiritual director. Someone who set the table and invited the whole congregation into reflecting and probing for God's work in our lives."

We pause again. I've now hit the bottom of my smoothie and set it down. An odd, potentially tangential question comes to my mind. "What about Nikki? What happened to her?"

J's eyes grow wide as she slurps her smoothie. Then she shoots back, "Oh, that's crazy. She started showing up like every week. I couldn't believe it. When it was regular youth group that was about fun, she wanted nothing to do with it. But once the Waiting Room started, she'd show up early."

"Did you ever ask her why?"

"I did, mainly because I was worried that she felt weird about people talking about her mom's story. And then because we invited both Bernard and Kathy to come to one of those early Waiting Rooms so we could talk deeper about what they experienced. So I asked Nikki if this was all OK, or if it felt weird."

"What did she say?"

"She said it felt weird but Good. Then she thought about it and said something I'll never forget. She said, 'It's important that I know who I am.'"

I return a surprised look. "What did that mean?"

Fourteen

An Identity Event

How Youth Ministry Affects Identity

MID-APRIL

I can't completely remember what Nikki exactly said next," J responds. "I'll never forget the 'It's important that I know who I am.' But then she said something else; it was something like beautifully weird, something I couldn't have imagined her to say in hundred years."

I laugh as J racks her brain for the words.

"What was it? It was something like, 'It's good for me to know about the mysteries that made me.' Yeah, I think that was it."

Now we both laugh. Not because the statement is ridiculous, but because it's surprising and beautiful, like delightfully hearing a five-your-old talk about photosynthesis.

Through the laughter, J says, "I'm not sure what that meant!"

But I think I might, and I start to wonder how this wrestling with the stories of open takes became impactful to Nikki's self-definition. So just as quickly as the words make me laugh, they draw me somewhere important. Nikki was confessing that this encounter with a story of an open take was pressing in on her being, affecting her identity.

Open Takes and Identity

To say that youth ministry is for exploring open takes with young people is intriguing, but it opens up more questions. Particularly, how can this work within the strong current of the cultural assumption that identity is constructed, which we explored in chapters 5 and 7? We saw in those chapters that the surplus of identity options has played a major part in stripping youth ministry of its purpose. Parents feel both deep concern and a sense of powerlessness when it comes to their child's self-chosen identity. Our cultural presumptions lead us to believe that identity is solely a self-chosen self-definition we perform, which then needs, and therefore seeks, recognition. For most middle-class parents, the tacit assumption is that youth ministry can play (maybe) a small but far from central role in a young person's performing *this is me*.

Yet this assumption is based on a cultural misconception of how identity is formed and therefore operates from a hidden closed spin. I believe if youth ministry is for open takes, it can avoid giving in to this misconception; it can play a central role in the formation of an identity. Youth ministry, in my mind, is far more equipped than most other *things* for this kind of identity work—yet to see how we'll have to explore the misconception and the hidden closed spin.

First a look at the cultural misconception. Even in the cultural description of chapters 5 and 7, we said it's a distortion to assume that identity is solely an internal decision born from a self-enclosed feel. Assuming that identity is an individual performance leads to a frantic drive for recognition that looks more like Luther's *incurvatus in se* (to be turned in on oneself) than flourishing, often producing *ressentiment* more than a communion of joy born from humility and mercy (virtues that are transformed by the cross).

And yet most middle-class parents, even those connected to our congregations, see recognition as essential to achieving the hypergood of happiness. They'll contend that their child will only be happy if he has a clear identity through received recognition. Who has time for church when you're racing for recognition from a tennis coach, debate competition, and all those college recruiters? Even parents like the Rodriguez-Eriksons fall into this trap, because they concede to the misconception that identity is a self-enclosed individual performance that, because it is performed, necessitates some level of recognition. They don't see that holding to the good of identity through recognition tends to make a life well lived more about immanent winning than the calls of the transcendent Good.

Ironically, it's the need for recognition that shows that this is a misconception. Identity is never self-enclosed; it is always formed through some kind of conversation (and often with much more than words, since we enter into conversation through practicing rituals, through nonverbal body language, and more). As much as we might assume that identity is an internal task, no identity is discovered in a vacuum; we cannot truly find ourselves without finding ourselves with someone. All identities come out of some kind of exchange. The very necessity of this exchange opens up the possibility that discovering an identity can give us ourselves by taking us out of ourselves.

This is the profound claim of the gospel, and it's why the Christian faith claims such a deep identity in Christ that it can be put in ontological language (Gal. 2:20: "I no longer live, but Christ lives in me"). There is such an exchange at the heart of the Christian life that your identity becomes Christ. Youth ministry, then, is for Jesus Christ, because through open takes it invites young people to find their identity exchanged for Christ. And it is a joyful exchange,[1] as Luther would say, because Jesus takes on the identity of death and sin and gives you his very being of new life. In finding ourselves in discourse with the living Jesus (in prayer, confession, worship, preaching, singing, etc.), we're taken out of ourselves, only to be given ourselves back, now with our identity in Christ.

At its deepest level this illustrates that identity is always a coming out of your *self* so you might have your *self*. We can only know ourselves, and therefore have a firm identity, in and through communities and collectives of discourse (to be in Christ is always a communal reality of shared open takes).[2] The kind of recognition pursuits represented in Demi Lovato are like yelling matches. They, too, are forms of discourse, just bad ones that seek a collective of fans and haters through performance. In this form of identity discourse I try to scream my identity louder than you, so more eyeballs are on me, producing the kind of communal experience that is felt not as joy but rather as a sense of having fans.

Most parents downgrade youth ministry because their child is too busy discovering their identity through their many *things*. But ironically, a youth ministry like J's Waiting Room gives young people a community (particularly an intergenerational community) of discourse beyond the competition of recognition but full of affirmation. And this is more fundamental to identity than any other *thing*. Youth ministry, then, can be for identity when its focus is on the communion of persons sharing in the lives of one another through discourse. In the anxiety of the slowdown, young people more than ever need affirming communities of discourse to which to belong. J's youth ministry of

1. This is often translated as "happy exchange," but I believe it's better, particularly for pursuits of my argument, to call it a joyful exchange.
2. This is why the church is theologically essential for Reformation theologians. Because of the centrality of discourse (word) in the theological system, the community becomes theologically essential.

intergenerational discourse is born in the hospital waiting room and becomes much more.

This takes us to the hidden closed spin. When we presume that identity is a self-enclosed decision, absent communities of discourse, and solely our own choice, we buffer the self from transcendence. We even mock the necessity to be moved outside our self to know our self. We find it safer to spin things closed, giving us a sense of control in a culture that feels out of control with identity options. When identity is simply for being happy, and happiness is won by performing for recognition, we concede that the self cannot (and should not) ever lose itself in something more (Charles Taylor calls this "the eclipse of grace"[3]). In this hidden closed spin, transformation becomes something to fear, because transformation reorders the self, often over against its own volition but never without its full participation.

Taylor explains that a good litmus test for discerning if you're moved by an open take or bound in a closed spin, whether grace has been eclipsed or is still a live option, is to notice your reaction to Saint Francis.[4] Saint Francis of Assisi was born the child of a wealthy merchant with a solid identity in the privilege of his father's house. Yet unlike the rich young ruler, after direct discourse with Jesus through a vision, Francis gave it all up, radically transformed. Francis lived with a deep sense that God was calling him to something and that he'd only live if he sought it, abandoning all he had to find this calling. Taylor's point is that if you hear Francis's story of transformation and are overcome with an anxious stab of iciness or eye-rolling about the stupidity of some people, you're more than likely operating within a closed spin. This closed spin walls you off from the possibility of transformation, putting you in a cage of your own making. Yet if you hear this story (hopefully told much better than I just relayed it) and you're nervously open to what it could mean for you, for what it connotes about reality, and if you're moved in wonder, fear, and admiration for how deeply the human spirit can be transformed, then your take is more than likely an open one. And what it is open to is transformation of identity itself.

What Taylor is showing us with this little litmus test is not only a way to explore whether we're moved by open takes or closed spins, but that the transformation that delivers a new identity is storied. Taylor can show us whether we have an open take or closed spin by our feel, our response, to a story. Story is the form of the test, because story is essential to transformation. Identity

3. Taylor, *A Secular Age* (Cambridge, MA: Belknap, 2007), 222–25.
4. Taylor, *Secular Age*, 729–64.

necessitates conversation, and the form of this discourse that holds potent potential to transform is most often the storying of our lived events. It is in hearing the stories of Bernard's and Kathy's lived experiences and their open takes on them that young people are confronted with something that presses in on their own identities.

To have an identity I need a story about myself. My identity is the story of the events I live through. But to have a story about myself I must hear and share in the stories of others. In the waiting room and then the Waiting Room, the told narratives of Bernard and Kathy transfer their own open takes to the young people. We are transformed—our identity forged and reforged—in and through narratives, and these narrative open takes now invite the young people into an identity event.

Identity Event: The First Way

It's first an identity event because these stories have pressed deeply into the being of Bernard and Kathy. The stories are captivating because the listener intuitively knows, *feels*, that in confessing these events Bernard's and Kathy's humanity is revealed. This is what can make these kinds of experiences risky and able to be used for all sorts of spiritually abusive ends. But nevertheless the telling of these open-take stories is the remembering again (and living again) of events that Bernard and Kathy identify with. They both have their identities in and through these events, not through an internal quest for recognition. To know Kathy, to really see her, is to encounter her through the narratable events of her lost baby, her crushing anxiety, and the joyful arrival of Nikki. When Kathy tells this story, revealing her identity by revealing this event of the death experience, J really sees her for the first time. J now understands why Kathy so desperately wants Nikki to feel connected to the church, and why Kathy at times holds Nikki too close. The event of loss and struggle presses in on Kathy's being, making her at times overprotective. Like the rich young ruler, Kathy wants Nikki to be good without risk, succumbing at times to a closed spin. Yet in this occasion of retelling—and therefore remembering—the event of her loss, her spirit is awakened again to the Good. She reembodies, through narration, her open take, surprising everybody by confessing it.

Through their narratives Bernard and Kathy disclose their personhood as gift. It's most often story that unveils personhood, because persons are found in and through relational events. Story is the most primary vehicle of such relational events. The young people see Bernard's and Kathy's personhood because they encounter their narratives through the embodied experience of their testimony.[5] It becomes an event of joy because, through revealed personhood, persons share in the lives of other persons. It becomes an experience of joy because it is an encounter with the living God who is the Good of persons in the union of joy. It is an experience of the living Christ, for the event of shared personhood through the cross takes us into the triune communion of God's own being, which has the ambiance of joy. The confession of their death experiences—Bernard's guilt and Kathy's broken heart—and the encounters within them are the substance of their open takes. The movements of cross to resurrection shape Bernard's and Kathy's open takes. But to understand how this can be, we have to step back and dig a little deeper into how identity and events are interrelated.

Identity and Events

As we said, we have our identity through events we identify with. Events are episodes, occurrences, or happenings in time and space. Yet most of my life, like 90 percent of it, consists of episodes, occurrences, and happenings that make little impact on my self-definition. For instance, today I'll go for a run, talk with a friend, walk the dog, listen to a podcast, and get the washing machine fixed. These happenings are inseparable from cultural practices, so in a real way they shape me, but in the end they offer little direct impact on my felt sense of *this is me*. If the whole of my life is only a bundle of occurrences and happenings, and none of them become something more, it'll be hard for me to form a distinct sense of who I am and develop a clear identity. I'll be rudderless, just a cork bobbing in a meaningless sea of episodes, happenings, and occurrences. Alone, these episodes, happenings, and occurrences offer little to my felt sense of who I am, because a week from today most of these occurrences and happenings will be foggy at best, disappearing into the passing of time, leaving little to no direct impact on my interpretation of my being.

Yet at some point there will be an episode, occurrence, or happening that becomes an *event*. What turns an episode, occurrence, or happening into an event is concern.[6] And this turn is initiated through some evaluation next to

5. I'm pushing on the edges of Amanda Hontz Drury's wonderful book *Saying Is Believing: The Necessity of Testimony in Adolescent Spiritual Development* (Downers Grove, IL: IVP Academic, 2015).

6. Concern has something to do with feel and emotion. Robert Roberts says, "I have proposed that emotions are concern-based construals, and I regard this proposal as an example of Christian psychology. . . . So an emotion is a way of 'seeing' things, when this 'seeing' is grounded in

goods, or even the Good. When I become concerned with the meaning of an episode, occurrence, or happening, moved to reflect on it and interpret it and therefore strongly evaluate it,[7] the occurrence or happening has the potential to become an event.[8]

But an important final step is needed—and with what we've said above, you should be able to guess it. Pushed by concern and strong evaluation,[9] I'm moved consciously or unconsciously to shape the happening into a story. As a matter of fact, it's not as sequential as I've just described it. I can give an occurrence concern and strong evaluation only by beginning to give it some narrative shape.[10] In other words, if one of these happenings is to become an event, it will have to encounter me in such a way that it becomes a story—because stories often link to other parts of my narrative sense of myself. So an event, then, is always narratable to others or to ourselves, either consciously

---

a concern; and a concern is a disposition to have a range of emotions." *Spiritual Emotions: A Psychology of Christian Virtues* (Grand Rapids: Eerdmans, 2007), 11–12.

7. Strong evaluation is essential to Taylor's position, though he confirms in a response at the end of his Festschrift that he recognizes that the word *evaluation* is confusing, giving a heavier conception of cognitive reasoning than he wishes to connote. See Taylor, "Charles Taylor Replies," in *Philosophy in an Age of Pluralism: The Philosophy of Charles Taylor in Questions*, ed. James Tully (Cambridge: Cambridge University Press, 1994), 213–56.

8. Even those events I refuse to remember, but which continue to exist behind my back, work this way. My refusal to remember them affirms my concern about them. I'm so concerned that I wish not to remember this or that event; I've stuck it down somewhere deep in my subconscious because of its heavy concern. I've strongly evaluated it and have chosen at some deep subconscious level to ignore it rather than to story it for others to see, know, and share in. What can make this so painful, and sometimes debilitating, is that the refusal to acknowledge or even remember an event keeps us from sharing that story with others. As a result, the negative (traumatic) event tells secret stories to the self that the self cannot be loved, known, or cared for. It is only after storying the event that we can find some healing—hence the importance of all sorts of psychological therapies.

9. Taylor explains strong evaluation further: "I have spoken of these strong evaluations as assessments, but they are anchored in feelings, emotions, aspirations; and could not motivate us unless they were. Such are our moral and aesthetic intuitions about given acts and possibilities, our remorse or sense of worthiness, our longings to be good, noble, pure, or whatever. In giving the strongly evaluative assessment, we are giving the import to which the feeling relates. Our moral revulsion before an act of spite is our affective awareness of the act as having an import of moral baseness." *Human Agency and Language: Philosophical Papers 1* (Cambridge: Cambridge University Press, 1999), 67.

10. Most often this narrative shaping is done with others. Someone with cognitive impairments is likewise pulled into the deep narrative shape of concern and evaluation. The caregiver and the one cared for create a deep bond through narration, concern, and evaluation. This is part of the great breakthrough of Jean Vanier: those living with a disability and those who befriend them are transformed, for we're given new identity events through a new narrative of caring and being cared for. Our actions take on new concern, and we evaluate the meaning of our lives in a very different way.

spoken or subconsciously denied,[11] but never without it being in the shape of some story we tell others or ourselves.[12]

Kathy, for instance, has a handful of events she identifies with that become her identity. To know her—or, more profoundly, to share in her life and encounter her being—you, too, have to experience these events. The event of her promotion to vice president or the event of Nikki's birth is a part (a sentence, paragraph, or even chapter) of the story of who she is. And you can only share in her life as you share in these events. And you can only share in these past events, encountering Kathy's being, by entering a story (as we'll see, story moves across time, and we have our being, *Sein*, always in time, *Zeit*). But you can share in these events only through Kathy's free gift of narrating them to you, telling you the story of who she is. She unveils her identity not by abstractly answering the question *What is your identity?* or even *Who are you?* but by telling stories of events with which she identifies.

Youth ministry hack: this is why it works much better in small groups to ask a young person to tell you about their most meaningful accomplishment or saddest day, and then to ask them to tell who they are. No one can really answer the question of who he or she is without telling you stories of events—unless a person has completely given himself over to the pursuit of performative recognition and has branded himself so extensively that, when asked, he can launch into a pitch like "I'm the playboy gangsta that you better recognize." Rather, to know a (young) person, we should gently invite her to narrate her events. When asked about the saddest day she's experienced, she'll confess an event: "My saddest day was when my grandma died. We were really close because my mom left when I was eight. My grandma was such a strong woman; I hope I'm like her when I grow up." These are two very different statements, the second a rich narrative—so rich you can't help but have follow-up questions, wanting more of the story. It unveils and invites the hearer into the events that this young person identifies with, producing a moment of shared personhood that most often is felt as being surprised by joy.

11. This way of claiming the authority of Scripture stands in contrast to the positivistic scientific perspective of conservative Protestantism. The Bible is authoritative because God is an event. As an event, God can be known only in and through narratives of God's acts in time and space. Therefore, the Bible is essential in recording and telling the narrative events of God's being. Hearing these stories, we too are invited into an identity event, having our own identity, in and through these events of God's action that are narratives, transferred to our own being.

12. Clearly some stories are fundamentally false, and we too often live out of false stories. This, in part, is what it means to be living in a sinful/broken world.

The Practicality of Events

Events, then, are concrete and practical. Because events must be narratable, they have to be located in time and space. The stories of the events that shape me, and that in turn I tell to others as the discourse that gives me my identity, must transpire in concrete places and times. Other people can only share in stories that are set within our "given" practical experience in time and space. When we ask the young person, "What is an event of your saddest moment?" she stories the concrete experience of her grandmother—her care for her and the pain of losing her in Hudson, Wisconsin, on July 17, 2018. The hearer can identify with these practical realities because they happened at a specific time and in a specific place. Imagine that instead the young person said, "My saddest moment was when my brother made us all sit on the front steps, and he was shaking and crying because the house was filling up with bugs and water was pouring out all the windows. That was so sad." The hearer would have no idea how to understand this story, no way of making sense of the supposed event, not sure if it really was an event because the hearer could not be sure whether it actually happened. Such a story would resist someone sharing in it. The only way such a tale could become an event is if it were interpreted.

In other words, dream states and LSD trips (Paul would even say speaking in tongues, 1 Cor. 14) can't be identity events, unless they are significantly interpreted and therefore translated back into our practical experience in time and space. Someone must turn the weird happening into an interpreted story that correlates with our being in the world. The young person might instead have said, "The summer I turned seven, my four-year-old brother got very ill, and his fever was so high that he hallucinated, and I didn't understand what was happening to him, and I thought he was dying. After the ambulance and the hospital, he would be OK, but that moment on the front steps was the saddest and most scared I have ever been."

To take this one step further, it isn't enough to just be practically in time and space. Nonlanguage animals, like cats and koala bears, too, are bound in time and space. They have *Sein* (being), to use the German word. But they have no *Dasein*, to use the famous word of the twentieth-century German philosopher Martin Heidegger. Cats and koalas have no real sense of being *there* (*da* means "there" in German—you just shove words together in German), because cats and koalas have no language, as far as we know, to form narratives.[13] They are not the kind of animals who tell stories. And therefore they have no events to identify with that might produce an identity, born from concern and strong evaluation, to state *this is me*.

13. This is why Heidegger says language is the house of being.

It is humans' unique ability to narrate our concerns and strong evaluations inside a particular happening, right *da*, while *being there*, that gives us the capacity—the necessity—to experience some of our happenings and occurrences as events in a story: "Everything changed when my grandma died." I may not always be fully conscious of all events that direct my identity, but if they direct it in any way, they have some links—sometimes hidden links—to the narratives in which I live out my life (this is why psychoanalysis and other psychological therapies can be very helpful; they help us consciously spot the hidden story out of which we are living). For I'm the kind of being who has *Dasein*. I'm the kind of creature who cares about my *Sein*, making me the kind of being who needs to story my happenings into events that shape me and describe me.

Narrating and Interpreting Identity Events

So to have an identity is to have some episodes, happenings, or occurrences become events I identify my being with, through storying these events into an interpretation of myself and the reality my self exists in. Even with this said, because of the necessity of interpretation, not all events are equal. Some may be interpreted as more essential to my self-definition than others. Some events are weightier than others. For instance, the birth of Nikki presses in more on Kathy's being than the event of the day she was promoted to vice president. The birth of Nikki is more central to Kathy's identity, evidenced by her deeper concern and evaluation and the overall detail of the narrative. Usually, the weightier the event (and therefore the more it demands interpretation), the more we identify with it, making it more central to our identity. The more Kathy identifies with the event of her infertility and Nikki's birth, the more the event not only becomes a major piece of her identity but also shapes her view of reality itself.

And this gets us back to open takes and closed spins. Narratable events forged through concern and strong evaluation can arise nowhere else than in time and space, in a direct lived and practical history.[14] This concrete location of events compels us to always be in interpretation, seeking for meaning. We can do this event-interpreting through an open take or closed spin, recognizing some mystery and transcendence in the unfolding of these events as we narrate them. Or not.

The deeper the concern, which leads to a stronger evaluation, the more detailed the story—and usually, the more heavily the event presses in on our

14. Again the connection to *Dasein*.

being. This pressing often leads to deeper interpretation of the event. The more someone interprets an event, I contend, the more it starts to crack things open. The event pleads to be interpreted through an open take. One reason middle-class people may be skeptical about transcendence, and default to a kind of functional naturalism, is that there are few spaces in our overly busy, exhausted lives to rest and to tell the stories of the events that make us.[15] We're too tired to be vulnerable enough to share these events that make us (enter Brené Brown). We're too tired to let these stories breathe and be interpreted. Yet when we do, we find that closed spins of those crucial events are inadequate. The more an event is narrated, the more it asks to be interpreted through an open take that reaches for transcendence.

As we narrate to others the events that we most identify with, we start to see connections and revelations that lead us more and more to open takes of reality. We can know reality only by experiencing it in and through the events we narrate as central to shaping us. If, in community, I'm invited to be brave enough to share the hidden, narratable events of a death experience, having others experience me through it, it will be nearly impossible for me to spin things closed. Telling my death experience to others who compassionately and empathically hear it, sharing in me through it, will be a concrete lived experience of transcendence.

When Kathy confesses her death experience, sharing the story of this event she so deeply identifies with, and how a new possibility comes from it, she can't help but have an open take on reality. Narrating the event of the death experience, having others share in it, opens her to see God's act within it. J is developing a youth ministry, right here in the hospital waiting room, that is not only forming the faith of young people but, in turn, forming the faith of the adults. This formation happens not through J's sheer talent but within the space to narrate such events and interpret them with and for the young people. When Kathy tells her story, she receives a gift: an experience of shared personhood that opens her to the mysterious reality of transcendence, calling her deeper into transformation.

Transforming Events

Transformation comes in and through the narrating of such identity events. For instance, turning to Bernard and his loss of his daughter, there is almost no way to live through an occurrence of this magnitude without concern and strong evaluation, which coalesce into a story about one's

15. Other than podcasts, which is why they've become so popular, and storytelling events like The Moth, which are so meaningful to many people.

being. Bernard loved that little girl (concern) and hates himself for not being there (strong evaluation), telling himself over and over again the story of his failure. He wishes he could escape the story, but the event of her loss presses deeply into his being, causing his being to identify with her loss even over against his will. This narrative of her loss surrounds and chokes him. Because this event overflows with meaning and the human being makes sense of meaning through story, Bernard can't help but be haunted by this story.

Even so, because this story chokes him, he can't tell it. He can't tell the story of this event he so deeply identifies his being with, because he fears the story will condemn him. It itches to come out, tormenting him like the ticking clock in the wall in John Bellairs's novel.[16] But he worries that to tell it will necessitate the negation of his being. The story haunts him, which pushes him deeper into drug use. The drugs are a strategy to escape the storied event of his transgression, which presses in on his being, defining his self (it then is no surprise that AA is about repeatedly narrating the stories that haunt you, and this has been shown to be powerfully therapeutic). Instead of bearing the negation, Bernard decides to slowly negate himself, hit by hit.

Bernard needs something from outside him to free him to tell this story and therefore have his personhood embraced as a new event. He's caught in his shame, unable to free himself. Facing the possibility that telling the story might negate him, he needs another to invite him to bravely narrate his experience.

Right inside this narratable experience of failure and betrayal that Bernard wished not to speak of, he has another happening, the potential of a new story line to add to the narrative of his failure. Bernard is shaken from sleep by a man who says, "Bernard, your baby girl is with me. Peace be with you." Having this second occurrence, Bernard can make sense of it in the logic of a closed spin or as an open take. It's logical, and even somewhat honest to the experience, for Bernard to assume he is only dreaming. Maybe it's all just a neurological misfire caused by the opiates.

Yet if he chooses the closed spin, the happening is stripped of meaning. What strips the meaning is that the closed spin upends the happening's narratability, therefore rendering its eventfulness counterfeit: "It was just a stupid dream." Rendering the event counterfeit makes it useless to have an identity impact, never freeing Bernard from negative evaluation by answering his concern. This new happening, then, thanks to the closed spin, is flattened under

16. See *The House with a Clock in Its Wall* (New York: Puffin Books, 1973).

the concern and evaluation of the past event, leaving Bernard with only a destructive self-definition and more reasons to get high.[17]

The occurrence discerned through an open take does something very different. Most primarily the openness allows for the possibility that the occurrence might become an event. There is no guarantee. Bernard might be open to the possibility but find it has no connection to his concerns, evaluating it as just a weird glitch, with no need to connect it with a fuller story. At a pub or campfire, he might remember and tell it to a few friends: "I swear I saw a figure in a crack house once." The listeners would all be shocked. It would be a great ghost story but lack any possibility of being an identity event. It might pry their closedness open for a minute; some drunk guy might even say, "I totally believe in crap like that." But it more than likely would never reach the level of transformation: its occurrence wouldn't seem to press into Bernard's being, change the way he's in the world, or connect with his concern and strong evaluation. Someone might even say, "You don't seem like the kind of person [i.e., you don't have an identity] that's had something like that happen to you."

But, of course, this isn't what happens to Bernard. Rather, the experience addresses directly a concern (his love for his daughter) and strong evaluation ("I'm worthless for letting her down"), making it feel ever more real, affecting his being-in-the-world enough for him to stumble into the Tuesday morning Bible study. There Bernard is given a space to tell the story that haunts him, to vulnerably feel the grace to articulate the tale he worries will negate him in shame. When he tells this story, his shame is held by the older women in the group, and they invite him to tell more. And the more he does, confessing his concern and strong evaluation in and through his death experience, the more the event with which he identifies is open to the possibility of transcendence. The more he interprets that event with the women, the more he sees amazing providence, care, and the possibility of forgiveness. Through his narration, his broken person is shared in by the personhood of these women. His identity is transformed—he is now in Christ—because in the confession of this storied event, Jesus will make Bernard's events part of Jesus's own story, giving his resurrection humanity to Bernard. And Bernard believes it's true because these older women, in this musty church basement, embody it. They identify

17. The logic I'm sketching out here, while not necessarily intending it, connects with Gabor Maté's research on addiction. In his important book *In the Realm of Hungry Ghosts: Close Encounters with Addiction* (Berkeley: North Atlantic Books, 2010), he explores how drug addiction has little to do with the chemical constitution of the drug but mostly (giving him my language) with isolating events that press in on our persons, leading us to seek the escape of the drug rather than bear the loneliness induced by unshared painful events.

with him through this narrative of a death experience, manifesting in their presence new life—new identity.

Identity Event: The Second Way

These stories, in being told, become an identity event in a second way. Through listening to the told tales of open takes, young people are given narrative lenses through which to see their own lives. And this seeing has the potential to stretch wide, inviting young people to use these very stories, and the experience of encountering them (as an encounter with personhood), as events of their own identity. The age of authenticity asserts that a high (for some the highest) good is to be original. The ethic of the age of authenticity claims that every human being should find his or her own unique way of being human. Yet too often this drive for self-determined uniqueness obscures the fact that we always use narratives from outside of us, even other people's stories, to form our identities. (A superfan of an athlete usually is so because the fan is not only moved by the athlete's skill but is also using the athlete's stories of his or her own events to provide narratives for the fan's own identity.)

There is actually no one, superfan or not, who *doesn't* live in and through someone else's stories (hence, the big business of Ancestry.com). There is no human being who is so original, so free, such an Übermensch, that he or she doesn't live out of the stories of others' events. There simply is no way to be the kind of deeply interpretive animals we are without leaning on forms of shared cultural narratives—for example, to understand our world. This fact is what makes our present society so fraught, thrusting us into culture wars. Different communities have very different narrative interpretations of happenings, identifying with different stories and using the narratives of these events to claim their own *this is me*. We are the kind of beings that thirst for stories to make sense of our world.

We are such language animals who have our being through narrative that we are always porous to stories getting inside us. They seep into us from everywhere. We're deeply affected by our cultural locale, because every cultural milieu is formed by layers of competing, contrasting, complementary, and concealed narratives that leak into our beings, shaping our concern and strong evaluations. The reality of these seeping stories means that if parents are truly concerned for their child's identity, involving them in a youth ministry like J's will be more impactful for an identity than another *thing*.

Yet most middle-class parents, even churchgoing ones, sense that this is too risky. What feels threatening is that they know somewhere deep down that the more their child is exposed to such direct stories, the more they're exposed to open takes. And the more they're exposed to the open takes of transcendence, the more receptive they are to being shifted radically off the track of the *summum bonum* of happiness and toward a very different conception of a flourishing life, maybe one even closer to Francis of Assisi! Better, then, to stick with a youth ministry that will settle for just a youth group with a lead counselor of fun at the helm, keeping youth ministry as just another *thing*. And better yet to invest in the closed-spin (or at least open-take-ignoring) activities of basketball, piano, and debate. Though these *things* lack the depth of narrative to produce open takes that might transform, that's precisely why they're worth it. They feel much safer.

Yet when youth ministry creates space for a community of storytelling, like J does, it become inextricably about identity, because our identities are inseparable from narrative events. Experiencing the story of another's events can become our own event. In a youth ministry like J's, our identities can be directly affected by another's events because the events powerfully encounter us as "pure" story. Hearing Bernard's and Kathy's open takes has an impact on young peoples' identity because it comes as pure narrated event.

By "pure," I mean it comes to them directly—intentionally—as a story of an event that now, in hearing, becomes an event for young people themselves. (This is what makes story so much more powerful in forming identity than the *thing*, as we described in chapters 5 and 7.) The young people in the waiting room experience the event of hearing about Bernard's and Kathy's events. And the location is part of the event too: being in the hospital waiting room (being there, *Dasein*)[18] is a kind of happening that demands a story. So the young people hearing Bernard's and Kathy's events is an event itself, within the event of sharing in the death experience of Lorena and her mom.

My point is that the events of another can be transferred directly to us. Encountering the story of another's event, and that person's open take on it, can be as powerfully transformational as experiencing an event of transcendence ourselves. Or we could say it this way: hearing the narrative of an event like Kathy's can become for us an event that presses in on our own being, forming our identity around it.

As a matter of fact, a reverberating reality occurs in the telling of this kind of event. The more Kathy shares it, the more she identifies with it, further shaping her own identity. But to tell it, she needs others to experience her

---

18. It was the *Dasein*, the being there, that led Bernard and Kathy to share their stories in the first place. If they weren't there, having a sense of their being there, more than likely neither would have shared.

doing so. As these young people hear her story, they identify with it, confessing that it affects their own self-definition. And going one step further, as the young people are affected by Kathy's story, it reverberates back to Kathy and adds to the story's "eventfulness" for her, encouraging her to identify with the event even further because she can now see it even more as an experience of transcendence, for it has connected her personhood to the personhood of these young people as a tangible feeling of joy.[19] Again, we see that youth ministry can have an impact on the faith formation of adults by inviting them to share the story of their events, giving the adults the gift of young people as the audience to receive and interpret their stories.

Bernard and Kathy reveal their being when they tell their stories. This revealing of being through story is why J feels like it's a holy moment, like the group is treading on the Good (it is in this moment that she finds herself saying, "Youth ministry is for joy"). Through the storied confession of this event, a place of shared being is created, as a new event. Bernard's and Kathy's events, shared through story, press in on the young people's own being, impacting their being by moving the young people into concern and strong evaluation. But in these moments of confessed events around the death of a child and miscarriage, how can J see joy?

In chapter 12, I explained that you can discern joy over happiness by joy's ability to produce a narrative that bears burdens. Happiness has a much harder time rising distinctly above all the other episodes, happenings, and occurrences in my life. Happiness is most often just a positive vibe painted on the surplus of episodes, happenings, and occurrences that wash over me. It's of course much better to have all these happenings painted with happiness than not.

After all, to extend the analogy, most of our lives are just waves of episodes, happenings, and occurrences. Better to have them all be happy, lapping waves than choppy, rough seas. Too often this is the core concern of middle-class parents. They want their child to be happy within the constant current of episodes, happenings, and occurrences. But none of these happy occurrences can actually produce a meaningful identity, because they're not weighty enough to press in on the child's being and leave a distinct identity mark that would open them to rich meaning in the world. They're not weighty enough because they are only happy happenings and not events that

---

19. I have no space to delve into this in the text, but there is also the possibility that in telling your story many times you can begin to feel disconnected from it. This happens often to traveling preachers and speakers. But I contend that one of the reasons this happens, and even leads some to be cynical, is that they are not in community with those to whom they repeatedly tell this narrative. Therefore they lack the direct and continued experience of how the story impacts the *Dasein* of others, allowing the retelling to separate itself from the teller's *Dasein*.

necessitate story. Joy, unlike happiness, is the feeling of an event. Joy is the feel of being directly connected to being, through a communion of narration, given to you as a Good gift.

And this is so because there is no experience that becomes an event that is not storied and held in some person-to-person encounter. Story is a kind of mysterious time machine that brings past events into the now of encounter. The direct personal event of Jesus can meet our being; he is unveiled to us in and through our sharing in the storied personhood of another. Because an identity event is always storied, it can unveil being across time. And where persons proclaim Jesus to persons, in and through a ministry of loving care, Jesus is concretely present. So we are disciples, ones who follow the person of Jesus, when we identify our being with the events (life, death, and resurrection) of Jesus's personhood. As we identify deeply with these events, the shape of these events informs our own being.

Coated Events

Kathy's event can do this because all events, to be events, must be storied. Events, by definition, must be coated in narrative. Even when it's my own event, which I experience directly, it needs to be coated in narrative for it to affect my being and shape my identity (*Dasein* needs narrative, for we are beings in time who have the distinct ability to bring the past into the present, to direct a future). It's the event's narrative necessity that allows it, like a gelcap pill, to quickly reach to the depth of identity. What makes events so potent is that their narrative necessity allows them to press themselves as markedly into the being of the one who hears about the event as one who directly experiences it. The story of event makes even past events continually alive, affecting our being through narration.

It's the narrative necessity of events that makes them deeply transferable. Hearing your event can call my own being into such identification that it can transform me, giving a new narrative shape to my own being-in-the-world. Think of Paul. He experienced the event of Jesus's arrival on the road to Damascus, thrusting him into a death experience through judgment and blindness ("Saul, Saul . . . I am Jesus, whom you are persecuting," Acts 9:4–5). Paul so deeply identifies with this event that it recasts his identity. He is no longer Saul but Paul, transformed and given new direction, new purposeful action in the world—but only after he can narrate this experience to Ananias.[20] (In the hospital waiting room, the young people play the important

---

20. I have a particular interest in Ananias. I think he plays a very important part in being hearer of Paul's narrative. For my discussion of this story, see part 2 of *Faith Formation in a*

role of Ananias to Bernard and Kathy, and the young people are ministered to as they minister to Bernard and Kathy by giving concern to their events, evaluating them, and therefore opening their own being to be affected—even transformed—by them.)

After narrating his event to Ananias, Paul preaches over and again about the event of his encounter with the living Jesus, narrating it alongside the story of the apostles and prophets. Paul goes first to the Jews, linking the narrated event of his encounter with Jesus with the story of Israel, inviting those who hear him to encounter this same Jesus by identifying with his event of encounter. They, too, can be *in* Christ, by identifying their own being with the event of Jesus's crucifixion, in and through Paul's own event of cross and resurrection on the road to Damascus, and in Judas's house on the street called Straight.

Hearing or reading others' stories of how Jesus arrived to them can become for us a direct event of identifying our own being with Jesus. Paul tells his communities to share in Christ by sharing in his story, by encountering the presence of Jesus in and through this event of hearing about Paul's experience with Jesus on the Damascus Road. And in hearing this event, giving it concern and strong evaluation, this event can press into your own being too. Through story, the hearer, too, can identify with this event, having her own being in and through it. Through this story she, too, can meet the resurrected Christ with the same immediacy that Paul does.[21]

Interpreted Death Experiences

But we should be clear. To claim that story can move across time is *not* to lock our encounter with Jesus in some naturalistic narrative theory. We cannot meld God's agency with a psychological state or neurological reality. Rather, this movement of identification with event is also profoundly about God's own action. We identify our being with Jesus's own being (being in Christ) by identifying with Jesus's storied events of death and resurrection. This is how we're given Jesus's very being as our own.

But our events matter too.

The God revealed in Jesus Christ is a living God who, as living, has a story that we must identify with.[22] But also, because this God lives, this God identifies with *our* events. This God is a minister who acts. In other words, this God

---

Secular Age: Responding to the Church's Obsession with Youthfulness (Grand Rapids: Baker Academic, 2017).

21. Obviously not in the same form.

22. This is why the biblical text is normative and has authority. It delivers these stories we're invited to interpret next to our own events.

has events because this God acts in time and space—God identifies with the events of exodus and resurrection, as Robert Jenson says,[23] which causes these historical happenings to spill over with narrative meaning, able to be retold and reinterpreted to become events of our identity across time.

This means that because this is a God who identifies with events, ministering to us through them, this God upholds our own personhood by arriving in *our* events. God calls us to identify with the event of God's action, but never without God promising to identify God's very being with our own events too[24]—with Bernard's shame and Kathy's suffering. We're justified by faith alone, allowing our identity to be in Christ, because Jesus not only gives us his own events to identify with as a gift but also encounters us with the gift of his own personhood by identifying with our own events.

This is why the confession of the death experience, which moves us into a *theologia crucis*, is so important and central to the confession of the follower of Christ (the rich young ruler couldn't enter the event of the death experience and therefore couldn't follow Jesus). When Bernard and Kathy share the events of their own death experiences, which press in on their being, knowingly or not they offer a story of an event that God himself identifies with. Because the Father so deeply identifies with the event of the Son's death—and because the Son dies, ministered to so fully in death by the Spirit that the Son is made alive—at the center of God's very trinitarian being is the event of death that is overcome with new life.

This means that all those who confess a death experience as an event that presses in on their being, having their identity in and through an identification with a death experience, find that the God made known in Jesus Christ identifies with them. This God whose being is identified with the death experience of Jesus reaches out and ministers to all in a death experience, sharing in their event of failing a daughter or losing a child. In sharing the event of the death experience, God invites them to confess this death experience so the event might be storied and shared in, interpreted inside a community of loving persons who are the body of the resurrected Christ.[25] God gives both

23. Jenson builds his whole theology around this point. See particularly *The Triune Identity: God according to the Gospel* (Eugene, OR: Wipf & Stock, 2002), 21–102.

24. This identification is God's ministry. God identifies with our event for the sake of ministry, to minister to us, to be our shepherd. See my *Pastor in a Secular Age: Ministry to People Who No Longer Need a God* (Grand Rapids: Baker Academic, 2019) for much more on this.

25. Craig Dykstra offer helpful connections between these points and the church: "The importance of the church for the moral life is not just the fact that it might provide an arena for social role-taking. Its importance lies in its character as a particular community that holds particular convictions, stories, language, rituals, and forms of action in common. The church, through its scripture, tradition, and theology, provides a history and a moral and spiritual

Bernard and Kathy a new event of having their personhood shared in through the confession of a death experience to these young people. The union of personhood through the narration of an event of a death experience becomes a sacramental experience of sharing in the very being of God. J is showing us that youth ministry can be for a sacramental experience called joy, where persons are transformed through the narration of their events of loss.

This is what Paul sees and tells his community in Corinth: through the foolishness of confessed events of weakness and death, the power of God comes to transform our identities so deeply that we come to be in Christ. Not only do Jesus's events become our own identity, but our painful and broken events press in on God's being, becoming part of God's own story. So we are always in Christ as a deep ontological reality—because it is about *Dasein*—but never through the annihilation of our distinct selves. God embraces us in love because God has made space for our own events in God's own life, making our events profoundly, beautifully, and amazingly part of God's own story. We can share in the joy of the communion of the Trinity because our events, through the cross and resurrection, are made events in God's own story.

The confession of the death experience, then, does two things at once. It stories this event, allowing others to share in our being by sharing in this story that we so deeply identify with. We are ministered to by hearing this story. In turn, and second, it does more: it shapes our very identity in the form of Christ. The moments when Bernard and Kathy confess their death experiences are profound because they unveil their being in the shape of Jesus's own being: if they die like Christ, they will be made alive like him (Rom. 6:8). Confessing the death experience to the young people in the hospital waiting room becomes an event the community can claim God identifies with, allowing the story to be so deeply shared in that it impacts the identity of the young people who hear it. Experiencing the story of Bernard and Kathy's events has the power to shape the way the young people interpret their own being in the world.

Interpreting Open Takes

Interpretation is the key that turns a tale of a happening or occurrence into a heard event that can have an impact on my own identity. As we said above, happenings are made into events through concern, strong evaluation, and narration. This movement assumes the centrality of interpretation. As language animals who have *Dasein*, we're the kind of beings always in interpretation. But for a story to become an identity event for a hearer, the hearer must be

---

vocabulary." *Vision and Character: A Christian Educator's Alternative to Kohlberg* (New York: Paulist Press, 1981), 57.

invited into direct interpretation. We are always susceptible to stories, but clearly not every story we hear transforms us or even engages us, pressing in on our being, to potentially form our identity. Some tales we disregard (rightly or not) as not worthy of our attention. Other times we're too busy seeking other goods to discern if a story is an encounter with a call from the Good. We then allow some stories to pass into mere happenings, because we don't give them the attention of interpretation.

Interpretation is essential for these shared stories to become identity events for the young people who hear them. It isn't enough to just hear a story; through interpretation we must feel it, walking into it as a way of discerning the shape of reality and our inextricable location within it. The stories that do press in on our being, becoming a shared event, do so through some kind of interpretation.

For instance, Bernard tries hard to forget about his failure to be there for his daughter. He tries to obliterate this story, but he can't because it interprets his being. It haunts him because the narrative event interprets his being as a failure and betrayer. He tries to smother this interpretation, but it creeps out over his being, making assertions about the constitution of his being.

What is so powerful about Bernard's story for the young people, what keeps them from overlooking it, is that Bernard invites them directly into his interpretation, confessing how the story interprets him. But in doing so, he allows the young people the space to interpret it as well. Bernard lets the young people into the interpretation that he held after he received the phone call from his daughter's mother—that he was a failure who needed more drugs to forget this story and its condemning interpretation of his being. But he also invites the young people into his interpretation of the event of the man who shook him awake. The authority of his story rests solely in his interpretation and the way that interpretation has directed his being-in-the-world. "It must have really been Jesus," some young people contend. These young people confess this interpretation because it led Bernard to the Tuesday morning Bible study, giving him a direct experience of the Good in and through confession and communion.

This brings us back to open takes and closed spins. To have an open take or a closed spin is to be in interpretation. Both are forms of interpretation. But spins tend to regulate narratives for fear that a told story will knock things off-kilter. Closed spins are a form of interpretation that tends to eliminate connections and therefore flatten narratives. Open takes, however, embrace a story as the only way to communicate our open experience with reality, seeking connections across reality that we narrate to others. When Kathy says as a responsive interpretation to Bernard's story, "I had an experience like that," and "That's why I came today. Waiting rooms are holy places to me," we're drawn into connections. The connection of all these narratable events delivers a deep sense of openness, even a direct taste of transcendence. When these events are shared, new possibilities, eerie coincidences, and beautiful connections are recognized. And because of the richness of the narratives, these events invite young people to identify with them, to explore the story of their own identity around such open takes to transcendence that they now experience through Bernard's and Kathy's stories.

The young people are now on much more solid ground than fun can bring us to, for inside the telling of these tales of open takes, these young people have been made into interpreters and evaluators. They're empowered to ask, *Do I buy the story? How do I make sense of it? Is this a story of the Good? Does it open us up to the Good? How is God acting in it?*

The young people are invited not to swallow Bernard's and Kathy's open-take narratives whole but to interpret and evaluate them.[26] J is stumbling into something significant. Youth ministry isn't about giving young people the answer, prodding them to accept propositions. Instead, it asks them to interpret and evaluate narratives. As their pastor, J invites them to offer their interpretation to questions like, What do I think of Bernard's take? What do I think is going on in Kathy's story? How do I encounter Bernard's and Kathy's personhood as it's revealed through their takes? Could these stories be true? What else could explain them? What does this say about reality? What kind of world do we live in? What do these stories say about me, about what is good, about what is a good life? Is there something Good inside these stories that calls out to me? What could that mean? What does it want from me? Is my life directed toward the Good? And what kind of God is Good enough to come to Bernard and Kathy like this?[27]

Young people now are asked to do something deeply important: to wrestle directly with the shape of reality in and through the narrative claims of Bernard's and Kathy's humble stories. When takes are offered, they can never be offered as wielded clubs, using even supposedly open takes to shame people for lacking an experience like Bernard's or Kathy's. This is why the story

---

26. In the early chapters of *Human Agency and Language*, Taylor discusses the importance of both evaluation and interpretation.

27. A vexing question that reveals a part of our secular age is a mix of the theodicy and the "fairness" questions. For instance, someone hearing this story may be tempted to ask, "But why didn't God come to me like this? That isn't fair!" But this is a deeply modern problem that equates fairness with equality. Rather, these events, even if they happened directly to just one person, are for all people. That's why they're in narrative shape, to be given as a gift to the community. Before modernity, few people would need such stories to only be true if they themselves consumed the happening.

most often starts inside the death experience and is given to a community as an event of grace, as a gift.

As the young people hear Bernard's and Kathy's interpretations of their events of a death experience at the event of Lorena's sickness, they're invited themselves to enter the death experience (the cross) and interpret reality within it. It's in interpretation that these stories weigh heavily, able to press them into the being of those hearing them, and become identifying events of their own identity.

As J finishes her smoothie, this is just what she tells me. "This is what we do in the Waiting Room. We interpret stories. We help each other see our lives next to God's saving work. That's my main focus—not fun anymore, but to offer and invite young people to interpret stories alongside one another and the adults of the church. It all started in the waiting room; that's why I give so much credit to Bernard. He shared his story, and the young people started interpreting it. I tell people that we no longer do youth group but we do meet to interpret stories, to see our stories as part of God's story to save the world. One of the young people or an adult from the congregation shares a story, or I've even brought in stories from books and articles, once a film, and even sometimes stories from the Christian tradition, like Augustine. We talk about Augustine's story, all with the direct purpose of interpreting stories. I made a lot of mistakes at the beginning. There were a lot of Waiting Rooms that were me painfully babbling, and we've had a lot of nights of not-so-well-told stories. But as time has gone on, I've started to lay out a biblical text as *the* interpretive lens to use to look at the stories we've heard and now need to interpret. I've grown through a lot of trying and retrying. But my failing and using bad stories encourages others to try."

She continues, "Youth ministry, for us, is about actively interpreting stories, seeing our stories as part of God's working in the world. Young people aren't just receivers of something; they must be actively engaged in interpretation, in being detectives of reality. We now even have some young people who are hardcore atheists showing up, because they to want to interpret our stories with us. We're happy to have them; we're all just here to interpret these stories. But we're unapologetic that we interpret these stories as a part of God's own story. This is how we start forming our identities in Christ and seeking a good life. It gives us a well of meaning. It becomes an experience of mystery. I was a little scared at first because I wasn't in control, but it's changed all of us. We've started to do confirmation this way—telling parents that confirmation is about interpreting the core stories of our faith, the central stories of our tradition, inviting young people to wrestle with them, interpreting them next to their own story."

J tells me that she now sees her responsibility not as creating a youth group of fun but as providing a space for these stories to be interpreted, inviting young people into being open takers. It's only through an open take that we can seek the Good. We need an open take to reality itself to seek the kind of Good that turns death into life. This turning death into life is the very drama of God's act to save. Our stories start with the confession of a death experience, because we seek to interpret our stories inside the drama of God's saving action.

As we stand to leave the smoothie shop, I'm secretly wishing J would offer to get me one of those Waiting Room T-shirts. I discard my cup, thinking about how teenage atheists are being drawn to J's midweek meeting to wrestle with the meaning of a good life next to the drama of God's moving to bring life out of death. Dialogue around the narration of open takes seems like an interesting and appropriate approach to evangelism in the age of authenticity.

Yet these thoughts get me thinking more about discipleship. Youth ministry is for joy, because youth ministry seeks the Good in and through the narratives of open takes shaped around cross and resurrection, interpreting our stories next to the drama of God's act to save. But what about practice? We are language animals who can only have an identity through story. But these stories are always directed toward some moral horizon, some seeking for the good. We can't live without some *summum bonum*. If culturally we've slowed young people down to make sure they never derail but stay securely on tracks toward the *summum bonum* of happiness, how do we challenge this? After all, none of the parents I interviewed went to a webinar on making happiness your family's highest good. Rather, it was through unconscious cultural practices that they not only were placed securely on these happiness tracks themselves, but also slowed down the growing up of their children to make sure they never risked derailment.

So I ask J, "What about practice? Do you have a place in your ministry for the classic Christian practices?"

"Oh yeah," responds J as she grabs her keys and moves toward her car. "First Monday of May. Come check it out. Email me."

Fifteen

Holding Vigil

Youth Ministry and Cruciform Practices

MAY

'm late. I hate being late, but I couldn't help it. I'm ambushed by bumper-to-bumper traffic. I left after rush hour but forgot that in Minnesota we jokingly have two seasons, bone-chilling winter and road construction. May feels too early for the dawn of road construction season, but here it is—94 westbound is down to one lane. This means the forecast is a harsh one for the coming summer of roadwork.

I don't do well with traffic. I'm an impatient person with an active imagination. Sitting caged and captured on a freeway has a particular way of getting under my skin, leading me to play tortuous imaginative games about where I'd be if the paved river were free-flowing. Frozen in place, I get restless and annoyed, quickly becoming unforgiving, unkind, prideful, and downright misanthropic. I spend the boxed-in gridlock yelling at all the stupid people who nose their way in front of me and all those dumb city officials who think it's a wise idea to close lanes on a Monday evening.

When I get to J's church, I feel intoxicated with tension. I'm sure if someone got close enough, they could smell it on my breath. I bet I'd blow a 1.0 on the annoyance Breathalyzer, a solid reading of "jerk." But my tension quickly turns to confusion, even anxiety. All is quiet in the church. I walk around, looking for J's group. But there is no sign of them. Everything is still, at peace. I check the calendar on my phone and then reread J's email.

Yes, it's May 3; I'm where I'm supposed to be. Armed with that razor-thin confidence, I try downstairs.

Surprised, I find about forty people lying and sitting in stillness on the carpeted floor of the all-purpose room. It looks at first glance like some are sleeping. Others are breathing in deeply, and still others are staring at a projection of a fourth-century icon. This is what I was looking for, what I was swearing my way across town to encounter.

J had explained in her email that on the first Monday of every month the youth host a vigil. The kids actually call it The Vig, texting each other with "R u goin to The Vig?" At first J just called it Vigil, but the young people started adding *The* in front. I like the *The*—it has a sense of reverence, and it should as a vigil. This is a set-aside time for people to comport their bodies and minds toward the open take of the transcendent God, who breaks in to identify with their events, giving them the event of God's action as the story of their own being.

In the same email, J told me that she called it Vigil not only because they would hold this time to wait, using classic Christian practices to do so, but also because she wanted to remind herself that she was done trying to compete for young people's time and energy. She wasn't willing to go back to her pre-hospital-waiting-room paranoia, anxious about getting kids to show, hoping they'd choose youth group over soccer. She wasn't going to allow particularly this gathering to just be lumped together with all the other *things* that young people do, just another option on the menu of activities. Rather, this would be a time of vigil—that would be its purpose, period. It would continue the experience of the hospital waiting room, when adults and young people gathered to wait, bent their bodies toward the hope of God's future, and experienced the joy of carrying each other's burdens. Their waiting was an active engagement in prayer and silence.

Now in the church basement they'd continue to hold a space, interceding for others, by comporting their bodies to the coming of God. Whoever showed up would do so for the sake of others, for the sake of offering a ministry of intercession to all those who couldn't be there, led out to follow God's calling in other places. The point was to remember our need for each other. Those seeking happiness as their *summum bonum* overlook how deeply they're connected and in need of others. The Vig would offer distinct ways to both remember and practice being directed toward the *summum bonum* of the Good in and through following Jesus. Even if you couldn't be present, if you were busy with other activities, you were aware that others were interceding for you, upholding you—reminding you, even as you were busy in your *thing*, to seek the Good.

J explains that it was no longer about missing something; that wasn't why a young person should come. The point wasn't to get young people to show up. The point was to help them live out their faith in the world, to discern Jesus's calling to follow him in the world, to follow him as they seek the Good. This time of gathering at The Vig was for supporting and directing those not present, holding vigil for them to seek the *summum bonum* of the Good.

As a matter of fact, as I sit and take in my first moment of The Vig, I quickly spot another projector scrolling names. The names appear to be mostly those of young people, but not exclusively. Lines read, "Denard, Lacrosse Regionals," "Karla, preparing for finals," "Ted, traveling for work," "Marcie, at her dad's this week." These people who can't be present are not absent but drawn to the center of The Vig. We're called to pray specifically for them, asking for wisdom as they seek the Good, following Jesus's call. Their absence isn't scorned and their presence is not forgotten (out of sight equals out of mind is as true at church youth groups as anywhere). Rather, the point of The Vig is to uphold and embrace those called out in the world, as the community puts them on their mind, praying for them, asking God to lead them in conforming their lives to the story of Jesus in these very moments that have led them beyond the community.

Those who are present intercede for them, praying for them as they're out busy in other activities. And to do this for each other is Good; it is to seek a different *summum bonum* than happiness. It is Good for those busy young people prepping for a test to know that others are praying for them, reminding them even in this moment to reach for an open take, seeking what is Good. The point, J says, is not to compete for young people's time but to wrap them in intercession wherever they go. It's become an amazing practice that connects them. Every few weeks J gets a short text story that keeps her relationally connected to the young people. They text and say, "For The Vig—super stressed, big test," "For The Vig—depressed, breaksville with boyfriend, try to make it, but maybe too sad." And in the last few months J's even gotten texts like, "For the Waiting Room—amazing thing happened with friend on hockey trip, need to tell the story." If a few weeks go by and J hasn't seen a young person or received an update for The Vig, she'll reach out. So the gatherings that anchor J's ministry are the weekly Waiting Room and The Vig, monthly.

As I take my place in The Vig, I allow the silence to meet my hot tension and red burning anxiety. Neither are a match for the gentle power of the stillness. My tension is smoothed as I'm held by the silence, like a lonely infant finding herself back in her mother's arms. Then a wave of peace meets me. Washed by it, my anxiety is carried away. The silence re-forms, calling into question

negative emotions and practices that accompanied my stuckness in gridlock.
The silence and stillness lead me to wonder why I was in such a hurry. *Did it
really matter?* In the silence I can hear the ever-quiet but poignant whisper of
the Good. The stillness starts to challenge all my supposed goods that lead
me to see happiness as my *summum bonum*.

Taking a breath, I look further around the room. If I had to guess, I'd say
about twenty-five of the forty are young people, mostly high school students,
but I see at least a few smaller children. The other fifteen or so are adults. J is
indeed done with youth group but is doing amazing youth ministry. Both the
Waiting Room and The Vig are youth-centric, even youth led, but necessitate
the participation of adults and children. I'm not speaking of a need for adults
to volunteer and help with the program. It's the very personhood of the adults
that's needed. Their stories, intercession, and intentional participation in the
practices are vital, alongside the ownership and investment of the young people.

Silence, Death, and the Good

The stillness is my friend, a salve of peace and perspective. But I'm unpracticed, and after just a few short minutes I become painfully aware of this.
The silence is soothing at first, like cold water running over the burn of my
hot traffic-induced frustration, but soon it becomes heavy. My impatience is
back, and now it's directed toward silence itself. It starts to hurt, like running
cold water over a burn for too long. But the group doesn't display any of the
jitteriness I'm feeling. They've been doing The Vig for over a year now. J tells
me later that the length of silence has grown, month by month.

As we debrief my experience over lunch the following Wednesday, J says,
"Both the young people and the adults are super busy. The rest, solitude, and
silence have been so life-giving to them. There are times in the year when the
juniors and seniors just come and sleep; they lie down and fall right to sleep.
Some even arrive in PJs."

I laugh. But J's got a much larger point to make. "I'd say it's more beautiful
than funny. Here are these kids in a community who allow themselves to be vulnerable, to sleep as the adults of this community watch over them and intercede
for them, holding vigil, lifting their fatigue to God." J's right. It is beautiful.

She has more to say. "But I think the silence does something else. It gets
us all—parents, young people, and others—to ask, 'For what?' We use the
silence to interpret. We ask: What is the point of all this busyness? What is so

good about these kids being up all night trying to get into this or that school? Is getting into the right college really going to make you happy? I mean, is being happy really the point of life? What is a good life? The silence seems to shift our view of things."

In this small but profound way, J is inviting people to shift off the Epicurean tracks and onto a form of eudaimonic tracks. As with the ancients, this happens through practice. But as we'll see, like Luther's *summum bonum*, it is the Good gift of Jesus Christ. The Vig is about the practice of cruciform virtue.[1]

As J explains how the silence itself condemns the group's false *summum bonum*, I realize she's right; it's no giggling matter. The silence itself is participation in a death experience. It's a virtue, but a cruciform one. The silence is a death experience that can open us up to the Good. It can call us into questioning what we've been living for, getting us in touch with our own finitude. J tells me that the silence has grown from five to forty-five minutes over the last fifteen months. The silence is the embodied shape of narrative that starts in a death experience, that moves from cross to resurrection. Being still is a virtue that isn't necessarily built on your own skill or holiness, but rather encourages you to face the boredom and stillness that preaches your need for salvation. It opens you to longing for the gift of grace. The silence is the placing of the cross as the central experience of the community.

But in the moment in which I'm experiencing the silence, these important thoughts are far from me. Because I'm unpracticed, it's hard to contemplate my finitude. I'm unable to bear the boredom enough to breathe in this small but real death experience. I keep trying to pull myself off the cross, to avoid the death experience and look for other goods to distract me. I'm unable to enter death to experience a taste of the transformation of new life, to bend my body and mind toward the Good.

1. For a significant project that draws together Luther, practice, and youth ministry, see Bård Eirik Hallesby Norheim, *Practicing Baptism: Christian Practices and the Presence of Christ* (Eugene, OR: Pickwick, 2014). Here is a helpful example of his work: "In the context of ministry this difference may be important in relation to how the experience of suffering and (radical) evil is approached both in preaching and in pastoral care. Whereas Luther would point at Christian practices as tools to fight the Devil, the Christian practices paradigm underlines that Christian practices are tools for growth and transformation. This marks a radical difference. Although Luther is in many ways a stranger to a post modern reader, at the same time his willingness to address evil strikes a chord: *Practicing baptism is a matter of life and death*. A complex and nuanced baptismal anthropology offers a more realistic and direct approach to this theme. For a generation who have grown up with terror attacks as a part of everyday reality a more complex anthropology may serve as an important and critical resource" (166).

I have to stop myself from reaching for my phone a dozen times in a short two-minute stretch. I notice that everyone else has their phones locked in little packs, which I learn later are called Yondr cases. J tells me that both young people and parents have told her they started coming to The Vig just to be able to lock up their phones for an hour and a half. Being late, I missed the Yondr case and now have to fight the temptation to avoid my small death experience, and bear my boredom, without the esthesis of my iPhone.

Moving into Gratitude

I swear I'm almost sweating from keeping the still silence. My spirit feels deep, muscle-shaking fatigue, like a fifth grader trying to break one minute on the flexed-arm hang. I'm relieved that after forty-five minutes (of which I only endured twenty) a small child, maybe about eight, stands and says, "It is time for our walk of gratitude."

Keeping the silence, people line up at four large labyrinths that have been painted on the carpet. They take turns walking them. On the screen, replacing the fourth-century icon, is Romans 5:8, "But God demonstrates his own love for us in this: While we were still sinners, Christ died for us." People are encouraged to walk into the labyrinth and repeat this verse over and over as they do. Then as they walk out, they bring to mind a relationship they are grateful for, contemplating the gift of the relationship as they walk. They end by contemplating one of the names that was on the screen. In gratitude they pray for one person, connecting their person to this absent one, thanking God for this person who is beloved.

Gratitude is the response to a gift, the gift that God alone acts to justify us, freeing us from death for new life.[2] Gratitude is a cruciform virtue, too, because we can only be grateful in the disposition of a gift receiver, in recognition that we are in need[3]—and in that need have received the blessing of our daily bread from the hand of another who bestows value and love on us.

2. Christopher Peterson and Martin E. P. Seligman say, "Gratitude is a sense of thankfulness and joy in response to receiving a gift, whether the gift be a tangible benefit from a specific other or a moment of peaceful bliss evoked by natural beauty." *Character Strengths and Virtues: A Handbook and Classification* (New York: Oxford University Press, 2004), 554.

3. "Gratitude is the self-accepting acceptance of God's gift; it is the healthy being-at-one with myself as poor and weak and unworthy. And so genuine gratitude to God practically guarantees compassion. To the person who is filled with thankfulness to God in Jesus Christ, compassion is not a duty to which he forces himself more or less against his will; being outgoing, self-giving,

In the disposition of the gift receiver, we taste the Good, coming to see that while we were dead in our sin, the Father, through the Son in the Spirit, gave us the salvation of new life. When expressing gratitude, we recognize that there are others who hold our being, others who bear our burdens. Gratitude is an expressed form of joy. The only appropriate response to God's saving act is gratitude. We share this gratitude from the locale of the cross; it's from within the death experience that we express the deep gratitude for new life.[4]

Luther almost cracked from trying so hard to hit the heights of holiness, to master all the virtues without equivocation. But release and freedom came in the revelation that Jesus alone is virtuous, and this virtuous Jesus has been given to us through the gift of faith. Out of love this gift of this virtuous Jesus comes to us in the opposite, in the cross. Meeting us in our own death experiences with the gift of his person, he joyfully exchanges our impossibility of keeping the virtues and finding the Good with his own person. We are in Christ not through our effort but by the pure gift of the Father to give to us the Son through the Spirit. Our response can only be gratitude, because we have experienced joy. But it's deeper than this. Gratitude doesn't simply follow joy; it produces it by orienting our being to the gift of God's act for us. Faith begins and ends in the practice of gratitude.[5]

Like silence, then, gratitude is a virtue transformed through the cross. We find ourselves in gratitude not through effort but in and through the confession of a death experience, encountering the Good in the middle of our impossibility. Gratitude is something that can be practiced, but it must be done so at the foot of the cross, in confession that you are in need, praying for your daily bread and the mercy of forgiveness.[6]

---

is 'natural.'" Robert Roberts, *Spiritual Emotions: A Psychology of Christian Virtues* (Grand Rapids: Eerdmans, 2007), 191.

4. Chapter 3 of Matthew Myer Boulton's *God against Religion: Rethinking Christian Theology through Worship* (Grand Rapids: Eerdmans, 2008) provides a rich discussion of gratitude through Barth and Luther. I'm influenced by Boulton's perspective.

5. Christoph Schwöbel explains Luther's understanding of gratitude: "Humans are gifted creatures for which they owe God gratefulness, and as creatures who are addressed by God they are creatures who are called to respond to their creator and are made responsible for creation before God." "Like a Tree Planted by the Water: Human Flourishing and the Dynamics of Divine-Human Relationship," in *Envisioning the Good Life: Essays on God, Christ, and Human Flourishing*, ed. Matthew Croasmun, Zoran Grozdanov, and Ryan McAnnally-Linz (Eugene, OR: Cascade, 2017), 78. In his own words Luther says, "Behold, from faith thus flow forth love and joy in the Lord, and from love a joyful, willing, and free mind that serves one's neighbor willingly and takes no account of gratitude or ingratitude, of praise or blame, of gain or loss. For a man does not serve that he may put men under obligations." Luther, "The German Reformation," in *The Protestant Reformation*, ed. Hans Hillerbrand (New York: Harper Torchbooks, 1968), 22.

6. See Karl Barth's little book on the Lord's Prayer: *Prayer* (Philadelphia: Westminster, 1946).

Yet gratitude is much deeper than just an attitude adjustment. It is that which in itself is good (especially when you're a parent of a thirteen-year-old). But what allows gratitude to unveil the Good, and to invite us into a flourishing life transformed through the cross, is its relational dynamic. Practicing gratitude quickly takes young people from goods like "I'm grateful for my guitar," "I'm grateful for being all-conference," or "I'm grateful for my phone" to "I'm grateful for my mom's love because she's always there," "I'm grateful for my friend Nancy, who has stood beside me," "I'm grateful for my confirmation mentor, Al, because he listened," or "I'm grateful for my dad, who really sees me."

The practice of gratitude must begin somewhere, so expressions of thanks for objects are a start. But by continuing in the practice, encouraged to remember both our own and others' stories of cross and resurrection—that is, of narratives that begin in a death experience—gratitude becomes inextricably directed toward relationship. When we express gratitude for another who is ministering to us (gratitude for the blessing of God using us to minister to another), we are not only drawn deeply into an open take but also shifted toward the Good. Cruciform gratitude is the expressed feeling of another sharing in your death experience, freeing you from its determinative power to isolate. Gratitude is the blessing of communion with another, giving them your presence in their own death experience. Gratitude is being both Paul and Ananias, receiving and giving communion in and through the confession of a death experience (Acts 9).

When people narrate their open-take stories of a death experience, we often say, "Thank you for sharing," not because it has accomplished any task but because it has been Good. It has revealed a moment we can share in. It has freed us from isolation and given us the gift of communion. It has directed our own being off the Epicurean tracks, to spot a greater horizon than the *summum bonum* of happiness. It has oriented us toward a new take, to experience the Good and seek flourishing as the direction of our lives. Gratitude and joy are often interconnected because they are interlaced with communion.

Happiness is not contingent on gratitude. You can be happy with objects, even happy with the accomplishment of your evil schemes, without ever getting to the level of relationship. But to feel the joy of gratitude necessitates a community of communication. We are grateful when we find ourselves with another who gifts us with their presence. We say thank you and feel gratitude. In the gratitude of the overflowing love of the Trinity, God chooses to create. Human beings are gifted with life from the gratitude of God's own triune communion. Therefore, to be human is to be a communicating creature who says thank you to God and one another. A flourishing life is not a *happy* one but a *joyful* one, filled with words and acts of thanks. Therefore, saying thank you as a practice wraps us in gratitude that starts in the death experience of the need for others, giving us the Good of communion.

After ten to twelve minutes of people walking the labyrinth, the same eight-year-old says, "It's time to pass fives of thank-you." I awkwardly reach for my wallet, assuming this is a moment for the offering. Yet the next thing I know, I'm hearing the slaps of high fives as people walk around the room, breaking the now near hour of silence with loud, even celebratory, palm-on-palm contact, accompanied with the jubilant words "Thank you!" We're instructed to look each other in the eye, exchange a high five, and say "Thank you." The laughter starts immediately. It's fun but touches something deeper. The silly high fives are a practice of joy, a passing of the peace. People laugh, partly because it's stupidly hilarious to be high-fiving, but more so because it's hard not to feel the joy of gratitude when you're giving and receiving thank-yous. There is a felt peace, a Goodness to it all—silly, sure, but Good.

Practicing Humility

In the middle of the high fives, J interrupts, asking people to find a group to pray with, encouraging adults to invite a young person to pray. I find myself joining two high school students and a man who looks like he's in his early fifties. We exchange names. And then Rob, the middle-aged man, looks at Esther, a tenth grader, and says, "Esther, will you pray for me?" She does. After praying, Esther looks at Megan, a seventh grader, and says, "Megan, will you pray for me?"

I'm moved by it every time I see it. If you've ever watched news coverage of Pope Francis meeting crowds, you'll see an incredible practice. The holy pope, from whom all Catholics wish the blessing of prayer, most often turns the tables on the encounter. Instead of being the powerful one who bestows prayers like a holy vending machine, Francis more often looks at those he meets in the eyes—particularly children, the disabled, and prisoners—bows his head slightly, and says, "Will you pray for me?" And he leaves them with a "Remember to pray for me."

Francis is practicing the most primary of cruciform virtues, humility. And in our world of supposedly self-determined identities, desperate needs for social media recognition, and *ressentiment*, humility seems like an odd and yet attractive relic from a past age. People love Francis—even post-religious Europeans and American Protestants. I believe it's because they're drawn to his humility. Particularly in the age of authenticity, we fight humility. We despise it in one sense, yelling for strangers to recognize us. And yet in another sense we long for it; Kendrick Lamar tells us to "sit down / be humble."

For Luther, humility is the most central of cruciform virtues.[7] In his day Luther saw too many "holy" priests feigning humility, using humility as a weapon for power, like Grand Maester Pycelle in *Game of Thrones* using his fake limp and aching back as a way to secure his importance. Humility can so easily become a work and therefore a lie. People claim they're nothing as a way of securing their significance. Powerful people act humbly to keep their power. Worse yet, powerful people tell those with no power that they should be glad for poverty and paucity, for their humility makes them holy (cue Karl Marx rolling over in his grave). Forget full bellies and meaningful work; enjoy the prize of humility, for this world is nothing anyhow. Luther would call these "humilities of glory," disapproving in every way.

To avoid these distortions we have to understand humility as cruciform. If we do so, humility can invite us into communions of joy and tastes of the Good. But to avoid these distortions we need to return to the death experience and the reality of nothingness, starting again at the cross and allowing it to transform virtue.

Humility and nothingness are fundamentally inseparable, which is what keeps many of us avoiding it like bedbugs, fearing the transformation that nothingness promises. Yet when someone like Pope Francis so willingly and directly enters nothingness, his humility radiates to our spirit, witnessing to something Good. But this is a risk because there are false nothingnesses that produce fake humility, taking us far from the cruciform nature of the practice.

Miroslav Volf explains that there are three ways of understanding nothingness next to humility. The first two Luther rejects as distortions that lead only to a defeating and condemning sense of virtue. The first false nothingness is a social nothingness. It is not cruciform nothingness to assert, "I am nobody compared to others."[8] This is a false, unhelpful sense of humility. It either strangles self-worth (people with green eyes are not as important as people with blue eyes, but at least it makes you green-eyed people humble) or manipulates people into giving you recognition ("No, no, Trevor, you're not a loser! We all like you! Don't feel like you're nothing! We're sorry that

---

7. However, again, I doubt Luther would use the word *virtue*.
8. Miroslav Volf, "Humility and Joy" (unpublished paper, 2018), 14.

we didn't realize we were making you feel so bad. Here, have another piece of cake.")

Volf contends that Luther doesn't see humility as resting on an existential nothingness either. This second distortion of nothingness says, "I am nothing compared to what I should or could be."[9] The young Luther believed this unequivocally, returning over and over again to Staupitz, his confessor, not sure that he truly meant his confession. He always felt he could do better, reach for higher virtues, confess a little more, humble *himself* further. It made him manic, a prisoner to his ambitions for humility. And it does the same today. Parents trying to keep their high-achieving daughter humble remind her that she can always do better. Though she has all perfect scores, she could nevertheless get a point higher on her ACT. This doesn't make her humble as much as caught in circles of anxiety.

Volf explains that the kind of nothingness that leads to a cruciform humility is an ontological nothingness—which is the kind of nothingness that Luther embraces. This kind of ontological nothingness asserts that "along with all other human beings and the rest of creation, my own self is not the kind of [being] that could be something on its own."[10] In other words, I *need*, my being necessitates, others to pray for me, to love me, to hear my story, and for me to hear theirs. I cannot *be* without others, particularly Jesus Christ, who comes to me as a gift, praying for me. I cannot *be* without a friend who holds vigil and prays for me, as I do the same for her. Humility is not thinking you're a worm or a loser, but the confession that you *need a minister*. And because you need a minister, you are called to be a minister to others.[11] That's what J is doing; the invitation through direct discourse, "Will you pray for

9. Volf, "Humility and Joy," 14.

10. Volf, "Humility and Joy," 14.

11. Both Jennifer Herdt and Ryan McAnnally-Linz echo Volf's point. Herdt says, "What we might say, then, is that the humble person is fully aware of her strengths and weaknesses in relation to others, and of others' perceptions of her, but is neither inflated nor deflated by these. That is, her sense of self-worth is not dependent on these comparisons. They simply provide important information concerning what she should and should not aspire to in particular contexts. So what humility seems to involve is a relative independence of others' good regard, such that one is not dependent on that regard for one's sense of identity or self-confidence, even as one remains sensitive to others' regard or lack of regard insofar as that might make one aware of some previously unrecognized flaw or weakness. And the humble person's concern for comparison is not directed toward being better than others for the sake of being better than others. Comparison is rather directed toward becoming better than one presently is and toward acting as well as possible given one's present strengths and weaknesses. Attention is focused not on the self as such, but only insofar as various aspects of one's agency are significant for fulfilling one's task, one's vocation." Herdt, "The Lofty Vocation of the Humble" (unpublished consultation paper, Yale Center for Faith and Culture, 2017), 7. McAnnally-Linz adds, "On this kind of account, to be humble is to have a certain sort of assessment of oneself, often in

me?" is the practice of humility.[12] It is the leaning into the Good, seeking a life aimed toward something more than happiness, desiring to be formed, in this eudaimonic way, into Christ. But it isn't so much furious overachieving as a humble confession that you are in need of prayer to *be*. And when you are prayed for, it is joy, because it produces a communion of friendship that bears our burdens. Jennifer Herdt says, "Humility is indeed a virtue and thus necessary to living well. It is, moreover, a source of lasting joy."[13]

Humility is being formed into Christ, because God, too—uniquely in God's own freedom—chooses to bear ontological nothingness: humility is the constituting nature of God's own being. Luther believes this because of Philippians 2. The Christ hymn says, "Though he was in the form of God, [Jesus] did not count equality with God a thing to be grasped, but emptied himself, taking the form of a servant, being born in the likeness of men. And being found in human form he humbled himself and became obedient unto death, even death on a cross" (vv. 6–8 RSV). New Testament scholar Michael Gorman has argued that the "though" can be translated as "because."[14] In other words, we can read it as "because Jesus was in the form of God . . . he humbled himself . . ."[15] This seems to square with Luther. "Luther's God isn't a proud divinity, vacuuming up all the glory into the divine Majesty"[16] but a humble God who comes to us as a baby in a manger, saving us by dying for us, overcoming death with invitations into a community of love, storytelling, and prayer.

---

particular of one's talents and achievements or one's value." "An Unrecognizable Glory: Christian Humility in the Age of Authenticity" (PhD diss., Yale University, 2016), 187.

12. Humility is a call to be a minister in the world, sharing with God's own being by a fellowship of ministerial action. "I propose, instead, that we think of humility primarily as *a mode of tenacious devotion to God's will for and work in the world, especially as one submits the desire for honor, glory, privilege, and/or social standing to that devotion and is thus ready to bear dishonor, shame, loss of social standing, etc. and to forego or not insist upon the honors, status, etc. that one is (actually or supposedly) due.* Humility, on this view, is a mode of acceptance of a divine *commissioning* in service of the divine mission. It is that acceptance insofar as it overcomes fear of humiliation, resists the temptation to deviate from its service for the sake of acclaim or status, or makes one willing to forego the accessories of one's rightful status." McAnnally-Linz, "Unrecognizable Glory," 209.

13. Herdt, "Lofty Vocation of the Humble," 2.

14. See Michael J. Gorman, *Cruciformity: Paul's Narrative Spirituality of the Cross* (Grand Rapids: Eerdmans, 2001).

15. Stephen E. Fowl gives more texture: "In this respect self-emptying does not primarily represent a decision on the part of the preexistent Christ prior to the incarnation. Rather, self-emptying displays something crucial about the character of God. In refusing to use his participation in the glory of the God of Israel for his own advantage and adopting, instead, the disposition of self-emptying, which includes incarnation, obedience, crucifixion, and ultimately exaltation, Christ is actually displaying the form of God, making the glory of God manifest to humans." *Philippians*, Two Horizons New Testament Commentary (Grand Rapids: Eerdmans, 2005), 96.

16. Volf, "Humility and Joy," 17–18.

So humility is the central cruciform virtue because it not only comes in the opposite way from how we'd imagine but also forms us into the very being of God, who, though full of glory, has chosen for the sake of our Goodness to be our minister, to humbly reveal the fullness of God's being in the body of Jesus Christ, who is crucified and now alive.[17] To practice humility as onto-logical nothingness, asking for prayer, is to find our being sharing in the being of God. To practice humility is to be conformed to the very being of Jesus, who is the very form of God. Volf says it beautifully: "Humility of being is the fruit of trust in the humble God whose nature is to create something out of nothing. . . . Humility in acting—which is nothing but the other-oriented side of the humility of being—is participation in the movement of the humble God toward the lowly, in passing God's gifts to others who need them."[18]

And so I turn to Megan and ask her if she'll pray for me. I receive her prayer as a ministry of friendship. Through this asking for prayer, I confess my ontological nothingness. I humbly ask this seventh grader to be there for me, to minister to me, to allow me to minister to others, as Rob asks me to pray for him. I'm invited into a communion that can only be experienced as joy, for I'm participating in the Good.

"Our Father, who art in heaven," J begins, praying aloud over the mic. People in their groups finish praying for one another and join in the Lord's Prayer. Together we build to a crescendo: "In the name of the Father, the Son, and the Holy Spirit. *Amen!*" Everyone cheers and then starts chanting, "DQ time! DQ time!"

I'm shocked, as frozen as a Mister Misty, as people quickly head out of the room. Esther touches my elbow and says, "Are you coming to Dairy Queen? We all go to Dairy Queen after The Vig."

17. Roberts echoes this directly: "I agree both that humility is central to human goodness, and that confronting death can foster it." *Spiritual Emotions*, 73.

18. Volf, "Humility and Joy," 18.

Conclusion

Friendship and DQ

MAY

I nod my head and then find my way to my car.

I'm late again, but this time it's because of my own violation. I need to check in with home, but more honestly it's my introvertedness. It feels less exposing to slide into the middle of this DQ gathering, when I can be sure that the few people I know will be there, rather than to show up early and have to partake in that awkward milling around that makes us introverts wish the earth would open up and swallow us whole.

When I arrive, there's a group of at least twenty-five people eating Blizzards and cones and laughing. *Thank goodness*—I win the introvert lottery. I immediately see Lorena, and even better, she sees me. Smiling brightly, she waves me over.

"Hi!" she says.

"Good to see you," I respond, the relief of my introverted nerves making me a little too exuberant.

"Were you at The Vig?" Lorena asks.

"Yeah, I didn't see you. Were you there?" I ask.

"I usually am, but I couldn't make it tonight. We had a track meet."

"I didn't know you ran track."

"I don't. I mean, I don't anymore. My doctors won't let me . . . or my mom won't. But I'm the team manager."

"Cool" is the best response I can muster, my mind shamefully shifting to my need for an Oreo Blizzard.

Lorena continues, "But even when you can't make it to The Vig, you try to get to DQ."

Just then, J appears with a chocolate dipped cone in hand, the top already cracked and leveled to about half. "Everyone's here tonight," she says, pointing out Bernard, Kathy, Nikki, Tannon, and even Lorena's mom. I can only smile; I feel like I know these people. It's like seeing in the flesh characters from a novel I've been reading. My introverted awkwardness disappears inside this warm thought.

"So why DQ?" I ask J.

"Because it's delicious," J responds in a tone of *duh*.

I laugh. "Sure, but why right after The Vig? I mean, my experience was that after the Lord's Prayer things weren't over. It seems like The Vig doesn't end until after DQ."

"It doesn't," J responds with a confident directness. "It really doesn't. I mean, sure, some people need to go, particularly parents with small kids who need to get them to bed. And, sure, we add a few people like Lorena tonight. But this is a spiritual practice!"

I nod my head with a smile, ear to ear, mistaking J's comments for a joke. "I agree, I think DQ is always a spiritual experience."

J kindly receives my confused joke and then adds, "No, I'm serious. This is a spiritual practice of friendship, and it's central to what we do. Youth ministry can only be for joy in and through friendship.[1] And what I've learned is that friendship can't just be for entertaining fun; it has to be practiced. It's a way of participating in the Good. It may be our most direct way of following Jesus, who promises to call us 'friend.' Joy is the feeling of being in a friendship that carries your burdens. That takes practice. And that reworks the point of life. And definitely youth ministry."

I think to myself, *That takes a summum bonum broader and richer than happiness.*

Philippians

Stephen E. Fowl ends his commentary on Philippians with a postscript titled "Theological Horizons of Philippians."[2] In it he reminds us that this letter

1. See Kenda Creasy Dean and Wes Ellis, "The Joy of Untamed Friendship" (lecture, Yale Youth Ministry Institute Lunch and Lecture Series, Yale Divinity School, New Haven, CT, November 2, 2016), available at https://youtu.be/cp-Qt8sdNxE.

2. Stephen E. Fowl, *Philippians*, Two Horizons New Testament Commentary (Grand Rapids: Eerdmans, 2005), 233–35.

Paul writes to the Philippians is a friendship letter. It takes the ancient form of a friendship letter, and friendship itself is its central theological thrust. Paul is reminding the church in Philippi that friendship is central to the Christian life, and therefore friendship must be directly practiced.

For Paul, friendship is a dynamic reality. It's not only a practice but also the kind of practice that escapes being a means to another end. Friendship itself is the disposition of one who is in Christ, a description of being a follower of Christ, an articulation of someone who has tasted the Good. Thomas Aquinas in his *Summa Theologiae* goes so far as to claim that friendship is so much an end and not a means that we were created for friendship with God—God created humanity to be God's friend.[3] Therefore, friendship is the state of our reconciled and redeemed being, because it's central to what it means to be in God's image. We experience the Good, God even calling us creatures "Good," because we are made for friendship. We find ourselves living good lives, flourishing as we were made to do, not when we're religious or recognized or even happy, but when we're affirmed as friend and gifted with friendship. It's in walking with God in the cool of the garden, laughing with friends over a Peanut Buster Parfait. The person whose being has been transformed—bearing the marks of cruciform virtue—is in the world as a friend, not a religious vanguard or a connoisseur of happiness. Often our lives are most full of the Good when we are called by and calling God and others "friend."[4]

Yet too often, especially with young people, we assume that friendship is a means to another end, to other goods, asserting that we want our kids to

3. See *Summa Theologiae* I-II.65.5. Jennifer Herdt adds, "Indeed, for Aquinas charity, the infused theological virtue that becomes the form guiding and directing all Christian virtues, just *is* friendship with God. It is God communicating God's own goodness to human beings in such a way that they themselves become capable of *amicitia*, of self-giving friendship, with God and one another. Thomas is guided here by scripture, notably by Jesus' farewell discourse in the Gospel of John 'I will not now call you servants . . . but My friends' (John 15.15). 1 Cor. I.9: 'God is faithful: by Whom you are called unto the fellowship of His Son.' Human beings, he tells us, are invited into a fellowship and communication (*conversatio*) with God that can be imperfectly experienced now but that will be eschatologically perfected (II-II.23.1 ad 1; 23.3). Befriended by God, we begin to love all that is loved by our friend. Hence, out of charity our friendship extends to all, even enemies and sinners. God's befriending of us, then, frees us for a humility that fosters and invites friendship with others. That this is so helps us understand why human friendship, too, is not simply fostered by humility but also the gift that can make friendship possible." "The Lofty Vocation of the Humble" (unpublished consultation paper, Yale Center for Faith and Culture, 2017), 10.

4. This is the moral language for why I have argued, in *Revisiting Relational Youth Ministry* (Downers Grove, IL: IVP Books, 2007) and other places, that ministry is *not* about influence but about place-sharing, where the relationship is the end. Friendship is fundamental in the economy of God.

have friends *so they'll be happy*. Youth ministry needs to focus on friendship so young people participate, and everyone is happy with our program, youth choosing religion over other activities.[5] But seeing friendship as a means to an end of happiness can only lead to all sorts of frenemy conflicts in the rush for the higher good of performative identity recognition.[6] It can only obscure the eudaimonic way of practiced friendship, which seeks no ladder to elitist holiness but a Good life formed in the humble gratitude of shared life. When friendship is a means for winning recognition and an identity to be happy, it becomes pocked with all sorts of *Sorry, I'm not sorry* statements.

Friendship is powerful and beautiful because, like a reflex, it leads us into the life of another, to receive and give ministry, to give and receive a gift. Friendship is our deepest move of sharing in the happenings of others. There is no way to be a friend other than to share in happenings, occurrences, episodes, and moments of another. When something happens to us, we feel compelled to tell a friend, to have this friend share in our being by sharing in the narration of our experience. Facebook is worth $500 billion thanks to the human spirit's insatiable desire to reach out to a friend and share our happenings. But the reaching out itself doesn't solidify a friendship. What makes someone a true friend—and more than just a "friend" on Facebook—is that they embrace the shared happening with concern.

The reason Facebook can boomerang on us and actually be a zone that undercuts friendship is that it overwhelms us with happenings, cutting off our ability for concern. Actually, being bombarded with happenings and occurrences nonstop, twenty-four hours a day, leads me in my overwhelmed state to not give a rip. I no longer want to embrace other's happenings with concern, which would force me into strong evaluation of my own narrative of the world. So I resist the postings of others' happenings and occurrences,

---

5. "Aristotle said that without friends no one would choose to live. It wasn't just because human beings are social creatures who find most things more enjoyable when they can be shared with others or because there is no way any of us could make it through life without friends to whom we could turn. All that is true, but the most important reason we need friends, Aristotle insisted, is because a life of goodness . . . depends on having certain kinds of relationships." Paul J. Wadell, *Happiness and the Christian Moral Life: An Introduction to Christian Ethics* (Lanham, MD: Rowman & Littlefield, 2008), 25.

6. Alasdair MacIntyre reorders recognition through the kinds of friends we've been discussing: "It is in and through the relationships of friends that the particularity of each and the distinctive value of each as being this particular individual with her or his own distinctive good to achieve is accorded recognition. And we each of us need this recognition, if we are to pursue our own good effectively within networks of giving and receiving. It is not only for the achievement of our common good that we are dependent on the other members of our communities, but we depend too on some particular others to achieve most of our individual goods." *Dependent Rational Animals: Why Human Beings Need the Virtues* (Chicago: Open Court, 1999), 161.

either feeling like they taunt me with how great their life is going, or assuming they're trying to convert me to some ideological position. Hence, Facebook and other social media sites become ovens cooking *ressentiment* to seven hundred degrees, providing me the tools to spread my *ressentiment* to others with concern fatigue, possessing a strong evaluation of hating some ideology. We've seen of late that Facebook does a much better job of creating comrades in the culture wars than friends in community.

Back to Paul, Philippians, and Kenosis

Paul in his letter to Philippians helps us escape *ressentiment* and the utilitarian use of friendship by calling us to the very kenotic being of Jesus himself. Friendship is an end in itself. It is kenotic, which is the shape of God's own being. Friendship is a practice that creates a rich context for us to live out the other cruciform virtues of humility, gratitude, and even stillness.[7] Friendship as an end is a gift. It is grace, which calls us into action, to form our lives in such a way that we are good friends, entering the Good through friendship itself (not disconnected happiness). Paul is telling us that disciples, those who follow Jesus Christ, are Good friends. To make our *summum bonum* Jesus Christ, as Luther contends, is to be in the world as a good friend; it is to seek the Good through friendship. It is to have a flourishing Good life in and through friendship. The disciple lives a Good life by being a Good friend, practicing humility and gratitude in the concrete location of friendship.

J is so insightful. DQ is of essential importance; it is the confirmation that the other practices were indeed directed toward, even participating in, Jesus Christ. This is because directing our being toward Christ in this eudaimonic way of practice doesn't necessarily (primarily) produce stout holiness or stoic virtue like Socrates possessed, but produces a spirit (a participation in the Spirit) of friendship. Friendship is the confirmation that our practices are conforming us to Christ. Therefore, to evaluate our youth ministries isn't to say, "Oh yes, our kids are reading their Bibles until they pass out." Or, "Yes our kids are crying when they worship." Or, "Yes, our kids pray until their knees are bloody." These kinds of results in and of themselves would

---

7. Herdt connects this to humility: "Humility also stands in a special relationship with friendship. Where pride isolates, humility paves the way for friendship. For the prideful engage in just the kind of comparisons with others for which the humble have no need. The prideful are focused on themselves and their status, and hence cannot but regard their friends through the lens of perceived inferiority or superiority, as those who enhance our standing by way of association, or whose subordinate status feeds our sense of self-esteem. But we might also just as appropriately say that friendship fosters humility." "Lofty Vocation of the Humble," 10.

not confirm that a eudaimonic movement toward the *summum bonum* of Jesus Christ is on track. They would only affirm that we're on the track of the Pharisees. Rather, it is friendship that confirms we're aimed toward the Good and following Jesus Christ as our *summum bonum*, that we are living faithfully as those reconciled, as those returned to friendship with God. The peace of stillness, gratitude, and humility—these cruciform virtues—is only appropriately lived out in friendship, with a celebration at DQ. In the life of a disciple, friendship is a hypergood because, again to echo Thomas, it is what we're created for, to be God's friend.

We are made for friendship. All human beings, even us introverts, have longings—even needs—for friendship. But what makes friendship particularly cruciform, leading directly into encounter with the living Jesus, is, not surprisingly, the death experience. Cruciform friendship is fashioned out of a willingness to bear each other's burdens—in kenosis, out of humility and gratitude, to minister to your neighbor. Friendship is the context in which others share in our events. It's the place where we participate in stories, both by telling others the stories of our events and by hearing others tell their own stories. Friendship is the most direct locale for working out an identity. In friendship we share in the events of others, taking on the very action of God, who identifies with our events of death experiences through God's own death experience on the cross. Christ makes us God's friends by God's participation in and through our death experiences, giving us the tangible take of reconciliation and sanctification as the joy of being God's friend. We are called to join with others who are God's friends, and we become a community of friends. This community tells stories and seeks the Good life by conforming to the cross through silence, gratitude, humility, and ultimately friendship. And because it is on the practice of friendship that all other cruciform practices rest,[8] joy is the manifest disposition. Joy is the outward sign that we are in Christ, that we are friends with God, that we are sent into the world to be ministers in and through friendship.[9]

8. Because friendship is the most fundamental of hypostatic practices, it delivers personhood, the direct form of God in the Second Person of the Trinity. God desires friendship so deeply that he sends the Son.

9. Fowl connects this to Philippians: "Given this abundance of references to joy and rejoicing in the epistle, it is not surprising that joy should play a significant role in Christian friendship. In the light of what I have already said, I would argue that joy and rejoicing are not so much ends in themselves as byproducts of the proper working of Christian friendships, what one should expect in the midst of a common life ordered in a manner worthy of the gospel of Christ." *Philippians*, 234.

Nearing the bottom of my Oreo Blizzard, I realize that my nine-month journey is coming to an end. I started in September, thrown into cognitive dissonance. I wasn't sure how I'd answer "youth ministry is for _____." The answer to this question only became more opaque as fall gave way to winter. I talked to parents and realized that youth ministry is lost in a new slowdown, where identity is self-chosen, recognition sought, and happiness the *summum bonum*. Yet the dark winter brought me to J and her claim that youth ministry is for joy. Making youth ministry about joy in the slowdown of growing up gives us a rich alternative perspective on the good life. The slowdown is here because parents want their children to have a good life. J was addressing the slowdown by focusing direct attention on the Good, claiming that youth ministry is for joy.

Over the past few months this seemingly odd phrase has now encompassed a universe. I've discovered how identity is forged through events of storytelling, how joy is a story. I've discovered the need for youth ministry to narrate open takes bending toward transcendence, and the importance of cruciform practices shifting us away from happiness to the Good, recovering a cruciform eudaimonic disposition.

Talking with J, I realize that to say that youth ministry is for joy is actually to say that youth ministry is for many things. It is for storytelling, humility, openness to transcendence, the Good, and friendship with one another and God through Jesus Christ. But the shorthand for all this, the tangible feeling of it all, is that youth ministry is for joy. And it is joy that we offer overly busy, anxious, fragile young people.

Those who have gathered together in friendship to tell stories and identify with each other's events, bending their lives in practice toward the Good of God's own cruciform love, having their identities in being God's friends— this community bears each other's burdens and experiences lives of joy. As Fowl says in light of Philippians, "Joy and rejoicing in the Lord, then, are the fruits of Christian friendships in Good working order."[10] I'd only add this: joy in friendship and rejoicing in the *summum bonum* of Jesus Christ are what youth ministry is for.

May it be, in and through Jesus Christ our Lord, who is the Goodness of God.

---

10. Fowl, *Philippians*, 235 (capital G added by me).